Philosophy

5.25

DIRECTIVES AND NORMS

International Library of Philosophy and Scientific Method

DIRECTIVES
and
NORMS

by

ALF ROSS

LONDON
ROUTLEDGE & KEGAN PAUL
NEW YORK : HUMANITIES PRESS

First published 1968
by Routledge & Kegan Paul Ltd.
Broadway House, 68–74 Carter Lane
London, E.C.4

Printed in Great Britain
by Western Printing Services Ltd.
Bristol

Library of Congress Catalog Card No 67–28027

SBN 7100 3635 3

CONTENTS

v

CONTENTS

vi

CONTENTS

PREFACE

I am highly indebted to Mr. Brian Loar who has revised or, more exactly, completely rewritten my own English manuscript and I tender him my sincere thanks for his invaluable services. As it has been necessary to make subsequent additions and alterations he should not, however, be made responsible for any linguistic shortcomings.

The Danish *Rask-Ørsted Foundation* has contributed to the costs involved in producing the manuscript in English, for which help I am most grateful.

Copenhagen 1967

ALF ROSS

I

INTRODUCTION

Traditionally a distinction has been made between 'theoretical' and 'practical' discourse. It remains undecided, however, what the subject of this distinction is, and what is its foundation.

The opinion has long been current that a fundamental distinction has to be drawn between 'theoretical' and 'practical' utterances or speech-acts. The former class is thought to include 'assertions' and 'statements'; the latter, 'imperatives', 'evaluations' and 'normative expressions'. It has been held in consequence that only the former can be true or false, and that they alone can therefore be discussed by logic. Imperatives, it is said, express a volitional attitude taken up by their author, and thus have no truth-value. This view, however, has not prevented philosophers from thinking with Kant, that there are imperatives which express moral principles having absolute, categorical validity—imperatives which are neither subjective nor arbitrary, but issue *a priori* from man's practical reason, and are self-evidently apprehended by rational intuition; nor from holding, with the adherents of an ethics based on 'objective' values, that we can cognize these values and derive from them valid moral imperatives.

In its original form the distinction was drawn within a transcendentalist epistemology, which postulated the existence of separate cognitive faculties or rational powers.

The same distinction is made in different words by contemporary 'analytical' or 'linguistic' philosophy. Following Hare and others, many philosophers distinguish between *descriptive* and *prescriptive* language or discourse.[1] Some, however, still use the terms 'theoretical' and 'practical' (or 'non-theoretical'), though without any transcendentalist implications;[2] and others speak of 'Seinsurteile' ('is'-judgments) and 'Sollensurteile' ('ought'-judgments).[3] In whatever terminology, these distinctions come to the same thing so far as they concern the question of the extent to which something that is said can be appraised as true or false.

It remains undecided, however, what the subject of this distinction is, and what is its foundation. Hare, for example, speaks about 'prescriptive *language*' and mentions 'the ordinary imperative *sentence*' as its simplest form. This may seem to imply that the distinction is one between grammatical phenomena. But Hare expressly stresses that the distinction is not one of grammatical form; it concerns, rather, the *meanings* conveyed by the different grammatical forms, which he calls 'statements' and 'commands'. The distinction, accordingly, might be thought to be semantical. On the other hand it may be urged against this interpretation that Hare points out that the distinctive feature of prescriptive language is its *function*, which is to guide conduct; but the distinction in that case would belong to pragmatics.[4]

When such an ambiguity is found in Hare it is safe to assume that the problem which concerns us needs clarification on a general level of enquiry. It goes without saying that so long as it is not clear *what* is being classified, the problem *how* or by what criteria it is to be classified can be no nearer solution.

The distinction between descriptive and prescriptive discourse (or whatever expressions one may prefer to use provisionally to mark this distinction) is clearly in some sense a linguistic one. Accordingly, the first step toward clarification must consist in an account of the different levels of linguistic analysis, so that we may be aware of the different possibilities open to us. The best way to do this, I believe, is first to explain the distinction between language and discourse, and then to analyse the phenomenon which is called *a speech-act* or *locutionary act*. Although this elementary

---

[1] R. M. Hare, *The Language of Morals* (1952), pp. 1ff., 18ff.

[2] E.g., P. H. Nowell-Smith, *Ethics* (1954), pp. 11ff., 95ff.; R. Edgley, 'Practical Reason', *Mind* (1965), pp. 174ff.

[3] E.g., Hans Kelsen, *General Theory of Law and State* (1946), pp. 37, 46, 110ff., 164, a.o.

[4] *Op. cit.*, pp. 1–2, 4–5.

analysis will be familiar to many of my readers I believe it necessary to start from the bottom.

§ 2

Speech is the concrete linguistic phenomenon. A speech-act is (1) *a phonetic sequence* (2) *of correct syntactic structure* (3) *with semantic meaning and* (4) *pragmatic function.*
Our distinction between language and discourse is the same as the well-known distinction between *la langue* and *la parole* made by the Swiss linguist Ferdinand de Saussure. The following explanation of that distinction is borrowed from Bertil Malmberg:

By *la langue* Saussure meant the linguistic system itself, that is, the totality of all the rules which in a particular linguistic community regulate the use of sounds and forms and the use of syntactical and lexical means of expression. In other words, *la langue* is the superindividual linguistic system, an abstraction whose existence is the very condition of understanding between people. By *la parole*, on the other hand, Saussure meant the concrete act of speech, i.e., the language as it is actualized by a speaker at a particular time. *La parole* is an individual phenomenon, *la langue* a social one. *La langue* is the foundation of *la parole*. If there were no accepted system of linguistic rules to be applied in speech the latter could not function as a means of contact between people. Conversely, we are able to study *la langue* only by observing concrete speech-acts or texts (i.e., *la parole*), and inferring the linguistic system from these. In other languages we find parallel expressions used to denote the distinction for which Saussure used the terms *langue* and *parole*: in German, *Sprache* and *Rede*; in English, *language* and *speech*; in Swedish, *språk* and *tal*; in Spanish, *lengua* and *habla*. But these terms have not established themselves to the same extent as the French ones used by Saussure.[1]

In this book I shall use the terms 'language' and 'speech'. By 'speech' is meant any concrete use of language, whether it occurs as speech in the narrow sense, that is, as a sequence of sounds (phonemes), or as a text, that is, as a sequence of characters (graphemes).

It is usual in logic to consider propositions as bearers of

---

[1] Bertil Malmberg, Nya vägar inom språkforskningen [*New Approaches within Linguistics*] (1959), p. 45. My translation.

unambiguously determined meaning, and therefore as true or false, without taking into account the speaker of the proposition and the circumstances of its utterance. Propositions considered in this way are abstractions and idealizations to be found, as Alfred N. Whitehead used to say, only in Heaven. In real life we find only concrete speech-acts, utterances made by certain individuals in certain circumstances, having a meaning dependent on the circumstances and often so vague that the clearcut alternative of truth or falsity does not apply. Consider for instance the famous dispute (in a Danish play) whether the moon is white or yellow (decided by the dictum: the moon has the colour which moons ought to have); or Austin's example: whether it is true that France is hexagonal.[1] The nearest approximation to the ideal 'propositions' of logic is found, I suppose, in sentences occurring in textbooks of exact science.

Speech is the immediate subject of linguistic analysis. It is only through speech that we can know the language—i.e., the totality of the actual or possible elements of expression and the rules for their combination into compound wholes. Speech can be soliloquy or dialogue. In dialogue there exists a relation of communication between one or more speakers or writers and one or more hearers or readers. Let us call the first class *senders* and the second *recipients*. The process of communication (or, more briefly, 'the communication') depends on more than linguistic factors. As is well known, the communications in relation both to the intention of the sender and the effect produced in the recipient, depends on its context, taken in a broad sense, that is, on the total concrete life-situation in which the communication occurs. The complete meaning of utterances like 'Peter, shut the door!', 'The King has died', or 'It is raining' varies a great deal according to the circumstance of the utterance. (Which Peter and what door is meant? Which king? Where and at what time is it raining?)

Soliloquy may be taken similarly, the sender and recipient being the same person at different times. I can, for example, take notes meant for myself at a later time. Nor is the continuous internal dialogue which we call thinking, or considering, or pondering, in principle different. In this case the time interval is shortened and the sending and reception of the utterance occur as consecutive components of the continuous stream of consciousness of one person.

[1] J. L. Austin, *How to do Things with Words* (1962), p. 142.

Speaking, like shutting a door or lighting a cigar, is a human act. And it is the elements of the locutionary *act* which determine the levels of linguistic analysis.

The locutionary act is essentially a phonetic act, i.e., the production of a sequence of sounds (or symbols for sounds). These sounds are psycho-physical phenomena. Phonetics and the general theory of communication attempt to record the sound-elements occurring in a particular language and to describe the processes by which the sounds are generated by a speaker, conveyed to another individual, and there received and apprehended. As a physical phenomenon, the phonetic act may produce effects quite outside the process of communication, e.g., when by shouting, someone causes an avalanche in the Alps.

Not every production of a series of phonetically recognizable sounds is, however, a speech-act. For the phonetic act must possess a structure which accords with the syntactical rules of the language concerned, i.e., the rules governing the ways in which the permitted linguistic elements may be combined into compound wholes. These rules include, first of all, the fundamental norms of the *structure of a language*, for example, the norms which exclude from Danish the occurrence of syllables spelt 'mdt', 'mgt', or 'mkt', or syllables beginning or ending with these combinations.[1] The syntactic rules include, secondly, the rules which govern the *structure of sentences* or grammatical syntax, according to which, for example, the word sequence 'That failed of boys yesterday because' does not count as a sentence. Finally, the *syntax of formal logic* rules out certain combinations of sentences, e.g, 'It is raining and it is not raining.'

Not every sentence whose structure is syntactically correct, however, constitutes an act of discourse. For this, it is further required that the sentence possess meaning. The following sentence (borrowed from Carnap), though grammatically correct, does not meet this last requirement: 'five per cent of the prime numbers, having as their father the concept of temperature and as their mother the number five, die, within a period of three years plus five pounds plus seven inches after their birth, of either typhoid fever or the square root of a democratic constitution.'[2]

---

[1] Louis Hjelmslev, *Sproget* [The Language] (1963), p. 37.
[2] Rudolf Carnap, *Einführung in die symbolische Logik* (1954), p. 76.

A phonetic sequence of correct syntactic structure having meaning constitutes a speech-act. As this act is not normally a reflex action, but a deliberate and purposive human act, it will normally be performed with the aim of producing certain effects. These effects will of course vary with the content of the locutionary act and will depend, most likely, on other factors as well. If it can be established that speech-acts of a certain kind, taken according to content, are calculated to produce in a standard recipient under standard conditions effects of a certain kind (e.g. cognitive, emotional, or volitional effects), these effects will be said to be the *function* of that type of locutionary act.

In accordance with this analysis of the locutionary act the levels of linguistic analysis may be described as follows, in order of increasing abstraction:

The *pragmatic analysis of language* (or simply *pragmatics*) is concerned with the act of discourse considered as a human act aimed at the production of certain effects.[1] It studies our use of linguistic tools, and how these function and are conditioned by their grammatical and semantic properties. Pragmatics abstracts from individual peculiarities and considers the act of discourse in standard communication, assuming a standard sender, a standard recipient, and a standard situation. It also abstracts from the non-linguistic features of communication. When pragmatics is taken together with the study of certain technical, psychological and other aspects of the process of communication, we may speak of a *general theory of communication*.[2]

The *semantic analysis of language* (or simply *semantics*) is the next step in order of abstraction. Semantics studies linguistic expressions as bearers or meaning, abstracting from their actual use in particular situations. Whereas pragmatics is concerned with the use and function of linguistic tools, semantics studies these tools as such and the properties which make them fitted to specific uses. The fundamental concepts of semantics are *meaning, sense, truth,* and *falsehood*.

In semantics I would also include semantic logic, especially the theory of the categories of predicates, which deals with the re-

---

[1] E.g., R. M. Martin, *Toward a Systematic Pragmatics* (1959).
[2] E.g., Miller, *Language and Communication* (1951); Colin Cherry, *On Human Communication* (1957).

quirements which must be met for a grammatically correct sentence to have meaning.[1]

The *syntactic analysis of language* (or simply *syntax*) is a further step in the progression toward abstraction, which disregards not only the function of a linguistic expression but also its meaning. Grammatical syntax is concerned with the rules which govern the construction of sentences, regardless of whether these sentences have meaning. Logical syntax borders on semantics; it abstracts from the actual meaning of linguistic expressions but not from the fact that they do have meaning and may therefore be true or false. This is the basis of the rules of combination with which traditional formal logic is concerned. When, for example, the combination 'It is raining (here and now) and it is not raining (here and now)' is ruled out it is not because this combination refers to the state of the weather. The incriminating feature is the way in which the words 'and' and 'not' are used in sentences and in combinations of sentences which have descriptive meaning and which are consequently true or false. Formal logic, then, does not operate with sentence-instances, but with sentence-variables. Instead of the sentences quoted we shall therefore write 'p & ~p', where 'p' stands for any true or false sentence with a descriptive meaning. Later in this book we shall deal with the question whether there exists a similar logic (deontic logic) governing sentences without truth-value.

§ 3

Indicative and directive speech are distinguished. It is the aim of this study to explicate the concepts 'directive' and 'norm' on the basis of this distinction, and to help lay a foundation for deontic logic.

The aim of this study is, in the first place, to work out a distinction between what I shall call *indicative* and *directive* discourse. The term 'indicative' is on a par with 'theoretical' and 'descriptive'. The first of these I shall not use, partly because of the taint it inherits from transcendentalist philosophy, and partly because it seems inappropriate for designating an utterance like 'Peter is shutting the door', suggesting, as it might, that this utterance is connected with a theory. The word 'descriptive' is likewise

---

[1] Cp. Jørgen Jørgensen, 'Some Remarks concerning Statements, Truth-Values, and Categories of Predicates', *Logique et Analyse* 1961, pp. 125ff.

unsuitable, since the distinction, as I shall later explain, does not depend on the utterance's describing anything.

'Directive' is on the same side of the distinction as 'practical' and 'prescriptive'. Neither of these latter terms will do, however, since the concept 'directive discourse' is not intended to cover all discourse currently called 'practical' or 'prescriptive'; value judgments, at any rate, fall outside its scope. Furthermore, the word 'prescriptive' seems inadequate for many types of utterance which it is intended to cover—for example friendly requests, advice, questions.

The distinction between indicative and directive speech is, consequently, not intended to be exhaustive. I am inclined to believe, though, that the distinction is fundamental in the sense that the phenomena denoted by the two concepts do fall on either side of a fundamental boundary. I have no idea whether an exhaustive classification would place some other types of discourse alongside indicatives. But it is implied by what I have said that some utterances other than directives (certainly, for example, evaluative utterances) belong on the same side as directives.

I exclude evaluative utterances[1] from the scope of 'directive speech' for the following reason. This study aims at explicating the concepts 'directive' and 'norm' as these function in the social sciences, especially in legal theory and ethology (by which I understand the study of conventional morality, folkways and related subjects). I wish in particular to investigate whether directives and norms are, like indicatives, subject to a logic. But I have found that the logical structure of value judgments is essentially different from that of directives and norms; hence the inclusion of evaluative utterances in this enquiry would be at best confusing.

It remains to explain the arrangement of this book. In Chapter II, indicative speech is examined in as much detail as is necessary as a background for the subsequent discussion, in Chapter III, of directive speech. In Chapter IV the concept 'norm' is examined, and in Chapter V the elements of a norm are analysed. The sixth and last Chapter treats of the fundamental problems of deontic logic.

[1] See below, p. 38, note 1.

II

INDICATIVE SPEECH

---

§ 4

The phrase is a linguistic figure which expresses the idea of (or describes) a topic.

Imagine a circle of mutes who sit around a large table on which there lie piles of letters which are to be put into frames. The mutes communicate with each other by filling in a frame in an appropriate way, showing it to the person for whom the message is meant. To avoid misunderstandings caused by filled-in frames lying around, without it being clear whether or not they are meant as communications, a rule has been adopted to the effect that a word-frame counts as a communication from A to B if and only if A, upon presenting the frame, rings a bell and points at B.

The mutes often fill in frames merely for practice' sake, and sometimes idly play with the letters and frames, or go off into reveries while continuing in an absent way to put letters into frames. It may happen that, upon becoming aware of the results of such activity, the mutes wonder whether these already made frames might be used for some purpose.

Let us suppose that a frame has been filled in this way with the sequence of letters 'mdt'. If the mutes are Danes the frame is useless, since the rules for the structure of the Danish language are such that this sequence can neither form a syllable nor occur at the beginning or end of a syllable. It is not that the combination does not now occur in Danish, but that it is excluded from the language by the structural rules which make Danish, precisely,

Danish. The mute cannot, therefore, even introduce 'mdt' as a new Danish word to which he has given sense.[1]

Suppose, now, that a frame is made consisting of the words (1) 'blue anemones'. Could it be used for any purpose? It could be used as, say, an answer to the question 'What kind of flowers do you have in your hand?'. The pragmatic context would in this case indicate that the expression 'blue anemones' is an abbreviation of the more complete expression (2) 'The flowers in my hand are blue anemones'. That (1) is an abbreviation of (2) means that, when uttered in this particular speech situation as an answer to this question, (1) will be taken by both sender and recipient to have the same meaning as (2). 'Blue anemones!' might also be an abbreviation of a vendor's offer. The question arises, however, whether the expression 'blue anemones' can be properly used in a situation in which there is no reason to take it as an abbreviation. Can the word combination 'blue anemones' function as a communication without any kind of implied extension?

It would obviously be rather exceptional if *A* said to *B* 'blue anemones' and nothing more. Such a communication seems somehow to lack substance; it contains no message. The puzzled recipient of the message might well ask 'Well, what about blue anemones?'. There is nevertheless a difference between this utterance and the utterance *tout court* of the sequence 'Peter because'. Whereas the latter completely lacks meaning, at least if we ignore the possibility of a very exceptional speech situation, the expression 'blue anemones' does have meaning. For it describes a *topic*, that is, it typically calls to mind the idea or thought of this topic in a standard recipient. 'Anemones' by itself denotes a topic, as does 'blue anemones' and even 'black anemones', though the latter denotes no existing flowers. We may call a word or word-combination describing a topic a *phrase*.

The phrase as a linguistic figure must be distinguished from the meaning-content it expresses, which is called an *idea*. The idea is the abstract meaning-content, not the thought of the topic as it occurs to some individual inside his private world of experiences. The thought of blue anemones is a psychological phenomenon. It must always be had by a particular person at a particular time. The idea of blue anemones, at the other hand, is a semantic phenomenon, i.e., the meaning content that in a given language

[1] Cp. above, p. 5, note 1.

10

is attached to the phrase 'blue anemones'. The same idea may often be expressed by different phrases. '*A*'s parents' and '*A*'s father and mother' express the same idea. The same is true of phrases in different languages which are translations of each other—i.e. are synonymous.[1]

The phrase's power to evoke the thought of some topic may be exploited on its own. For example one may imagine trying to soothe or hypnotize a patient by whispering 'Blue anemones, . . . drifting skies, . . . murmuring brooks'. Phrases are much used in poetry of some kinds, like the Japanese *haiku*, to work on the imagination not by describing fictional happenings or states of affairs, but by evoking pictures in the mind of the reader:

> *The bell of the temple*
> *a butterfly*
> *sleeping at rest*[2]

We may call the function of speech, in so far as it makes use exclusively of phrases, its *ideographic* function.

To use a phrase is one thing; to mention it, as I for example have just done, is another. To use a phrase is to utter it in communication; such an utterance *is* a phrase. The sentences in this book are not phrases, but are *about* phrases, in the same way as they are about many other things.

The words 'anemone' and 'blueness' both denote topics. The phrase 'blue anemones' denotes a composite topic which is characterized by the union of the properties 'being an anemone' and 'being blue'. While 'prime number' denotes a topic, the phrase 'blue prime number' is without meaning and describes no topic. The rules governing the permissible combination of simple phrases into compound phrases would be called *semantic logic*. It would include, for example, the theory of the categories of predicates and Russell's theory of types.

Apart from the rules of semantic logic, there are no limits to the possible complexity of phrases and the topics they denote. New elements of meaning can be continuously added. 'Door'

---

[1] My terminology is different from that used by Gottlob Frege in his paper 'The Thought: A Logical Inquiry', *Mind*, vol. LXV (1956), pp. 289ff. My term 'thought' corresponds, I believe, with his 'idea', and what he calls a 'thought' with my term 'proposition', see below § 5.

[2] *Haiku*. Translations [into Danish] by Hans-Joergen Nielsen (Copenhagen 1963). My translation.

denotes a topic, and so do 'shutting the door', 'shutting of the door by Peter', 'shutting of the door by Peter now', and so forth.

§ 5

A sentence in indicative discourse is a linguistic figure expressing a proposition (an indicative), which is the idea of a topic conceived as real.
Suppose that *A* has filled in one of our frames with the phrase 'shutting of the door by Peter' and another with the sentence 'Peter is shutting the door'. It seems obvious that the meanings of the two frames are different; they may be used to perform different functions. But what exactly is the difference?

Grammatically, the linguistic figure 'Peter is shutting the door' is a sentence. While the phrase describes a topic, the sentence describes a *state of affairs*, that is, a *topic thought of as real*.

This is evident if we analyse the phrase and the sentence. The phrase describes an act, Peter's act of shutting the door. The sentence is about the same topic, but in another way; for in it the topic is not only thought of, but thought of as *real*—in the sense of actually existing or being the case.[1]

I hope that I shall not be expected to explain in this connection what it means to think of something as real. It must suffice to point out that, since Kant, it has (or so it seems) come to be accepted that a real *Thaler* possesses no property that an imaginary one lacks. To call a topic real is not to ascribe to it a new property. 'Real' does not describe one property among others; it has not like other adjectives a predicative function. The word's peculiar semantic and logical function, and hence its meaning (but not any reference), can be defined only by indicating the conditions under which a topic can legitimately be called real. There is clearly a close connection between these conditions and the conditions under which the proposition corresponding to the topic may be called true.

This brings us to the further problem of whether there are different spheres of reality corresponding to different sets of truth-conditions and verification-procedures. I refer to the well-known and still much discussed distinction between analytic and synthetic propositions. It is usually said that the truth or falsity of analytic propositions depends immediately upon the rules of logical

---

[1] Cp. Adolf Phalén, 'Om omdömet' [On the Judgment] in *Festskrift tilägnad Hans Larsson* [*Festschrift dedicated to Hans Larsson*] (1927), pp. 159ff.

syntax, while that of synthetic propositions depends upon observation. A parallel distinction between logical-mathematical and physical reality can be made on the basis of this distinction between propositions. Physical reality may perhaps be further divided. This, at least, is the opinion of Jørgen Jørgensen, who distinguishes between everyday reality in which it is true that the grass is green and the sky is blue; objective or physical reality in which it is true that all things consist of colourless atoms; phenomenological reality in which objects change their relative position as I move among them; and the world of imagination in which it is true that Hamlet killed Polonius and Ophelia went mad.[1]

As with phrases, sentences as linguistic figures must be distinguished from their meanings. The 'meaning-content' of a sentence I shall call a *proposition* or *indicative*. As we have pointed out, the proposition differs from the phrase, in that the topic which both describe is conceived in the proposition as real. As an explication of this difference one might be tempted to say that the sentence:

'*Peter is shutting the door*'

is to be analysed into a phrase plus an expression indicating that the topic of the phrase is thought of as real:

'*(Shutting of the door by Peter now)* so it is.'[2]

But this analysis might easily lead, as it has done in the past, to the seriously mistaken view that the operator 'so it is' is to be equated with an assertion operator indicating that the proposition is accepted as true. But acceptance of a proposition as true is an act of use belonging to the pragmatic level, and has nothing to do with the task we are tackling here, which is to explain the content of the proposition, regardless of its truth.

It must be stressed that what distinguishes a proposition from an idea

---

[1] Cp. Jørgen Jørgensen, *Sandhed, Virkelighed og Fysikkens Metode* [*Truth, Reality and the Methods of Physics*] (1956), pp. 72ff.; 'Some Remarks concerning Statements, Truth-Values, and Categories of Predicates', *Logique et Analyse* 1961, pp. 125ff.—It is a mistake to say that the 'world of imagination' makes up a sphere of reality on a par with the other mentioned. The statement that Hamlet killed Polonius refers to 'everyday reality', namely to the fact that a literary, fabulating work exists, containing an episode in which a person named 'Hamlet' kills another person named 'Polonius'.

[2] Cf. Hare, *The Language of Morals* (1952), pp. 17ff.; Ingemar Hedenius 'Befalningssatser, normer och värdeutsagor' ['Commands, Norms and Value-propositions'] in *Nordisk Sommeruniversitet 1954 Verklighet och Beskrivelse* [*Nordic Summer University 1954: Reality and Description*] (1955), pp. 179–202.

(*i.e., the meaning-content of a sentence from that of a phrase*) *is a non-descriptive semantic element, the thought of reality. This factor must be distinguished both from 'nodding assent' to the sentence (or accepting the sentence: see § 6), (vid. Hare[1]) and from asserting it (see § 7).*[2] *For both these concepts denote acts, i.e. what can be done with a sentence, and are not, therefore, connected with the question of what a proposition is.*[3]

A proposition may be symbolized by the formula 'i(T)', where 'T' stands for a topic, and 'i' indicates that the topic is thought of as real.[4] What this means comes out most clearly when we merely consider a proposition without doing anything with it—that is without accepting or asserting it. *A* having made a frame with the words 'Peter is shutting the door', may sit contemplating it, considering whether he can accept it, or whether he wants to assert it, using it in a communication to *B*. In the latter case, as we have mentioned, he will have to ring a bell. In a similar way we may examine a proposition uttered by someone else without deciding on an attitude toward it and without asserting it. There is nevertheless more before our mind in this case than the thought of the topic; there is also the thought of a state of affairs, the topic as real. Imagine a detective puzzling over the solution of a crime. He may say to himself or others: 'Let us suppose that *N.N.* at time *t* in place *p* did *a* . . . etc.' He would be thinking of certain events as real without assuming or asserting them to be so. The purpose of such a procedure would be to see whether the supposed state of affairs, thought of as part of reality, hangs together with other states of affairs whose reality is taken for granted. A proposition considered in this way without being accepted or asserted is called a *hypothesis*. As is well known, such hypotheses play an important role in scientific thought.[5]

---

[1] *Op. cit.*, p. 18.

[2] Cf. Hedenius, *op. cit.*, pp. 181–2. I find the author's presentation of his ideas rather abstruse, but am inclined to believe that he in the main agrees with me.

[3] If this theorem is correct it is of far-reaching consequence as the foundation of a satisfactory analysis of the distinction between indicative and directive discourse. I return to this point below § 18, at the end.

[4] 'i' is thus not identical with the sign '⊢' commonly used as symbol of assertion.

[5] On the fabulating use of propositions see further below § 8. Gottlob Frege, who uses the term 'thought' for what I have called a 'proposition', has clearly demonstrated how 'thoughts' are used in speech-acts without any decision on their truth value, e.g. in interrogative sentences, fiction and hypothetical thinking. Frege, 'The Thought. A Logical Inquiry', *Mind*, vol. LXV (1956), pp. 289ff.; 'Negation' in *Translations from the Philosophical Writings of Gottlob Frege*, ed. by P. Geach and M. Black (1960), pp. 117ff.

In § 2, we pointed out that sentence formation is subject to the syntactical rules of the language which are of three kinds, grammatical, logical, semantical. There exists a problem about whether certain sentences which can in principle be neither verified nor falsified really do express propositions. I refer to 'metaphysical' sentences such as 'The world is governed by an invisible demon whose nature is inconceivable.' Logical positivism, as is well known, called such sentences meaningless. The terminology was unfortunate, since sentences of this kind do undoubtedly have a role in communication, and to this extent, at least, have meaning. The Vienna Circle's basic point, though, was not to define the concept of meaning, but to stamp metaphysical sentences as illegitimate in the realm of science. And this is certainly correct, since such untestable utterances cannot be included in a system of scientific propositions whose peculiar distinguishing mark is their intersubjective testability. It remains an open question whether such utterances, despite their fundamental untestability, may possess not only emotive but also descriptive meaning. I shall not discuss this problem.

§ 6

Accepting or rejecting a proposition as true or false is a soliloquistic act which has an adjudicative function.

Let us now consider what use can be made of a proposition expressed in a meaningful sentence, e.g., 'Peter is shutting the door'. (May I remind the reader that according to the plan of this book outlined in § 3 I am for the moment dealing only with indicative utterances.)

The most fundamental use, in a certain sense, to be made of a proposition is the act of deciding what attitude to adopt toward it, by either *accepting* or *rejecting* it. Accepting a proposition is the same as acknowledging it to be true; rejecting is the same as declining such acknowledgment. Acceptance is the act of establishing and expressing the mental state called *opinion, belief,* or *conviction*. The spontaneity of the act of acceptance or rejection may often make it seem that the act is caused by the belief, rather than that the belief is established by the act. In my room there are many things which I, in a sense, have become aware of and know about without having formulated and accepted propositions about them. If I were asked 'Is there a chair here?', 'Is there a painting hanging there?' I should without any hesitation accept the corresponding affirmative propositions. It may then seem misleading to say that my belief is established only when I accept the proposition. I am nevertheless inclined to hold that it is most to the point to maintain that a belief is established only when a proposition is formulated and accepted. One might add that the necessary and sufficient conditions of this act may be already present in such a way that I am *disposed* to accept without hesitation a certain proposition and to hold the corresponding opinion. In other cases the birth-pangs may be more protracted: one may hesitate, doubt, waver, and perhaps never reach a decision. As we have indicated in § 2, a proposition may have a meaning so vague that the clear cut alternative of truth or falsity does not apply. The two old aunts in the play by Gustav Wied may dispute for ever about the colour of the moon, since words like 'white' and 'yellow' possess in ordinary use no exact boundaries. Whether France is hexagonal is a question having no *true* answer. It is a fairly rough description which may be good enough for some purposes (perhaps military strategy), but not for others (e.g. geographical description). The current opinion that any proposition must be either true or false (whether we know it or not) holds only if the proposition is expressed so precisely that its testing can be carried out with unambiguous outcome. For different purposes, the sort of verification demanded is different, and consequently a proposition may be accepted in one context and rejected in another.

The acceptance of a proposition is a datable occurrence. A person X may accept the proposition p at time t_1, and reject it at time t_2. That X at time t accepts the proposition p is expressed by the formula

$$X_t \, acpt \, p = X_t \, acpt \, i(T)$$

Acceptance is an internal act. It occurs in soliloquies as the utterance to oneself, with consent, either of p, or else of a metalogical proposition about p, such as that p is true, or can be accepted. One may inform others of one's act of acceptance. The occurrence of the act of acceptance is empirically established by conventionally determined test criteria. X is counted as having accepted p if and only if he answers, within a fixed time, 'Yes' to the question whether p holds. The reliability of the answers may be tested by comparison with his other utterances and with his behaviour.[1] A proposition which is accepted is a *judgment*. It is illuminating, in the present connection, to recall the legal use of the expressions 'proposition' and 'judgment'. In some languages the word 'proposition' may denote the draft statute placed before a legislative assembly. The draft may be identical, word for word, with the stature carried, but as yet it is only a draft without 'force' as law. This force, or this integration into the system of 'the law in force' comes about only when the assembly registers a favourable attitude to the draft (proposition) by passing (accepting) it. In the same way, the proposition 'Peter is shutting the door' is only a 'draft', a proposal, a thought without 'force' or validity until I have adopted a favourable attitude toward the proposition by accepting it, and so integrating it into my system of 'valid' opinions. The word 'judgment' appropriately indicates that a decision has been made to accept or reject the 'claim' of the proposition and the term 'adjudicative' correspondingly points to the judging and appraising nature of acceptance.[2]

It is the acceptance of the proposition which Hare refers to as 'nodding assent' (though Hare speaks of 'sentences'). Hare, however, confuses the acceptance of the proposition with what is in

[1] Martin, *Toward a Systematic Pragmatics* (1959), pp. 10, 33ff.

[2] C. H. Langford and Marion Langford, 'Introduction to Logic', *Philosophy and Phenomenological Research*, 14 (1953–4), pp. 560–6, give an account of the concepts 'sentence', 'proposition' and 'judgment' that is closely related to my view. These authors, however, have not clearly realized the difference between an idea and a proposition, and this defect vitiates their analysis of a directive (see below, p. 71f.).

Jørgen Jørgensen, *Sandhed, Virkelighed og Fysikkens Metode* [*Truth, Reality and the Method of Physics*] (1956), pp. 71ff., on the other hand, seems to lack a clear understanding of the difference between a proposition and a judgment. Having discussed whether a judgment is the expression of an act of volition or a state of belief and having repudiated a definition on this basis, the author advances this definition: 'To judge is to predicate, that is to state that a certain subject matter in a more or less penetrating analysis can be shown to include or possess certain traits.' A proposition, however, is also a predication, and Jørgensen's definition therefore veils the essential feature of a judgment—unless one may interpret the term 'state' as containing an oblique reference to that believing acceptance which constitutes a judgment. That this has been Jørgensen's intended though not so clearly realized meaning is corroborated by what he writes on the next page: 'As already mentioned it would perhaps be most appropriate to define judgments as statements in which it is held or believed that something (the subject) is in such and such a way (the predicate).' The belief or acceptance that Jørgensen rejected in the first part of the passage he here expressly refers to. On the distinction between proposition and judgment, see also Jørgensen, *A Treatise of Formal Logic*, vol. III (1931), pp. 247–8, with note 13, containing references to Meinong, Mill, Russell, a.o.

fact part of its meaning, namely, its characteristic reference to reality. He speaks of the *phrastic* and the *neustic* as two parts of the sentence. The latter term is derived from a Greek verb which means 'to nod assent'. Nodding assent, though, is a non-linguistic act and not part of the meaning of the sentence. It is in fact contradictory to consider nodding assent both as a *part* of the sentence[1] (the neustic) and as an *act* performed *in relation to* the sentence. ('Nodding assent', Hare writes, 'is something that is done by anyone who uses a sentence in earnest.')[2]

Our beliefs are formed and articulated by the presentation, consideration, and acceptance or rejection of propositions in soliloquies, which is what *thinking* is. There may be a wordless thinking in pictures, but it is unquestionable that all higher thinking requires the medium of language in soliloquy and is communicable only by the use of language in dialogue. It is a popular fallacy to believe that thinking precedes linguistic expression. To think is to speak. Speech is man's most precious skill and language his most valuable instrument.

It is questionable whether it is appropriate to say that the consideration and acceptance or rejection of a proposition in soliloquy constitutes a use of the proposition. For it may be objected that the formulation of the proposition and its characterization as true or false is merely the production of the tool and discovery of its properties and not yet a use of that tool. The question is of no great importance. If by 'making use' of something we understand its being instrumental in a process aimed at the production of a desired effect, then it is correct to say that to accept a proposition is to make use of it. In considering the proposition and deciding on an attitude toward it, I engage in thinking, that is, I produce a desired effect which consists in the formulation and articulation of my beliefs, and in this process the proposition has been instrumental.

Language is used in soliloquy, then, to carry out the process called 'thinking'. The immediate effect of this process (its function) is the production of decisions or judgments, in which the claim of the proposition is either sustained or dismissed. This is the *adjudicative* function of discourse.

[1] 'I shall call . . . the part [of the sentence] that is different in the case of commands and statements ("yes" or "please") the *neustic*,' Hare, *The Language of Morals* (1952), p. 18.
[2] *Op. cit.*, p. 18.

§ 7

Asserting a proposition is an act of communication with an informative function, by virtue of the basic norm of communication.

The acceptance of a proposition is an internal act. It is distinct from the use of the proposition in communication with other members of the linguistic community. An act of communication is an external, social act whose standard objective is the production of a certain effect in the recipient; the production of this effect is its *function*. Accordingly, it is convenient to classify and describe acts of communication by their various functions.

I should like to point out, without becoming lost in the intricacies of the concept 'function', one most important aspect of that concept. The function of any tool should be determined by its *proper* effect, that is, the immediate effect to whose production the tool is directly suited. Any further intended effects in the subsequent causal chain are irrelevant. If this is not observed the peculiar features of the tool and of its use may go unmarked, and thus the concept of function will lose its point. The function of an axe is to be described in terms of its chopping function (dependent upon its edge and weight) and its hammering function (dependent upon its blunt surface and weight). It would, on the other hand, be unreasonable to talk about the 'inheritance acquiring' function of the axe because an axe may be used to kill a testator. The only connection between this effect and the axe's properties is by way of the immediate function of the axe; as an instrument of murder the axe has to be used either as a chopper or as a 'blunt instrument'. The function of language must likewise be specified in terms of the immediate effects which a linguistic instrument of a certain shape is especially suited to produce. Certain communications, for example, are suited to convey information, that is, to bring about as their immediate effect that the recipient accepts a certain proposition. This, then, is their function. It is inexpedient to specify the function of a type of utterance, and hence its classification, by the further intended effects caused by the conveyance of information. Authors often sin against this principle; Harald Ofstad, for example, defines the function of a piece of language in terms of all the effects of its utterance, and so distinguishes between its actual and its intended functions. There is, however, no set limit to the possible objectives of an utterance; it would seem, therefore, arbitrary to enumerate, as Ofstad does, a number of specific functions. In this way the essential distinctions become blurred. The utterance 'The house is burning!', says Ofstad, may have the intended function of getting people to run for water, and the actual function of making the hearers laugh. And 'Now the lemons are in bloom in Italy' may be used by a travel agency with the evaluative function of getting people to go to Italy. But why pick out exactly these, or other, functional effects? According to Ofstad's way of explaining the concept 'function', it would be easier to rule that any utterance may, according to the circumstances, have any function, intended or actual. But this abstract triviality does not illuminate what happens in communication. On the other hand, it *is* illuminating to say that the utterances 'The house is burning' and 'Now the lemons are in bloom in Italy' are specifically suited to convey information, and under standard conditions always do so. Further intended effects—to make people run for water or travel to Italy—are conditional upon and mediated by this fundamental and specific function of conveying information. This is the essential point; it should not be blurred by assigning to such utterances a hundred and seventeen, or indeed an unlimited number of, functions.[1]

A similar objection may be raised against Karl Bühler's doctrine that any utterance has a triple function as *symbol, symptom* and *signal*.[2] If *A* tells *B* that it is raining, it is said that this utterance has first the function of referring to or symbolizing a certain state of affairs. Secondly, the utterance is a symptom which expresses, to a greater or lesser degree according to the circumstances, a certain mental state of *A* which causes him to make the utterance (e.g. his depression at its continuing to rain). Finally, the utterance functions as a signal through its power to influence the actions of *B*; it may, for example, induce *B* to carry an umbrella.

To place these three functions on an equal footing blurs the essential fact, namely, that 'It is raining' has primarily and immediately an informative function; it functions as a symbol. Its two other functions are derived from and subsidiary to this, since both are brought about as a result of the conveyance of this information. Furthermore, such an analysis blurs the essential

---

[1] Harald Ofstad, *Innföring i Moralfilosofi* [*Introduction to Moral Philosophy*], vol. I (1964), pp. 74, 85, cf. pp. 41–42.
[2] Karl Bühler, *Sprachtheorie* (1934), p. 28.

distinction between informative utterances and utterances whose exclusive function is to express a mental state or to direct action.

I for my part shall classify the use to be made of a proposition in communication according to whether the appropriate effect in the recipient depends upon the proposition's being true or false. The use of the proposition which depends on this property—in the way that an axe's being used for chopping depends on its edge—is called its *assertion*. The relevant function is the *conveyance of information* (the *informative function*), that is to induce the recipient to accept the asserted proposition. Such a use of the proposition is an *assertion* or *statement*.

The informative process is a technique which enables us, by manipulating a certain instrument (discourse directed at other people) to produce a specific effect (their being informed). Our task is to explain how this is possible.

It is often difficult to see what is problematic in an everyday occurrence. There seems to be nothing puzzling, to be no challenge to the understanding, in the conveyance of information which occurs when the housemaid tells me that dinner is served or that Peter has shut the door. Further reflection, nevertheless, will show that the case is not so simple. Let me once more make use of the parable about the mutes at the letter table. Suppose that *A* has filled in a frame with the words 'Peter is shutting the door', and shows it to *B*. What facts are now before *B*, and how can they conceivably influence his thinking? The facts seem to amount, on the face of it, to nothing more than that *A* has been able to fashion correctly, according to syntactic rules of language, a frame with certain contents, and for some reason has wanted to show it to *B*. Why does not *B* react simply by patting *A* on the cheek and thinking 'Well done, my little friend!'?

If *A*'s intention amounts to nothing more than a desire to demonstrate his ability to produce a sentence, then *B* certainly has no reason to believe what is said, just as a teacher of foreign languages has no reason to believe what his students say when demonstrating their fluency. To make it possible to distinguish such situations from situations which do involve an intention to convey information, I have postulated that this intention is indicated in the parable by ringing a bell. The question is: Why does this make a difference? What factors, indicated by ringing the bell, are added to the simple demonstration of linguistic ability so that it becomes understandable that the communication is able to arouse in B the belief that Peter is shutting the door?

The answer to the problem is that circumstances must be such that B is brought to believe that A is trustworthy in two ways: (1) that A himself believes what he says, (subjective trustworthiness), and (2) that A is to some extent well informed about the matter (objective trustworthiness).

To the extent that B has reason to believe that these two conditions are satisfied he is willing to accept the proposition which A presents to him. The message will be accepted automatically if B's belief in A's trustworthiness is well established through personal knowledge of A. Such is the case when, for example, my wife announces to me that dinner is served. I have no reason to believe that she is lying or is uninformed about the matter. The situation is different when one or both of the conditions fail. When the accused in a trial pleads not guilty, we question not his objective, but his subjective, trustworthiness. The opposite holds when a Jehovah's Witness tells me about the imminent end of the world.

The communication will be successful if B believes that the two conditions are satisfied, whether or not they actually are. If they are not, the communication is false. If A is speaking in bad faith, the communication is a lie.

The question now arises how it is possible for B to form any idea of the trustworthiness of A. His position differs with regard to the two types of trustworthiness.

Whether A is to some extent informed about the subject-matter of his communication is estimated by standards appropriate to the individual case. We continually receive communications—instructions, news bulletins, advertisements, educational information, friendly gossip—and spontaneously take into account the competence of the sender, whether he is a well qualified expert, a skilled observer, a man of education and judgment, or whether he lacks the qualities necessary for forming a well-founded opinion on the matter at hand (consider, e.g., the layman's report on wonder treatments or supernatural experiences). Requirements for competence vary, of course, with the communication. Those concerning everyday conditions within the experience of the speaker will usually be accepted without question. The requirements become more exacting in proportion as the communication concerns matters which are beyond the scope of the ordinary man's judgment.

Regarding subjective reliability, on the other hand, we seem in most cases to possess no criterion to guide our judgment. If we have no private knowledge of the speaker's qualities and if the circumstances do not indicate that he has a special interest in telling or concealing the truth, how is the hearer able to form any opinion whether the speaker is to be trusted or not? What justifies the ordinary belief that, say, a stranger will tell me the correct time and not give me an answer at random? There is a problem here, for it *must* be the case that people generally trust the veracity of others. If this trust did not exist or were not justified, no communication would be possible. For if people did not in general speak the truth, but selected their communications according to other standards—say, the euphony of the sentence used—there would be no reason for believing communications. There would in consequence be no purpose in attempting to give information and the practice of informative communication would cease—indeed, it would never have arisen. Consequently we have to admit that neither personal knowledge of the speaker's veracity nor circumstantial evidence of his interest in telling the truth constitute ultimate reasons for believing a message. Ultimately any willingness to communicate the truth presupposes a general attitude of willingness to believe the message, and this attitude, again, is possible only on the condition that people in general do speak the truth. The point is that even lying, the misleading of people through false information, is possible only on the same condition. Lies exist only as parasites on truth; they are conceivable only as exceptions which depend on the norm they violate.

Since communication does take place, therefore, we are justified in concluding that people do in general speak the truth, unless special interests motivate them to act otherwise. Lying and telling the truth are not alternatives on an equal footing. Truthfulness must be the rule. The question, however, is, Why?

One may be tempted to answer this question by saying that people are educated to regard lying as morally wrong. But this is not an adequate explanation. For lying is a misuse of the institution of communication, and, as we have seen, depends on the generally successful functioning of the institution. The prohibition against lying cannot then be the foundation upon which the institution is built. Lying is like cheating at poker, which is possible only because of the existence of rules which define the normal play of the game. To cheat in any game is to make a 'move' which violates the constitutive rules of the game, with the intention that the other players, unaware of the violation, should take it as a regular move. The prohibition against cheating at poker, therefore, is identical with the prohibition against (surreptitiously) breaking the rules of poker, and this is the same as the prescription to play according to these rules. It is evident, consequently, that the prohibition against cheating cannot be the rule which constitutes poker, since it, on the contrary, presupposes by its very nature a constitutive rule or body of rules.[1]

Analogous remarks apply to the institution or 'game' of communication. The game must be constituted by a basic norm or body of norms which are more fundamental than the moral rule against lying, that is, against the misuse of the institution and violation of its constitutive norms.

The basic norm cannot itself be a prohibition against lying since lying is not possible as long as the basic norm is not established and the institution of giving information not functioning. As long as this is not the case, the opposite of telling the truth would not be lying, but what we may call, to coin a word, *fabulation*, that is the mere presentation of propositions without making any truth-claim. The basic norm, therefore, is a prohibition against fabulating or, to put it affirmatively, a demand that propositions should be used in communications only *qua* bearers of a truth-value and that, consequently, any communication should be taken to imply a truth-claim. Only when this norm has been commonly accepted is it possible to lie, that is to 'cheat' or mislead by saying something which is not true. During the time when children are not completely familiar with the institution of communication their not telling the truth is fabulation, not lying. Adults fabulate also, in fiction and in scientific hypotheses.

The fundamental conventional norm which rules out fabulation is not absolute. Fabulation is permitted on the condition that the speaker indicates explicitly or implicitly that he is fabulating. In

[1] For this reason I cannot agree with Isabel C. Hungerland, who regards the fundamental norms of communications as culture-bound and maintains the possibility of a culture in which saying what one doesn't believe (with intent to deceive) is taken as a normal, proper or right linguistic act for most people. 'Contextual Implication', *Inquiry*, 1960, pp. 211ff., 236-7.

the parable we supposed that there was a convention that the sender indicated his intention to inform by ringing a bell. In normal communication the case is exactly opposite; intention to assert the proposition, or make a statement, and to convey information is presumed. If the communication is not meant in this way, the speaker must indicate so. This indication may, however, arise from the situation itself. If the situation is not, according to convention, a 'stating situation' the presumption that the communication is intended as an assertion is weakened. A stating situation is created when, for example, B puts a question to A in such a way that it is evident that the question is meant seriously and not rhetorically. The examination of witnesses in court is an obvious case of serious intent. Similarly with an academic examination, but in an indirect way. When he asks 'When did Napoleon die?' the examiner wants information, not about Napoleon, but about what the student knows. Stating situations are created whenever people meet to receive information on educational, political or other matters, or for discussion. Information may be offered without any kind of request or expectation on the part of the recipient, when, for example, people are on 'speaking terms', and it is conventionally considered appropriate, or even obligatory, to talk and discuss (e.g., in family circles and social gatherings). On the other hand, when unrequested information is offered outside such conventionally defined stating situations, the utterance may seem odd, and it will depend on the circumstances whether it is to be taken as a statement or as a fabulation. If a stranger in the street tells me that Napoleon died in 1821 or that the whale is not a fish, I will certainly be perplexed and inclined to believe that the man is intoxicated and fabulating. Normal conventional barriers are, however, broken down if the speaker appears to believe that the addressee of his utterance has a great interest in certain information. Statements by a stranger that my house is on fire, or that my children have fallen through the ice, or that my soul is lost if I am not converted, are normally taken as seriously meant.[1]

An utterance of p is presumed to be an assertion of p. Let us review the cases in which this presumption does not hold. First of all, it does not hold when the proposition is used with a fabulating, and not an informative, function. The speaker, as we have

[1] On the criteria for a stating situation, see Hungerland, *op. cit.*, p. 224; Gerard A. Radnitzky, 'Performatives and Descriptions', *Inquiry*, 1962, pp. 12ff., 25ff.

said, is conventionally obliged to indicate non-seriousness, and is liable if he does not. Fabulating speech will be analysed below in § 8. Secondly, a proposition is not asserted when its use is not a piece of communication at all—when, for example, a telephone technician tests a connection, or a person with a speech defect performs therapeutic exercises. Finally, p is not asserted when it is mentioned. Like axes, houses and prime numbers propositions can be mentioned without being used. In this book I have mentioned the proposition 'Peter is shutting the door' many times—in this sentence itself, for example—but without ever using it. Vocabularies and grammars contain statements which mention propositions, e.g., the statement that the English sentence 'he is ill' should be translated in German as 'er ist krank'.

Utterances which have no statement-making or informative function are not to be confused, as is sometimes done,[1] with utterances which are statements but whose meaning, because of special circumstances, differs from the standard meaning of such utterances. Such is the case when, for example, an ironic tone of voice or winking of the eye, or the like indicates, that what is said is not to be taken in the usual way. When someone says ironically 'How ladylike she is!', he is making a statement to the effect that the lady is not ladylike.

Making a statement or asserting a proposition is, as we have said, a speech-act governed by a social norm. The norm does not *oblige* anyone to make a statement. It does oblige whoever issues a communication to say only what he believes to be the truth, unless he expressly or implicitly warns the recipient that his communication is not meant as a statement, as an author does when he calls his book a novel and on the back of the title-page tells the reader that the book is a work of fiction and that any seeming resemblance to real persons is purely coincidental. The purport of the norm is that in making a statement the speaker undertakes responsibility for his own good faith. When A asserts p he is taken to have asserted at the same time A *acpt* p and to be responsible for the truth of this last assertion. This means that if A lies and is detected he will be held responsible by the persons affected. He will be branded as a liar. The social reaction of disapproval will vary according to the consequences of his lying. It has been pointed out that there are degrees of acceptance; and in the same way a

[1] E.g., in Hungerland, *op. cit.*, p. 224.

speaker can give to his statement guarantees of varying strength. His guarantee is of the highest degree if he says that he *knows* the truth of what he is saying. If he makes reservations which indicate that he feels some doubt about the validity of the proposition, his guarantee is qualified. Consider, e.g., 'I am inclined to believe', 'I consider it probable' and similar clauses.

Because a statement creates expectations, or claims and corresponding responsibilities, it belongs to the group of linguistic acts which have been called *performative*. If this concept is to be of philosophical and not only linguistic interest, it should in my opinion be limited to the designation of locutionary acts which by virtue of a social norm create social relations of claims, obligations and responsibilities determined in accordance with the meaning content of the act.[1]

On the basis of the preceding analysis we are able, I believe, to give a better explanation than the current one of a logical problem discussed by Nowell-Smith and others under the labels 'contextual implication' and 'logical oddness'.

Suppose that *A* says 'It is raining, but I don't believe that it is.' There seems to be something wrong with such a statement. There is no logical contradiction, however, between the two connected propositions:

(1) *It is raining*, and
(2) *A does not believe that it is raining.*

Nowell-Smith analyses the statement by introducing the notion 'contextual implication' which he defines in this way: 'I shall say that a statement *p* contextually implies a statement *q* if anyone who knew the normal conventions of the language would be entitled to infer *q* from *p* in the context in which they occur.' On this principle, if *A* makes the statement that it is raining, the rest of us are entitled to infer that *A* believes it to be so. It is 'logically odd', therefore, if *A* at the same time asserts that it is raining, and that he does not believe that it is so.[2]

What Nowell-Smith has done, in my view, is to christen the phenomenon rather than explain it. Several questions arise to which he has given no answer. What sustains the inference from the fact that *A* says that it is raining to the conclusion that he believes that it is? What does it mean to say that we are 'entitled'

---

[1] On the concept of competence, see my *On Law and Justice*, pp. 202, 281ff.
[2] Nowell-Smith, *Ethics* (1954), pp. 80–81.

to make the inference even if in fact it proves not to hold? If A actually does not believe what he himself says (if, that is, he is lying), why then is it logically odd if he truthfully states this fact? The statement contradicts no other statement made by him, but only the inference we have incorrectly made.

The reason why Nowell-Smith's analysis is unsatisfactory is that it remains on the semantic level, operating with concepts like 'implication', 'inference', and 'contradiction'. A satisfactory analysis is possible only when the pragmatic aspects of the utterance are taken into account, when, that is, the utterance 'It is raining but I don't believe that it is' is considered not only according to its *meaning*, but as a *pragmatic speech-act* undertaken, as other human acts are, with a certain end in view.

We have shown that false as well as true communication is possible only on the basis of an effective social norm which imposes anyone who makes a statement or obligation to speak truthfully.[1] In virtue of this norm a statement made by A will produce in others the belief that A himself believes what he is saying, unless there are special reasons to suspect that he is lying. This belief is a necessary condition of achieving the aim of communication, viz. the giving of information. If B does not believe that A believes what he is saying, there is no reason why B should believe what A is telling him. If, then, A while telling B that it is raining, adds that he himself does not believe that it is (that, in fact, he is lying), he has destroyed by this second statement the mediate effect which was a necessary condition for the first statement achieving its aim—to be believed. Lying, like cheating in a game, is an act which can be undertaken only if concealed, only if, that is, the other party (in the communication or game) does not know about it. Cheating (or lying) involves getting the other party to accept a false move as if it were correct. To cheat (or lie) and at the same time to disclose this fact is a practical impossibility. In trying to do so, A would resemble a man building a house with one hand while tearing it down with the other, or a man who said 'There is one thing I want to keep secret from you and that is . . .'.

[1] It follows that I agree with Hungerland, *op. cit.*, pp. 224ff., 255, in the view that contextual implication is based on presumptions which are not inductively established but which function as principles of communication; and also in the view that the 'presumption of normality' is warranted only in a stating situation. Above at p. 24, note 1, I have argued that it is a mistake to regard the principles of communication as culture-bound.

No contradiction is involved, for contradiction is a relation that holds between the *meanings* of two sentences. What we are confronted with is a *teleological conflict between two acts*; the one act destroys the *telos* (goal) of the other act. To call it 'logically odd' to say at the same time that it is raining and that one does not believe that it is, is to say no more than that such behaviour is in some way puzzling or amazing—it does not explain why. What is puzzling is that the behaviour is quite futile—at any rate in so far as the speaker purports to be communicating and not, say, trying to be funny. I should prefer in such cases to speak of *pragmatic absurdity*.

§ 8

'Posing' a proposition is a speech-act which has a fabulating function.

There is a certain pragmatic use of a proposition which is not dependent on its being true or false, but only on its having meaning. Such a use may be called the *posing* of the proposition. May I remind the reader that the meaning of the proposition is such that it describes a state of affairs, that is, a topic thought of as real (see above § 5). The posed proposition is called either a *fiction*, or a *hypothesis*, the corresponding function of speech its *fabulating* function.

Fabulating speech includes every kind of fiction—novels, poems, dramatic performances, recitations, singing, the telling of anecdotes and stories etc.—as well as scientific and technical hypotheses.

The novel—to take a clear example—relates events that have happened to named persons at particular times and places—e.g., to Mr. James Smith in London in 1940. The propositions which make up the novel might have been true; but (and this is the peculiar feature of the novel) the author does not assert these propositions; he merely poses them. It clearly appears from the context that the author's intention is not to provide information about what is the case. The truth-value of what he says in the novel is immaterial; it will most often be false. His aim is not to record and report facts but to get the reader to imagine the described events and circumstances as though they were real. It is as if the novelist were to write 'Suppose that (   )', with the brackets surrounding the whole novel.

29

Though the truth-value of propositions in fabulating speech is immaterial, these propositions must, nevertheless, like all others be true or false. An historical novel will usually contain some true propositions. Novels about imaginary persons and happenings will contain only false ones. It is, say, not true that a Mr. James Smith committed murder in London in 1940.

Anecdotes are peculiar in this respect. While a story or joke about Kruschev may be completely and unquestionably fictitious, an anecdote purports to have some truth at its roots. The usual formula is something like 'It is said that . . .'. The anecdote refers back to some report which had the character of a statement, but at the same time it is understood that the narrator in no way guarantees the truth of the story. Its meaning and point lie not in its historical but in its poetic truth—the light it throws on its subject.

I shall not discuss the purpose and meaning of fabulating discourse in art, except to stress that even if its aim were to reveal a 'poetic truth' about man and his destiny, this 'truth' has nothing to do with truth in the ordinary sense. The truth-value of propositions in fiction remains irrelevant to their purpose.

The case is however different with fabulating discourse in science—i.e., with scientific hypotheses. It is true that here too propositions are posed and not asserted. But here, in posing a proposition, we do not imply that its truth-value is of no consequence, but only that it is unknown. The proposition is posed as a step in the process of advancing to the determination of its truth-value—i.e., the decision whether it shall be raised to the status of a confirmed theory or rejected as falsified. This sort of fabulation aims, then, at ceasing to be mere fabulation. The same is the case with technical or practical fabrication, e.g., the hypotheses which a detective constructs while trying to solve a mystery.

It is well known that hypotheses play an important role in scientific thought. The opinion has often been held, especially by Vaihinger in his *Philosophie des Als-ob* (*The Philosophy of As-If*), that fictions too play such a role. Fictions are also widely considered to have played and to play even now an important part in the evolution of law, both in legislation and in the practice of the courts. These views are erroneous, in my opinion, and are based upon an untenable conception of what a fiction is.

A fiction is commonly defined as a consciously false assumption.

30

What, though, is an *assumption*? If it is supposed to be a proposition which has been accepted, then its definition is a *contradictio in adjecto*. It implies that the same person at the same time believes the same proposition to be both true and false. If 'assumption' is taken to mean the same as 'assertion', and if awareness of the proposition's falsity is concealed by the speaker, a fiction seems identical with a lie. This, obviously, is not what is meant. The only remaining possibility would seem to be that a fiction is a proposition which is both asserted and accompanied by an indication that the speaker does not believe it to be true. That is, a fiction would be a statement of the kind 'It is raining but I don't believe that it is'. Utterances of this kind, as we have seen in § 7, are pragmatic absurdities, and we can reject out of hand the notion that they have an important role in scientific thought.

I cannot now consider in detail the fallacies of the *As-If* philosophy. But a few words may be said about the assumed use of fictions in legal practice. What has made people speak of legal 'fictions' is the fact that artificial devices are sometimes used in the drafting of statutes and in court decisions. A statute, for example, may say that movable oil tanks shall for some purposes be considered real property, or that women shall in certain connections be considered as men. This is a matter of expediency in drafting and involves no false statements. What is said is simply that in some circumstances movable oil tanks are to be treated according to the laws that apply to real property, and that women are for some purposes to be treated according to the laws that apply to men. The device conveniently avoids an otherwise necessary enumeration of laws. There is no reason to speak of false assumptions, or of anything fictitious. It makes no difference if such a ruling is expressed in the form of an assertion, as when in older Roman law it was said that 'the wife is her husband's daughter'.

Similar remarks apply to the use of the same device which is made in judicial decisions with the aim of adapting the law to changing social conditions. This has been the case especially in England.[1] For instance, some privileges which applied originally to the clergy alone have been extended to others on the ground that they should be considered as clergymen. In another instance, British criminal jurisdiction has been taken to include some acts committed outside British territory, on the grounds that the

[1] Lon L. Fuller, 'Legal Fictions', 25 *Ill. L.R.* (1930), pp. 363, 513ff., and pp. 877ff.

delinquent, while physically absent, has been deemed 'constructively present', if the immediate effects of his action took place within British territory. These cases, likewise, involve no false assertions; it is laid down merely, that lay persons are at times to be treated according to rules which have hitherto applied only to clergy, and that persons outside British territory shall in some circumstances be held responsible in the same way as those inside the territory.

The behaviour of judges, on the other hand, when this technique is used, may be said to imply a fiction, in the sense of a statement known by the speaker to be untrue, but which is not a lie. It is a time-honoured convention that the sole task of the judge is to apply an existing law, and not to create new law by adapting it to changed conditions. But anyone with some knowledge of the actual functioning of the courts, especially judges themselves, must know that the courts do play a part in changing the law. This is especially so in countries like England where legislation has traditionally played a modest role in the evolution of law. Nevertheless, the judges never openly admit that the convention is broken. When a new law is in fact created by the judge, he *pretends in his acts* (in his verbal acts, i.e., by using the legal device in question) that the law is unchanged. He merely extends the word 'clergy' to cover some lay persons, and the term 'territorial presence' to cover some cases where the crime was committed outside the territory. The judge makes believe that he is not changing the law, though in fact he is and knows that he is. He pretends that his actions accord with the official convention that his task is merely to apply the existing law; but all the same he and the rest of us know that this is not true. The fiction, then, lies not in the judge's judicial reasoning—that lay persons are to be considered clergy—but in the assertion implied by his actions, namely, that the judge does not change the law.

Such *make-belief actions* (which are, of course, not the same as false *statements*) are in social life quite common. I will merely call attention to this fact without explaining it. The most obvious examples are those which follow unintentional violations of social taboos. If a gentleman happens to witness a lady relieving herself in the woods, both parties, while aware of what has happened, will completely ignore it and in their subsequent behaviour pretend that nothing has happened. In our social dealings we consistently behave in ways which express or presuppose deceptive pictures of the world. In polite society we display toward others a respect and benevolence which everyone knows cannot be taken at face value. We often avoid calling things by their real names, and we spare the feelings of ourselves and others by pretending that what we well know to be the case is not so.

Behaviour of this kind does, then, imply what may be called a fiction, that is, a consciously unreliable statement which is not a lie since conventionally it is not to be taken at face value. But a fiction taken in this sense cannot be assimilated to the formula 'It is raining but I don't believe that it is', which is, to repeat, a pragmatic absurdity. The difference between a fiction and a lie is not that in the former the untruth of the statement is disclosed. For this would deny the fiction its social function, which is to keep up appearances. On the face of it, the implied statement is presented in the same way as any other statement. The distinguishing mark of the fiction appears to me to be that in these situations the basic norm of communication does not apply. Convention allows these statements to be uttered without any belief in their truth. They may be true and they may not; they cannot be used, consequently, either to evoke belief or to deceive. It is more to the point to call them *unreliable* rather than false. Whether they are true or false is left open; but we go on behaving and speaking as if they were true. When a letter is signed 'sincerely yours', 'your obedient servant', or when even more excessive phrases are used to express the writer's affection and respect, nobody acquainted with the ruling conventions would rely on their truth-value and feel deceived if there should prove to be little behind the fine-sounding words. They are not lies because they are not expected to convey information. They cannot be regarded as counterfeit coins because they are not circulated as good currency. Why people go on this way is a social-psychological question falling outside my field of investigation.

III

DIRECTIVE SPEECH

§ 9

A sentence in directive speech is a linguistic form which expresses a directive, that is, an action-idea conceived as a pattern of behaviour.

Consider an utterance addressed by A to Peter:

(1) 'Peter, shut the door',

and compare it with the utterance

(2) 'Peter is shutting the door'.

(1) is a straightforward example of utterances usually called 'prescriptive' or, in my terminology, 'directive'. In what way does (1) differ from (2)?

In § 5 we saw that the utterance (2) may be analysed semantically as a description of a state of affairs, that is, an expression of a topic conceived as real. It may be transcribed as:

(3) ('Shutting of the door by Peter) so it is.'

The bracketed expression is a phrase which describes a topic; the operator signifies that the topic is thought of as real. It is obvious that the directive utterance (1) likewise contains reference to the topic described by the phrase 'shutting of the door by Peter'. The difference between (1) and (2) must then lie in the operator; in (1) the topic is not thought of as real. Another operator seems to be called for:

(4) '(Shutting of the door by Peter) so it ought to be.'

A natural development of this approach would be to say that just as the meaning content of (2) is a *proposition* which may be symbolized 'i(T)' so the meaning content of (1) is a *direcitve* properly symbolized 'd(T)', where 'd' stands for the specific directive element 'so it ought to be'.

34

There may, though, be some danger of confusion in this manner of speaking if some fallacies are not expressly guarded against. Understanding what is meant when we say that in a proposition the topic is conceived as real presents no difficulty; for the thought of something as real corresponds to the thought of a proposition as *true*. Even if a distinction is required among the separate spheres of reality which correspond to different verification procedures, we can easily abstract from the proposition the reference to reality as the meaning component that is decisive when we make up our mind whether to accept the proposition as true or reject it as false. For my part, I find it impossible to understand, correspondingly, what it means to say, not that the topic is real, but that it ought to be real and that it has therefore a peculiar relation to reality. It is an empirical fact, however, that directive utterances are used to influence behaviour and that they succeed in this to a great extent without any mediate passing of information. (While the statement 'Your children have fallen through the ice' may influence behaviour it does so mediately by giving information.) I shall subsequently return to the question of the motivational mechanism by which A's utterance releases a behavioural response in B. What I shall try to show is that in all cases the effective motivating force lies not in the utterance itself, but in the circumstances in which the directive is uttered. The linguistic expression does no more than describe a topic, here a certain type of behaviour; or we might say that it presents an *action-idea* to the hearer. The situation will provide the impetus to act according to the action-idea; this will vary with the type of directive, whether it be a command, a request, a piece of advice, an exhortation, a rule of a game, or a legal rule. No common meaning element can be found in this multitude of directives to which the operator 'd' in the formula 'd(T)' refers, corresponding to the reference to reality in the indicative utterance.

If the formula 'd(T)' is used, then, parallel to the formula 'i(T)', it must be stressed that the operator 'd' ('so it ought to be') does not express a semantic element common to all directives. Its function is to indicate that the action-idea which is the topic is presented as a pattern of behaviour, and not that it is thought of as real. The action-idea has no motivating force of its own, but if B is motivated to do what A says, the action idea tells him *how* to act. One can turn the steering wheel of a car and not go anywhere.

When the motor is running and the clutch put in, however, the turning of the wheel will determine the direction in which the car goes. In a similar way, the words of a statute are in themselves without any motivating force; exactly the same words in an un-passed draft are without any effect. It is only when the words occur in such a way that they make use of law-abiding citizens' allegiance to the constitution, and constitutionally-voted laws, that they determine our actual direction.

The directive, like the indicative, must be distinguished, as meaning content, from the linguistic form which expresses it. Different linguistic forms may express the same directive, and *vice versa*. Certain linguistic forms are, however, especially suited to the expression of directives. Such is the case, most obviously, with sentences in the *imperative mood* ('Peter, shut the door'). Other types of sentence contain words—verbs, nouns, and adjectives— which have specifically directive meaning, and which we shall call *deontic expressions*. Examples are: the verb expressions 'ought to', 'have to', 'must', 'are obliged to', 'are bound to', 'owe', 'are forbidden to', 'are permitted to', 'have a right to', the nouns 'duty', 'right', 'claim', etc. No purpose is served by attempting to compile an exhaustive list; for although these expressions are especially loaded with directive meaning, there is no necessary connection between expression and function. On the one hand, they may occur in utterances with indicative meaning; on the other hand directives may easily be expressed in sentences that neither are in the imperative mood nor contain deontic terms.

The first possibility is presented in propositions which describe normative states of affairs. Sentences in legal theory which state what is actually the law are of this kind. The following sentence might occur in a legal treatise:

> Apart from warranty, a person selling goods he knows to be dangerous, in cases where the buyer would presumably be ignorant of the danger, is under a duty to warn the buyer that special care is necessary . . .[1]

This is not a directive, but a statement to the effect that the corresponding directive is part of English law. It will often depend on context whether an utterance which contains a deontic expression is meant as an indicative or as a directive. A policeman may

[1] *Stevens's Elements of Mercantile Law* (11 ed., 1950), p. 286.

say 'Parking is forbidden here'; this must be taken as a directive. The policeman is not stating the fact that the norm exists, but applying the norm by directing one to remove his car. If, on the other hand, one is visiting a friend, and he utters the same words, they will be taken as information to the effect that police regulations prohibit parking in this place. One may answer the friend: 'Well, never mind' but this kind of answer will be out of place if given to a policeman. The policeman is not giving information about the existence of a certain regulation but is bringing it to bear on the offender, cp. below § 12.[1]

Legal language also affords examples of directives which are expressed neither in the imperative mood nor in sentences containing deontic expressions. The Danish criminal code says that whoever kills another man is imprisoned for five years to life; and the constitution states that the King orders the promulgation and execution of statutes. If said in an appropriate tone of voice, the utterance 'You will shut the door now' expresses a directive, not an indicative.

We have given as an example of a directive the utterance, among others, 'Peter, shut the door'; we have, though, not examined the limits of the scope of the concept 'directive'. This question is especially important in relation to value-judgments, that is, utterances in which something—love, democracy, liberty, the fulfilment of needs—is called good or valuable. Such utterances resemble directives in that they are not primarily statements (which give information) but directly aim at directing action. That something is good or valuable implies that it would be good or valuable for it to exist or to be brought into existence. If liberty is of value, then it is good if liberty is achieved in the life of a community. This again implies an incitement to act in such a way that the existence of liberty is safeguarded. Value-judgments differ, however, from directives in that they present no definite pattern of behaviour. For while value-judgments express *pro* and *contra* attitudes which may urge the furthering of some ends, they express no decision on the means to these ends, nor are they able to balance against each other ends which are in conflict. Nothing is the only

---

[1] This distinction is related to that made by H. L. A. Hart between the external and the internal aspects of rules and the corresponding distinction between external and internal assertions concerning rules, see *Concept of Law* (1961), pp. vii, 55, 86–87, 99, 106, 143, 197.

thing of value in the world. That liberty is of value does not mean that one ought to achieve it at all cost. Directives describe a pattern of behaviour (e.g., 'shutting of the door by Peter'). Value-judgments describe some goal (e.g., the realization of liberty in the life of a community) which in integration with other goal-determinants should guide our actions. This difference between directives and value-judgments has, I feel, consequences in their respective logics. I have therefore decided to exclude value-judgments from the scope of this enquiry.[1]

§ 10

The class of directives called 'personal' includes as a subclass 'speaker-interested' directives, which include (1) sanctioned commands and invitations, (2) authoritative commands and invitations, and (3) sympathy-conditioned requests.

The mark of the directive is that it describes a pattern of behaviour and, in appropriate circumstances, evokes in the person to whom the directive is addressed the response of carrying out this pattern. In this section we shall attempt to explain how this is possible; and we shall, accordingly, distinguish among different types of directives in so far as they correspond to differences in situation and motivation. Though a systematic and exhaustive classification is hardly possible, I have attempted to arrange types of directive in some sort of order within a conceptual framework.

A *personal* directive has a clearly defined sender and recipient, for example, John's command to Peter to shut the door. In what follows, let us call the sender (speaker) A and the recipient (hearer) B. Personal directives have three subclasses: *speaker-interested*, *hearer-interested*, and *disinterested* directives. The first of these include those directives whose aim is that B undertake a particular act which is in A's interest; directives falling in the second class aim to produce actions which it is in B's interest to perform; and those in the third actions which are not specifically in the interest of either party. Here I shall discuss speaker-interested directives.

An 'interested' act is one whose effect, if successful, is to satisfy the agent. Felt needs are rooted in biological mechanisms of self-

[1] On the distinction between evaluative and prescriptive (directive) uses of 'ought' see e.g. Ruth Barcan Marcus in *Mind*, vol. LXXV (1966), p. 581, with reference to Paul W. Taylor, *Normative Discourse* (1961).

regulation (needs in the biological sense). An interested act is not necessarily selfish, for among human needs is the need of helping others. 'Disinterested' acts are those whose intended effects do not satisfy needs of the agent; they spring, rather, from imperative impulses whose motivation is completely independent of the satisfaction of needs. Instances include acts induced by hypnotism or suggestion, and acts undertaken out of a sense of duty.

There are those, I know, who would like to define the concept 'need' so comprehensively that it becomes a tautology to say that a human act springs from a need or aims at the satisfaction of a need. This is a difference of terminology which should not be allowed to obscure the fact that there does exist an essential difference between what I have called interested and disinterested acts. For a further discussion of this distinction I take the liberty of referring the reader to my book *On Law and Justice*, sections 84 and 85.

Speaker-interested directives, as we have said, aim at the production of an act which *A* wants *B* to perform because it is in *A*'s interest that he do so. The following further distinctions within this type of act may be made on the basis of what particular motivating force in *B* the directive appeals to.

(1) *Sanctioned directives*

A directive is sanctioned if it is obvious from the context of the directive (including what *A* might say) that *A* intends to and is able to respond to *B*'s actions in such a way that (a) if *B* does not comply with the directive he will be punished by pain, losses, or frustration, or (b) if *B* does comply with the directive he will be rewarded, that is, conditions will be made more agreeable for him than they otherwise would have been. If *B* believes that the situation is of this kind, then there has been produced in him a motivation to comply with the directive, which is in that case said to be *effective*. This does not mean that *B* will actually comply with the directive, since this motivation may be outweighed by others.

Punishment and reward, the levers through which sanctioned directives operate, will be called collectively *sanctions*. According to the circumstances and the particular sanctions applied directives will be produced, experienced and labelled in different ways.

If the punishment is severe and the resulting motivation is

opposed by other strong motives, interested or disinterested, the directive will be experienced as a *coercive (or compulsory) order or command*, and compliance with it as coerced or compelled. A typical case is a gangster's holding up the personnel of a bank; or a member of the resistance being tortured to make him reveal secrets. Such situations are characterized by the extreme severity of the punishment and its illegality. It is only a difference of degree if the punishment is less severe or not illegal. Similarly, a man who is forced to act in a way he considers detestable and immoral under the threat of legal prosecution will feel that he acts under compulsion. Hitler's Germany provides obvious examples. In more normal circumstances, however, a legally sanctioned directive will be felt to be a *valid* claim, which is to be complied with not for fear of punishment (or at any rate not exclusively so) but from a disinterested sense of duty or respect for law and order. Such a situation will not be thought to be coercive—for example, A's suing B for payment of debt. If B recognizes the claim's justice, he will not regard his payment as coerced, whatever his dislike of parting with the money. He will, however, experience coercion if he considers the claim unjustified but knows that A's suit all the same will be successful as a result of misleading evidence.

A's directives to B may be backed by power of many different kinds. Apart from the already discussed cases of coercion both legal and illegal, penalties for non-compliance with directives will almost always be non-violent, since our laws do not tolerate the use of violence by private persons. Even so they may still be so severe that they are felt to be coercive. Such punishment will often take the form of the omission of favours ordinarily granted. Parents, for example, may compel their children by threatening to withdraw allowances. One party in a labour dispute may attempt coercion by refusing his cooperation (as in a lockout or strike). Rivals and customers may coerce a firm by a boycott—i.e. by withdrawing from normal business contacts. And between husband and wife the threat to break off cohabitation is an effective form of compulsion, since it strikes at sexual or economic needs or both.

As the sanction becomes less severe or takes the shape of rewards one no longer speaks of coercive or compulsory commands and orders, but of *invitations under pressure or enticement (sanctioned invitations)*. Such directives are often uttered by teachers to pupils

('Do your lessons or you shan't come to the cinema'); and also constantly by adults to each other. We all in many ways use pressure and enticement to influence the behaviour of others. The pressure may consist simply in the threat to display frustration, or dissatisfaction, or coolness to the other party; withdrawal of affection is perhaps one of the most effective sanctions which parents can use with children. Correspondingly, an enticement may consist simply in the prospect of appreciation, kindness, or praise. Or, of course, it may take more solid forms, as in commerce, whose whole nature may be thought of as consisting in sanctioned invitations: *do ut des*. Nor is this exchange necessarily of services and goods for money.

(2) *Authoritative directives*

A may be considered an authority by *B*, in the sense that *B* has an attitude of spontaneous obedience toward directives (of at least some kinds) which *A* issues to him. *B* complies, then, not because of any sanctions, but by virtue of a sovereign, disinterested drive which arises out of respect for *A*'s authority. *B* feels obliged to obey because of *A*'s *right* to command. *A*'s power or 'authority' is in itself, however, nothing but a projection of *B*'s attitude of submission.

Examples of such attitudes of submission to authority are found in the attitude of children to their parents and teachers, and the relation of some believers toward religious authorities, of the members of a group toward their leader or of good citizens toward recognized authorities in power.

According to the degree of strength and absoluteness with which the directive is issued and the authority displayed, it seems natural to distinguish between *authoritative commands* (*orders*) and *authoritative invitations*.

If by 'power' we understand the ability to direct the behaviour of others, an authority excerises power as much as a bank robber. The power is, however, of different kinds in the two situations. The bank robber, like anyone else who uses sanctioned directives, appeals to the interests of the other party, that is, his fear of sanctions of some kind. An authority, on the other hand, appeals not to the interests of the obedient subject but to something often considered more 'essential', belonging to a 'higher' order in man's 'nature' than his need-conditioned interests, namely, his faith in a force which is *valid*—i.e., which is binding on him in splendid independence of all that he likes and dislikes, of his interests, his fears, and his hopes. The ambiguity of the word 'power', both in ordinary speech and in philosophy reflects this distinction between sanction and authority. Used in contrast to law and justice ('might —or power—goes before right', 'power politics', etc.), power is conceived as coercive force, the ability to exercise violence. Used in such contexts as 'legislative power', 'judicial power' or 'the distribution of powers', the same word designates a legal status, the authority to promulgate valid directives. Those who have power, in this sense, are called, simply, 'authorities'.

It is obviously the case that there do exist such attitudes of sub-mission to authority; and it is unquestionable that they are highly important for community life—for no social order can depend solely on sanctions. No government could rule by fear and terror alone. Political organization would be impossible if at least a considerable number of citizens did not recognize their rulers as *authorities*. The idea that such feelings of validity and disinterested attitudes of respect toward established institutions are the very foundation of all politically organized life, of law and the existence of the state, has been a recurrent theme in all my studies of legal philosophy, to which I refer the reader.[1]

It is much more difficult to account for the genesis of these atti-tudes and inclinations. Though the scope of the present study does not call for such an account, I should like to mention briefly that historically there have been two radically opposed views on this question, a metaphysical-religious one and an empirical-critical one. According to the first, validity is a supersensible quality that belongs to a world of pure ideas, a realm of pure reason which is different and independent from the world of empirical phenomena. The insight of man in this world is thought to spring either from divine inspiration, or from pure reason conceived as a faculty of the human mind which gives it *a priori* cognition of what is valid. Views of the second kind hold that the experience of validity is an empirical psychological phenomenon on a par with other experi-ences and as such to be studied and explained by psychology. A possible though hardly complete explanation is that such attitudes

---

[1] *On Law and Justice* (1958), pp. 52ff., 160, 364ff.; *Towards a Realistic Jurisprudence* (1946), pp. 18f., Chapter IV; *Kritik der sogenannten praktischen Erkenntnis* (1933), Chapter XIII; *Theorie der Rechtsquellen* (1929), Chapter XIV, 5.

arise through the process called conditioning. For example, it is well known that military drill may be so constantly repeated that obedience occurs spontaneously, and not from fear of sanctions, which may even be removed. Parental authority may be similarly established by the conditioning which results from the application of effective sanctions. The same theory may presumably be extended to explain the attitude of citizens toward political authority: any regime *de facto* tends to develop into a regime *de jure*. Sanctions, however, cannot be completely eliminated from society. The citizen's obedience to the law depends upon a combination of motives in which disinterested respect is blended in various proportions with fear of the legal apparatus of coercion (the police, the courts, and other enforcing authorities.)

Directives which are based upon a mixture of sanctions and respect for authority are themselves of a correspondingly mixed nature.

(3) *Sympathy-conditioned directives*

We often try, in various ways, to influence people to do what we want without having at our disposal either sanctions or authority. Our hope is that without any pressure the other party will act according to our directives purely from sympathy and benevolence. Since compliance depends solely on the kindness of the hearer, such directives will have the form, not of commands, but of (courteous) *requests, suggestions, invitations, supplications,* or *entreaties.*

If the parties involved are tied to each other by friendship or affection, quite burdensome requests may be made. If not, requests will be limited to minor services, since our kindness to strangers is normally too feeble to override our selfish interests. We ask a stranger for directions or for the time (that is, for information) or a fellow-traveller to provide a match or to close the window or to help us with our luggage. The beggar asks for a few pennies (and tries, perhaps, to evoke sympathy by a display of misery) but would hardly be taken seriously if he asked for a thousand pounds. In exceptional circumstances someone in great distress may ask for important favours or services: in this case we speak of 'entreaties'. A person who entreats (or implores, or beseeches), tries to arouse sympathy by showing through his words, gestures, and importunity, how much the thing he asks for matters to him.

For example, an unhappy mother may plead with a dictator to spare her son.

§ 11

Personal directives which are hearer-interested include advice, warnings, recommendations, and directions for use.

The common feature of directives of this group is that the directive uttered by A to B concerns actions whose performance is in B's interest. The function of the directive is not, then, to create a motive for B's compliance, since that already exists. Its function rather, is to inform B what course of action A regards as best serving B's interests. If B thinks A better qualified to judge the matter correctly, this belief will count as a reason for compliance. We call such directives, *advice, warnings, recommendations, directions for use,* etc.

The reason why B believes A to be more able than B himself to assess what best serves B's interests may be that he credits A with greater knowledge or wisdom. 'Knowledge' here means knowledge of those particular matters which are relevant to the prediction of what will serve B's interests best. The sick man consults a doctor, one with legal troubles a lawyer, and one with technical problems an engineer. The more complicated life is, the more we need the expert. In asking the expert for advice, one has to provide information about the problem—that is, about one's situation and requirements and how one's interests are likely to be affected by various solutions. The expert has to use this information and his own knowledge in advising B what action best serves his interests. In other words, the function of the advice is to say how a person would act if he had A's knowledge and B's interests.

It is natural to ask whether directives of this kind are genuine directives, or whether they are logically reducible to informative statements. Sometimes they are. The printed direction 'Open the tin by using a coin' means no more than 'The tin is most easily opened by using a coin'. It makes no difference if the directive is formulated hypothetically with reference to a purpose: 'If you want to open the tin, use a coin.' The wording of this directive should not lead one to confuse it with a hypothetical directive in another sense, e.g., 'If it rains, stay at home'. The hypothetically worded instruction on the tin is not meant as a conditional command, request, or piece of advice. The man responsible for the instruction does not want to meddle in the affairs of the owner of the tin by telling him that he is to do such and such in the event that he has a desire to open the tin. There could, indeed, be many reasons why he should not act in this way. The instruction means nothing more than that using a coin is the simplest way of opening the tin. The same is the case with other directions for use, technical instructions and the like.[1] Certain reservations must be made, however, with regard to the words 'most easily 'and 'simplest'. In the examples given this phrase is of no consequence. Although the tin could obviously be opened in more unusual ways—for example, with chemicals or a blowlamp—the tin has been constructed in such a way that the coin is the normal implement for opening it. This is the content of the instruction. It would be different if the instruction offered several methods and put them in order of merit; then it would contain an element of directive advice not reducible to information.

It is only when the necessary information is simple and easily understood, and the problem to be solved plain and unambiguous, that the required assistance can take the shape of pure information. A doctor, for example, cannot possibly provide his patient with all the medical insight and information required for making a diagnosis and deciding on a treatment. The expert, consequently, has in most cases not only to place his technical knowledge at the disposal of his client, but also himself to evaluate the conflicting considerations which arise in the course of reaching a decision. For normally a choice has to be made between different approaches each of which has its own advantages and drawbacks. The consideration of these approaches has to be carried out with the client's purposes and interests in mind, as these are explained to the expert. The sick man will say that he wants to regain good health; but 'good health' is not an unambiguously determined state. Which, for example, is more important, to live long or to live well? Is it worth losing the use of one's limbs to forestall a painful disease of the joints? In these cases, the expert has to help

[1] This means that I cannot share the current view according to which a distinction must be made between the technical directive itself and an indicative on which it is based and which gives information about the connection between ends and means; see e.g., Georg Henrik von Wright, *Norm and Action* (1963), p. 10.

his client to decide upon the end itself; and his aim should be to reach the decision the client himself would make, in his situation, if he had the expert's insight and knowledge.[1]

B might seek *A*'s advice for another reason, namely, because he supposes *A* to be wiser than he believes himself to be. For the choice to be made will at times depend not so much upon knowledge as upon a sympathetic understanding of human problems, and wisdom in weighing conflicting interests. Although there now exist many expert and professional counsellors in social, family and personal affairs, some of our problems are better taken up with a wise and experienced friend than with an expert. We expect the wise man to have extensive experience, a deep understanding of human nature, and mature judgment; these qualities are achieved not by vocational training but by intelligence and character, developed and tempered in a life full of challenging tasks and experiences. There is a special point, therefore, in seeking advice from the wise when one's difficulties are of a moral nature. For moral problems are never solved by knowledge and technique alone. Even if a dogmatic moral system is accepted, and certain authorities are recognized to have privileged insight into the system, the solution of a conflict cannot be simply deduced from dogmas. It requires the consideration of many particular circumstances whose relative importance has to be weighed against the background of accepted values. It is just this that demands wisdom rather than knowledge.

Since advice is given in the interest of the recipient he will usually take the initiative by making a request which he expects to be complied with, either for a fee or out of kindness. Advice and recommendations may, of course, be offered uninvited. In this case, though, the 'advice' is quite often a disguised 'speaker-interested' directive; for example, when a father says to his child 'Now, my boy, I advise you to tidy up after yourself' this is hardly intended as mere advice. Most of the advice and recommendations with which advertisers flood us are more 'sender-interested' than 'recipient-interested'. The same is true of many warnings. They may be given solely in the interest of the recipient, informing him of the risk involved in a particular course of action. I may for example know of a dangerous current and warn others

---

[1] On the expert as adviser to the politician, see *On Law and Justice* (1958), pp. 315ff.; *Why Democracy?* (1952), pp. 152ff.

not to swim off a certain beach. If, however, the danger has been contrived by the sender himself, the 'warning' may be a politely disguised sanctioned, command or invitation; consider, for example, the householder's warning 'Beware of the dog'.

§ 12

Personal directives which are disinterested are called exhortations or admonitions.

The common feature of directives of this group is that the act concerned is not as such in the interest of either A or B. If one of the parties does have an interest, it is accidental. Even if a directive of this kind is prompted by some interest of one of the parties it may all the same function independently of this interest. The characteristic feature of the disinterested directive is that A, whatever his interests, submits that B ought to act according to some norm or norms accepted by both of them. There is in current usage no term covering all direction of this kind. We shall say that A *exhorts* (or admonishes) B. If the required act happens to be in A's interest, the directive is a combination of an exhortation and a claim. The pure exhortation arises solely from respect for a system of norms. It appeals, not to B's interests, but to B's respect for the the same norms. Various systems of norms may be brought to bear on B: the legal system of a community, the by-laws of an association, the rules of a game, moral principles, or the conventional rules of courtesy and decency, etc.

Disinterested directives are expressed in various linguistic forms. Deontic terms frequently occur (see above, § 9). Often, though, exhortative meaning appears more from context and tone of voice ('but you can't really . . .', 'you simply have to . . .', 'do you think it correct to . . .', 'you cannot in decency . . .', 'that is a bit thick', 'I could not imagine your doing . . .').

An exhortation indicates to B what is expected of him, what in a broad sense is his duty toward another person. The normative system which backs up the directive will often be such that there will correspond to B's duty the claim of another person C. The exhortation may then take the form of expressing C's claim against B. 'C is really entitled to damages' is synonymous with 'It is your duty to pay damages to C.'

Exhortations are not to be confused with statements which say what a particular norm prescribes. Such confusion is easy, since an exhortation and the corresponding statement of a norm may appear in the same linguistic dress. For example, in § 9 we pointed out that the utterance 'Parking is forbidden here' may, according to circumstances, be an exhortation or a statement.

Nor should exhortations be confused with the authoritative commands mentioned in § 10. It is true that exhortations and authoritative commands have the common feature that both are obeyed by B out of a sense of duty. The difference lies in the role of the speaker: If A issues an authoritative command he does so as an authority and the source of the directive, while if he issues an exhortation he only brings to bear on B what follows from a particular system of norms. A policeman, e.g., has no authority to issue parking prohibitions, he only brings existing prohibitions to bear on offenders. B's obedience arises, in the first case, out of his respect for the personal authority of the speaker, but in the second case it proceeds from his respect for an impersonal system of norms.

§ 13

Directives which are impersonal and heteronomous are called quasi-commands. They include (1) legal rules; and (2) conventional rules (conventional morality, courtesy and decency).

So far our concern has been with types of directives whose classification depends upon the situations in which they are issued and whose motivating force arises from those situations. They are, according to type:

> *Sanctioned commands and invitations*
> *Authoritative commands and invitations*
> *Requests* (neither sanctioned nor authoritative)
> *Advice*
> *Directions for use*
> *Exhortations.*

All of these are personal, in the sense that some person is necessarily presupposed as their issuer, and that their effect on the hearer depends on the directive's having been issued by this particular speaker. If anyone says that he has been commanded, requested, advised, directed, or exhorted to perform a particular act, one is entitled to ask by whom, and one would regard the answer 'no one' as unreasonable. A command, for example, presupposes a commander, on whose power or authority its effectiveness entirely depends. What would the expression 'Shut the door' mean if it were not bound up with a definite situation and a definite speaker? One cannot decide in the abstract on a proper attitude toward the directive 'Shut the door', whether, that is, to comply with it or not, in the same way that one can decide on the attitude to adopt toward a proposition ignoring the situation of its utterance and the person who asserts it. If the Ten Commandments are considered valid in themselves and not conditional upon the authority of a commanding God then they are no longer commands.

The same is true of the other personal directives, with perhaps some reservation in the case of directions for use and exhortations. If a direction is reducible to an informative statement my confidence in it, as with all informative utterances, will depend on my confidence in the subjective and objective trustworthiness of the speaker. My dependence on the speaker, however, diminishes to the extent that I can test the truth of the statement myself. Similarly for exhortations: a presupposed system of norms provides a criterion for deciding whether they are justified. The exhortation 'Pay your debts' may have sense without having a known source; one cannot assume that anonymous exhortations of this kind are without effect, for example, when posted up or handed out in the streets.

We must now consider directives of another type, namely, impersonal directives, which have no definite source and whose motivating force is therefore not dependent upon the power, authority or wisdom of any individual. Having no sender they have no recipient as such. We tell whom they concern solely from the wording of the directive itself, and not from a 'speaker-hearer' situation. Impersonal directives are of three types: *quasi-commands, the constitutive rules of a game, and autonomous moral principles*. This classification, like the previous ones, is based on those differences in the special contexts of each type of directive which give rise to the motivating force of the directive. The first group comprises those directives which are experienced as heteronomous, that is, directives which appear to an individual as a given, existing order imposing itself upon him independently of any acceptance or recognition on his part. Directives of the second group arise from mutual agreement and have a mixed autonomous-heteronomous nature. The last group is made up of those directives whose motivating force originates entirely from the subject's autonomous recognition of them.

Quasi-commands and genuine commands have this in common: they are both obeyed out of fear of sanctions, respect for authority, or some combination of these. But quasi-commands, unlike genuine commands, derive their authority not from any person but from an impersonal system of norms. Consider, for example, the prohibition against manslaughter in the Danish Criminal Code, 1930, section 237. Whoever contravenes this precription is liable to a penalty of imprisonment from five years to life. The directive is, then backed up by a severe sanction. At the same time habitual respect of law, justice, and morality produce a disinterested motive which combines with the fear of sanctions. To this extent, such a directive resembles a personal command which is backed up by both sanctions and authority. Who, however, is the author of this command? What person, that is, (1) formulates and issues the directive, (2) decides upon and carries out sanctions, and (3) is regarded by the subject as an authority? It is simply not the case that any single person or group of persons occupy such a position. The Criminal Code was passed in 1930, and most of those who took part in framing it have now died. Besides, no person who takes part in the framing and passing of a code or statute is in a position analogous to that of the issuer of a personal command. For the latter commands whatever he himself thinks fit; none of those who have a hand in legislation can do this. The content of a statute is very likely not completely satisfactory to any of the participating legislators. The law is made in a series of formal meetings in which many persons take part, none of them having the power to get exactly what he wants. The 'legislator', conceived as a single person like the issuer of a personal command, is a fiction; and yet people readily believe in him, because they are used to ascribing linguistic formulations and expressions of decisions to individuals.

Furthermore, those who take part in legislative procedures do so because they hold office, that is, because they have been legally invested with the power and competence to create laws. Finally, those who make the law have nothing to do with its enforcement.

It is the function of others to apply the sanctions (the police, the courts, and other enforcing authorities), and these also act in virtue of legal rules creating their offices and powers.

This brief account, though it could be considerably elaborated,[1] shows that the enforcing power and authority which sustain *legal rules* cannot be located in any individual or group of individuals, but can be ascribed only to the system—to the legal order as such. The motive to obey them is produced by the regular functioning of the legal machinery of enforcement, which presents itself to the individual, not as a threat accompanying a command, but as a fact which needs to be taken into account if one is to avoid the wheels of the machinery, much as the dangers of a physical environment must be taken into account and avoided. The authority which sustains legal directives—for example, a police order to move along—is derived not from the qualities of the police officer as a man, but from his office, which itself depends on the legal order that creates it.

Since legal prescriptions are not issued by any person in his individual capacity, they are not meant to serve the interests of any particular person. But because we are accustomed to the idea that a command benefits a definite person, it is usually assumed that the law serves the interest of a person called 'the community'. Like the concept 'legislator' this is a fiction corresponding to nothing in reality.[2]

I have chosen the expression 'quasi-command' to express both the affinity and the diversity between legal directives and personal commands.

What I have said about legal directives applies analogously to the directives implied in social conventions of *courtesy, decency* and *conventional* (or *public*, or *positive*) *morality*. Unlike legal directives, these do not make up an institutional order.

That the legal order is institutional means that among the legal rules are some, especially found in constitutional law, that create institutions, that is agencies empowered to create or enforce law. These institutions traditionally comprise a legislative assembly empowered especially to make general rules, the courts of justice

---

[1] See, e.g., Karl Olivecrona, 'The Imperative Element in the Law', *Rutgers Law Review*, vol. 18 (1964), pp. 794ff.; H. L. A. Hart, *The Concept of Law* (1961), pp. 18ff.; Hans Kelsen, *General Theory of Law and State* (1946), pp. 30ff., 62ff.; Axel Hägerström, *Inquiry into the Nature of Law and Morals* (1953), pp. 17ff., 56ff.
[2] Cf. *On Law and Justice* (1958), pp. 295ff.

empowered to make final judicial decisions, and the executive comprising a great number of various agencies for the implementation and enforcement of enacted law and judicial decisions. All these agencies appear to the individual as public authorities making up a legal machinery independent of his will and wishes. For this reason the law is regarded as a social institution, something ascribed to the society, not to the individual: the law is Danish law or British law, not the law of Smith or Jones.[1]

Convention differs from the law of the community or of the State, first in that its sanctions do not include physical coercion, the use of violence being a monopoly of the State. Its sanctions are rather such reactions as disapproval, ridicule, and ostracism. But the essential difference between convention and the law is that convention's sanctions are not organized institutionally; there are no authorities setting up conventions or imposing and applying to particular cases sanctions as the authoritative reaction from part of the society. Sanctions are administered individually, and it is always possible that what one section of society disapproves and censures another may approve and commend. Convention is therefore in principle an individual phenomenon. For this reason one cannot speak of 'Danish morality' as one speaks of 'Danish law'. If it is possible, nevertheless, to say fairly precisely what is *the* convention in a certain community or social group, this is so merely because the members of the group to some degree adopt the same values and react uniformly to violations of accepted standards. Such conformity makes convention something of a social phenomenon, endowing it with an over-individual existence similar to that of the law. The individual member of the group experiences the demands of convention as a social pressure—the group expects certain things of him, and exacts them by its unorganized but nevertheless uniform reactions; it is, to him, an external power which forces him to conform by the threat of punishment. In our complicated society common and customary patterns of behaviour are disintegrating to an increasing degree, with the result that conventions have become progressively

---

[1] This is not at variance with the idea of rights being ascribed to individuals. In using the concept of individual rights we describe what the legal order, in standard situations, implies with regard to the interests of a certain individual; see *On Law and Justice*, Chapter 6.

diffused and bound up with social levels and circles rather than with the community as a whole.

Conventions emanate neither from the commands of individuals, nor from legislators. They too can be classified as quasi-commands.

§ 14

Directives which are impersonal and heteronomous-autonomous include the rules of games and similar arrangements founded on agreement.

The parking rules laid down by the police are concerned with the activity of 'parking a car', that is, with leaving it unoccupied in a public street. These rules prescribe how a person who wants to park his car has to behave. The rules of chess seem, in a similar way, to be concerned with the acitivity of 'playing chess', and to prescribe how one who wants to play the game has to behave. The two sets of rules are, however, related to their respective activities in an essentially different way. The difference lies in how they 'concern' those activities. Parking a car is a 'natural' activity; by this I mean an activity whose performance is logically independent of any rules governing it. Cars were parked before parking regulations existed, and it would be an obvious absurdity if I said that I could not park my car because of the absence of parking regulations in this town. Playing chess, on the other hand, is not a 'natural' activity. To play chess is to undertake certain actions according to the rules of chess. The actions of the game consist in 'moves' which have no meaning or purpose except that they are rules of chess. A move is made by moving a piece of wood on a squared plane. That the piece of wood is a pawn and its displacement a 'move' can be understood only if the action is interpreted in terms of the rules of chess.

This essential difference can be expressed by calling parking rules *regulative* and the rules of chess *constitutive*.[1]

The rules of chess define the game of chess as an institution and provide the logically necessary conditions for the making of chess moves, that is, for the actual game in progress, in which the game

---

[1] After this was written I have found the same distinction made in John R. Searle, ' "Ought" and "Is" ', *Phil. Review*, vol. LXXIII (1964), pp. 43f., 55, and R. M. Hare, 'The Promising Game', *Revue Intern. de Philosophie*, 1964, pp. 398ff. See also B. J. Diggs, 'Rules and Utilitarianism', *American Philosophical Quarterly*, vol. I (1964), pp. 32ff., 38f.

as institution manifests itself. The rules of chess endow the actions performed in chess with their specific meaning as 'moves', integrate the actions of the two players into a coherent whole in such a way that the motive and meaning of a move made by one of the players are dependent on the moves made by the other party. Each player's moves determine how the other player may or must react. When A has made his move, B must make a move in turn, within a time limit, and the number of moves open to him depends on the move made by A. In this way the two men are united in a social community quite different from that of two men digging a ditch together.

The rules of chess, since they define the game, cannot, strictly speaking, be violated. A player may of course cheat by making an irregular move. But in that case what is going on is not, strictly speaking, chess. Cheating in chess requires passing off, undetected, an action as chess that is not really so.

No information is provided by the rules of chess about what motives prompt people to play chess. No doubt the game is usually played for its own sake, that is, for pleasure. But nothing prevents the game from being integrated into a wider pattern of behaviour and played for some ulterior purpose. This may be done at the behest of other people for example, by paying the players or offering a prize to the winner, or there may be natural reasons; if it is a fact that chess trains the mind, that too gives us a motive for playing it.

Why do those who play chess usually obey its rules without trying to cheat? The desire to win, by itself, provides a motive for cheating, especially if winning is lucrative. Why is this motive in most cases overridden? A sanction against cheating does exist in the possibility of its being met by the discontinuance of play, and by the moral indignation and protests. But these reactions arise from the spontaneous and disinterested sense of obligation felt by the players to play correctly, this feeling being so strong that the idea of cheating does not normally arise.

The rules of chess are therefore very different from commands. First of all, they are obeyed essentially neither through fear of sanctions nor through respect for authority. Secondly, no one beside the players themselves lays down and enforces the rules. A player feels himself bound in relation to his opponent, and to this extent the obligation is experienced as heteronomous, as demand from without. But if we consider the players collectively, nobody outside this circle has the right to interfere in the play, or to lay down and apply rules—an umpire derives his authority from the rules and from the players' recognition. To this extent, the obligation is experienced as autonomous, that is, as dependent entirely on the acceptance and acknowledgment of those taking part.

The two-sided character of the obligation as both heteronomous and autonomous is explained by the manner in which the rules come into force and bind the players. They do this by *common acceptance*, or *mutual agreement*. If two persons without further ceremony sit down to play chess, it is understood that the game is to be played according to the rules of chess as commonly accepted at that time and place. Often, however, some variants of play are expressly decided upon. For example, is the rule which permits taking *en passant* recognized? Is there a time limit within which a move must be made? Are the tournament rules about the touching of pieces to be observed?

The rules of chess are complied with *voluntarily* in the sense that the fear of sanctions is not an important motive. They are observed disinterestedly, through a spontaneous feeling of obligation, which does not derive from respect for any authority. It springs from the players' own acceptance or approval and is, as such, experienced as autonomous. Since, however, this acceptance is established by mutual agreement, the obligation is at the same time experienced as heteronomous, that is, as a claim due to the other party. Through this agreement the autonomy of the players has been restricted; he was free to enter the agreement or not, but once having done so, he is bound, and is prevented from a unilateral amendment of the rules.

What we have said of the constitutive nature of the rules of chess, and of the basis of effectiveness in mutual acceptance, holds analogously, with perhaps small modification, of other games— apart from one-man games. A 'rule of a game' must, I believe, be so defined that its constitutive nature is made part of its definition. Since, however, some other rules are also constitutive, a 'rule of a game' cannot be defined by this characteristic alone. With regard to pattern-bound dances (e.g., the minuet), I feel some hesitation. It is, I suppose, true that one cannot dance the minuet without following the rules which define this dance. On the other hand, we can hardly say that the dance's separate steps are senseless and incomprehensible without knowledge of the pattern of the dance. We would otherwise have to say, analogously, that the recipe for *Mrs. Smith's plum cake* is equally constitutive, since if it were not followed the result would not be *Mrs. Smith's plum cake*.

It is of more importance to notice that some legal or conventional rules of great consequence to the life of a community are constitutive rules. Consider, for example, the norms which constitute the acts we call 'making a promise', 'accepting a promise', 'breaking a promise', 'fulfilling a promise' or in short what may be called 'the promising game'. *Promising* is no more a natural act than is making a move in chess. Lawyers and philosophers have found difficulty in accounting for the logical make-up of a promise. What has at least become clear is that a promise is not merely a declaration of intention, whether this is taken to mean a piece of information about a certain volitional state of mind of the one promising, or the spontaneous expression of such a mental state. To say 'I promise that . . .' is neither to inform, nor to exclaim, nor to predict, nor to command. A promise is simply a promise and nothing else; it is an act constituted by the rules of promising in the same way as a move in chess is constituted by the rules of chess. The rules of promising define various steps ('moves') to be taken by the person promising and the person to whom the promise is made. According to how this 'game' is played obligations and claims arise and are extinguished. The salient point is that the promise, as a rule, obliges its issuer to act as the promissory declaration specifies.

In legal terminology a promise is called an *acte juridique*, or act-in-the-law, which aptly expresses that the promise is not a natural act but one constituted by legal rules. An act-in-the-law is a declaration which (normally) by virtue of constitutive legal rules produces legal effects according to its content. Other examples are wills, laws, judgments, and administrative acts. *Making a will, legislating, deciding a case, resolving*, are none of them natural acts; they are acts-in-the-law, conceivable only as constituted by legal rules.

In recent years logicians have much occupied themselves with the logical nature of promises. A promise has, for example, been called a performatory act of discourse. But in my opinion the essential has often been missed, namely, that a promise is an act-in-the-law constituted by legal or conventional norms.[1]

In § 7, we have explained that informative communications, false as well as true, are possible only by virtue of a fundamental social-conventional norm which forbids using propositions in a merely fabulating way, unless the hearer is warned that the proposition is not being asserted. This basic norm too is constitutive, for without it informative communication is impossible.

We have mentioned the rules of promising and the basic norm of informative communication in this connection to show that the rules of games are not the only constitutive rules. They differ from the rules of games in that their basis of effectiveness does not lie in mutual agreement. As legally or conventionally established they are quasi-commands.

§ 15

Impersonal directives which are autonomous comprise the principles and judgments of personal morality.

In all his social environments—his family, his school, his job— the growing child is continuously bombarded with directives issued by his family and teachers, and by convention, which he obeys out of fear or out of respect for authority or both. 'You mustn't hit anyone smaller than yourself' say his parents; and then 'Don't eat with your fork in your mouth', and 'Don't say "I is hungry" '. It seems to me most likely that these three directives are, to begin with, taken by the child in the same way. In his subsequent development the child will differentiate them as being moral, conventional and linguistic. I cannot here examine the interesting question of how this differentiation is effected, and on what it depends; and so I need not try to define the three

[1] J. L. Austin, 'Other Minds', *Proceedings of the Aristotelian Society*, vol. 20 (1946), reprinted in *Philosophical Papers* (1961), pp. 44ff., see pp. 67ff.; A. I. Melden, 'On Promising', *Mind*, vol. LXV (1956), pp. 49ff.; Austin, 'Performative Utterances', *Philosophical Papers* (1961); *How to do Things with Words* (1962); Hedenius, 'Performatives', *Theoria*, 1963, pp. 137ff.; cf. *On Law and Justice*, pp. 217ff.; Radnitzky, 'Performatives and Descriptions', *Inquiry*, 1962, pp. 12ff. The views of Hare, 'The Promising Game', *Revue Internationale de Philosophie*, 1964, pp. 398ff. and John R. Searle, ' "Ought" and "Is" ', *Phil. Review*, vol. LXXIII (1964), pp. 34ff., seem close to mine.

categories.[1] What follows will concern only those directives which are experienced as moral, however this last quality is to be described and defined.

In the child's earliest years, there is no question of his 'approving' the moral prescriptions which he is given. Their motivating force consists solely in his fear of sanctions and respect for authority; the content of the prescription as such, is therefore immaterial for his obedience. Parental authority may eventually be superseded by the authority of teachers and leaders, or by the impersonal authority of the legal order and convention ('What will people think!'). At this stage of development, morality will be experienced as a set of commands or quasi-commands which are ascribed to God, parents, leaders, or 'people', that is, the impersonal authority of the State and society.

There are, we may presume, many people whose morality remains of this authoritarian kind throughout their lives. To the question why morality should be obeyed their ultimate answer is: God wills it; the disobedient go to Hell; father and mother said so; everyone says so; what would Mrs. Smith say if I didn't behave?

It becomes necessary, at a certain level of development, to provide oneself with reasons why some prescriptions should be obeyed or why one *ought* to act in such and such a manner. One must first realize that the possibility of punishment or other sanctions makes it merely *prudent* and *sensible* to behave in a certain way, and does not make such behaviour *right*, or a *duty*. Then it must be understood that authority cannot provide an ultimate answer either, since it must be explained what makes an authority, and justifies the claim that it is *right* to obey its prescriptions. The reference to authority is decisive only if we presuppose some higher prescription to obey this authority. But how can this last prescription itself be justified?

If this line of reasoning is followed, we are driven to the conclusion that there can be authorities in morality only to the extent to which one gives them a foundation in values and ideals which one approves immediately and takes as directly binding. It is, then, one's own approval or evaluation, and not authority, which is the ultimate source of obligation or validity. One may, for example,

---

[1] Cf. *On Law and Justice*, pp. 364ff.; *Kritik der sogenannten praktischen Erkenntnis*, pp. 442ff.

regard God as an authority because he is all-loving and all-wise. But in this case one has independently and sovereignly accepted and approved love and wisdom as moral values, and made the authority of God dependent on and derived from these qualities.

Having gone so far it is difficult to avoid taking the last step. If the ultimate basis of critical morality is one's own approval—one's autonomy, there is no reason why one should not exercise this autonomy with regard to moral directives independently of all authority. With this step we arrive at *personal* or *autonomous morality*, the morality of conscience.[1] Its manifestation takes the form of more or less clearly conceived directives of a more or less singular or general character. I may, for example, say to myself: 'You ought to visit Peter, who is ill'; and I may back up this directive with the general rule that one ought to help and comfort those in distress. I cannot take up here the many problems of moral reasoning. My concern is to point out the general character of critical-moral directives and their basis of effectiveness.

These directives belong, obviously, to the class of impersonal directives; they have no issuer and no recipient as such. Unlike the quasi-commands, they are not derived from the anonymous power and authority of an established order. Nor do they resemble the rules of games; for they are not based on mutual agreement and they lack its attendant heteronomy. Their basis of effectiveness is the subject's own approval and acceptance; they are without qualification autonomous.

The survey of different types of directives which has been given in section 10 to 15 does not claim to be exhaustive.[2] Our classification was based on differences in the circumstances on which the effectiveness of the directive depends. This effectiveness is the power of the directive to motivate compliance. This is not the

---

[1] By this term I don't mean a morality spontaneously emanating from a 'sense of morality', but moral attitudes which I, after critical examination and mature consideration, am willing to accept, cf. *On Law and Justice*, p. 368.

[2] Cf. von Wright's list of six kinds or types of norms mentioned below in § 20 Nowell-Smith, *Ethics* (1954), p. 145, distinguishes between four main types of situations in which language is used for telling others what to do, namely cases of giving (1) instructions; (2) advice; (3) exhortations; and (4) commands. The classification does not seem in either case to be founded on any conceptual framework or any guiding theory on the basis of which the various types are distinguished and characterized.

same as actual compliance, since this motivation may be out-weighed by other forces.

We may sum up this survey in the following diagram:

Directives

Type	Linguistic-contextual manifestation	Whose interests are served by the compliance with the directive?	Source of effectiveness
A. Personal directives			
a. speaker-interested			
(1) sanctioned	command under threat; legal claim; invitation under pressure or entice-ment	the speaker's	fear of sanctions
(2) authoritative	pure command or invitation	the speaker's	respect for authority
(3) sympathy-conditioned	requests; sugges-tion; invitation; supplication; entreaty	the speaker's	the hearer's sym-pathy for the speaker
b. hearer-interested	advice; warning; recommendation; directions	the hearer's	the hearer's self-interest, along with his reliance on the knowledge or wis-dom of the speaker
c. disinterested	exhortation	no one's	respect for a sys-tem of norms
B. Impersonal directives			
a. quasi-commands (heteronomous)	law and conven-tion	society's	fear of sanctions and respect for impersonal authority
b. Constitutive rules based on mutual agree-ment (autono-mous-heterono-mous)	rules of games	no one's	agreement and mutual approval
c. the autono-mous directives of morality	moral principles and judgments	no one's	one's own approval

§ 16

Acceptance is a soliloquistic act whose function is adjudicative. It occurs only with regard to the autonomous directives of morality. According to the non-cognitive view, acceptance is constitutive.

Considering a proposition as a linguistic tool we have, in Chapter II of this book, discerned the following steps in the production and use of this tool:

(1) to produce it correctly in accordance with syntactical rules of various kinds;

(2) to consider it without making any use of it;

(3) to talk about it without making any use of it, especially to talk about it discussing what use one possibly could make of it;

(4) to use it but not in any process of communication, e.g. in therapeutic speech exercises;

(5) to use it in soliloquy by accepting or rejecting it with an adjudicative function;

(6) to use it in communication by asserting it with informative function;

(7) to use it in communication by posing it with fabulating function.

Let us now consider the question whether on all levels similar statements can be made with regard to directives.

It seems obvious that this question must be answered in the affirmative as to the levels (1), (2), (3), and (4). In this section I deal with level 5, that is the question whether, with regard to directives, an attitude-deciding act occurs, analogous to that of accepting a proposition. In § 17 I shall deal with levels 6 and 7, the use of directives in communication with others.

It is a highly disputed question whether an act analogous to acceptance of propositions occurs as regards directives. If the comparison is to be fruitful, we must first briefly indicate what are the salient features of 'accepting a proposition'. Most important is the fact that the acceptance of a proposition is *declaratory*, and not *constitutive*. That is to say, the acceptance of the proposition is not a volitional act which endows the proposition with its truth value in the way that, for example, recognition and acceptance are essential for one to be a member of an exclusive club. The truth (or falsity) of a proposition is assumed to be a property of the proposition itself; acceptance of the proposition is merely the recognition that this property is present. Acceptance may be achieved with more or less difficulty, and may be more or less well-founded. Our own acceptance of the proposition often relies merely on its acceptance by others, and we assume that these others have good reasons for their acceptance. Acceptance is never final; it may always be re-examined. Despite these complications, the proposition is taken to be either true or false (provided that it is sufficiently testable; see §§ 2 and 6). The 'objectivity' of cognition consists in the fact that whether a proposition is true or false depends on what it says and not on any attitude which some individual may take up toward it. The possibility of this objectivity rests on the existence of procedures for testing the truth of the proposition which are independent of the subjective peculiarities of any individuals. This is, however, an ideal which is only approximated in varying degrees, and objectivity is therefore not absolute, but relative to the available procedures of verification (cf. above §§ 2 and 6). But although our attempts to achieve the ideal of objectivity and to overcome subjectivity are imperfect, we do not give up the assumption that a proposition, expressed with sufficient precision, is either true or false—though we may not be able to tell for sure which it is. This assumption is what defines the concept of objectivity in cognition. That it is not an unreasonable one is borne out by the fact that we have succeeded in both science and everyday life in indicating procedures of verification which eliminate subjective factors almost completely, and which create to that extent agreement. People agree in everyday life about the correct description of physical objects and their positions—there is a house here, a table and a chair there. The few who do not generally agree are called mad and perhaps locked up. The extent of disagreement in science is easily overestimated, because evolving science is always closely concerned with disputes over questions at the frontiers, and because any scientific theory, no matter how well established, may at any time be re-examined and reformulated more precisely.

The question is whether there is, in the case of directives, any inherent property corresponding to the truth or falsity of propositions, and ascertained by a similar attitude-deciding act.

It seems to me obvious that at least some directives are not accepted or rejected on such a basis. If a gangster orders 'Hand over the money or I'll shoot', one may be said to accept or reject this order in the sense that one must decide to obey or to defy it.[1] But it can hardly be maintained that this acceptance or rejection is like the acceptance or rejection of a proposition as true.[2] The decision whether to obey is an act of volition; it depends on the situation and not on the discovery of some property inherent in the directive 'Hand over the money'.

Nor is the case different if the directive is an authoritative command, e.g., an order given by parents to their children. It is true that such a directive is felt to have a validity not possessed by the coercive order. But this validity is not inherent in the directive; it is derived from the personal position of the speaker. Furthermore, the impulse to obey arises so automatically and spontaneously that there is no room for deliberation and a definite decision on the attitude to be adopted.

Something similar is true, I believe, of all other personal directives, and of quasi-commands and the rules of games.[3] When we consider autonomous moral directives, however, the picture changes. Their source of effectiveness is, as we have seen neither fear of sanctions, nor respect for authority, nor any other situation-bound factor, but solely the subject's own approval of what the directive prescribes. It is not, then, *prima facie* unreasonable to compare the approval of a moral principle with the acceptance of a

---

[1] Thus Hare, *The Language of Morals* (1952), pp. 19–20: 'If I said "shut the door" and you answered "Aye, aye sir" this . . . would be a sign of assent . . . If we assent to a statement we are said to be sincere in our assent if and only if we believe that it is true (believe what the speaker has said). If, on the other hand, we assent to a second-person command addressed to ourselves, we are said to be sincere in our assent if and only if we do or resolve to do what the speaker has told us to do.'

[2] Whereas it is natural to say that a man who believes a statement to be true assents to this statement, it seems to me contrary to current use to say—as Hare does (see the previous note)—that the threatened bank employees have assented to the gangster's order.

[3] Below, in § 21, it is explained that the existence of a social norm is dependent on the fact that the norm is generally felt as binding by its subjects. This feeling or attitude is usually the unconscious outcome of the training and conditioning of the individual during his education and growth in the group. It may happen in extraordinary situations—e.g. under revolutions—that an attitude of allegiance is the outcome of a decision which has the character of *acknowledgment* or *acceptance*. The 'validity' derived from this acceptance, however, even in this situation, is experienced not as inherent in the norm itself, but as derived from the authority or authorities behind the social-political order. For a dissenting opinion, see Hart, *The Concept of Law* (1961), p. 56; cf. my review of this book in *Yale Law Journal*, vol. 71 (1962), pp. 1185ff., 1188.

proposition. Moral approval would on this construction be conceived as an attitude-deciding act in which a moral directive is *accepted as valid*; and validity is to be taken as a property of directives and consequently independent of the situation in which the directive is experienced and of the person deciding. 'Validity' is thought, in short, to be analogous to truth.

This interpretation seems to be supported by our own unanalysed experience. Consider, for example, moral directives like 'I ought to visit Peter, since he is ill', 'Thou shalt not kill', 'Love thy neighbour as thyself'. Just as one considers a proposition and decides, on more or less solid grounds, to accept or reject it, so one may reflect on these moral directives and, on more or less solid grounds, accept or reject them as valid or invalid. And it seems natural to take the acceptance of a moral directive as declaratory, that is, to say that the directive is accepted because it is valid and not valid because it is accepted. Validity is hence conceived to be a property of the directive itself which we can become aware of. Since this 'cognition' has its immediate expression in directives which are recognized as valid, it is called 'practical' or 'moral', as opposed to the 'theoretical' cognition of propositions.

Against this interpretation, however, it may be argued that the acceptance of a moral directive is actually constitutive; that is, acceptance is a subjective attitude which constitutes the validity of the directive. There exists, according to this view, no specific moral cognition. In support of this view it must be pointed out that objectivity, as we have seen, is possible only if there are test procedures which eliminate subjective dependency; and that for the alleged moral cognition no such procedures have ever been indicated. The supporters of the theory of moral cognition usually take validity to be accessible to an intuition experienced by the conscience. But an intuition is entirely subjective; it is a *dictum* which precludes intersubjective reasoning and argument. To proclaim the objectivity of a subjective experience is empty backing for any theory; objectivity without objective (intersubjective) procedures is an absurdity. The plea that intuition is rooted in a power of reason which is inherent in human nature, or the claim that it is a revelation of the voice of God in our hearts which therefore transcends subjective arbitrariness, are patently no more than hollow metaphysical phrases, made to order for the sole purpose of defending the belief in moral objectivity. The faith of the cognitivist should be further shaken by the psychological analysis of the moral consciousness, its genesis, and evolution, which shows how the faith in a faculty of moral cognition satisfies pervasive religious and metaphysical needs and so has the function of relieving man from the burden of responsibility.[1]

Cognitivism and non-cognitivism are thus the two main positions in moral philosophy. We cannot, of course, examine this controversy in detail, but it seems reasonable to point out what is *not* implied in the non-cognitivist position, so that we may be spared the misunderstandings and distortions, so common in this area of discussion, with which it is hard to be patient.

First of all, the view has no connection with *moral nihilism*, in the usual sense of the rejection of all moral principles and values whatsoever, the opinion that everything is permitted or that there is no law but the law of might. I and other adherents of non-cognitivism have often emphasized that this doctrine is a meta-ethical theory about the nature of moral judgment and that there is neither a logical nor a psychological connection between this theory and the actual morality of its supporters. In particular, its supporters are in no way prevented from taking up the attitude which we have called the acceptance of a moral principle.[2] The non-cognivitivist philosopher as such lives as anybody else; he is no better and no worse than the rest of us. Like others he accepts

---

[1] The question of the existence of a specific practical cognition is the main subject of my book *Kritik der sogenannten praktischen Erkenntnis* (1933). See also my paper 'On the Logical Nature of Propositions of Value', *Theoria*, 1945, pp. 172ff.; *On Law and Justice* (1958), Chapter XI.

[2] E.g., Gunnar Oxenstierna, *Vad är Uppsalafilosofien?* [*What is Uppsala Philosophy?*] (1938), p. 57; Hedenius, 'Ueber den alogischen Character der sogenannten Werturteile', *Theoria*, 1939, pp. 314ff.; *Om rätt och moral* [*On law and morals*] (1941), pp. 35, 40ff., 110–13, 162ff.; Alf Ross, *Why Democracy?* (1952), pp. 92–114. If I may be allowed to quote the last mentioned work: 'It may be objected that anyone who, in this fashion, denies that values can be determined scientifically thereby cuts himself off from making a choice between good and evil and must end up in an indifferent passivity, but this objection is foolish. Because a point of view is a point of view and not a scientific truth, it naturally does not follow from this that one cannot have some point of view. I know very well what I shall stand for and fight for. Only I do not imagine myself, or try to make others believe, that it can be scientifically proved that my point of view is the "right" one.' That non-cognitivism has nothing to do with moral nihilism was the theme of a discussion in 1946 between the sociologist Theodor Geiger and myself; see *Juristen*, 1946, pp. 259ff. and 319ff. In my review of Frede Castberg, *Freedom of Speech in the West*, *Nordisk administrativt Tidsskrift*, 1960, pp. 224ff., I tried to weed out a similar misunderstanding in Castberg.

some moral directives (principles, rules, judgments) and rejects others. His only difference from the cognitivist is that he believes his acceptance to be constitutive of the validity of the moral directive, and not declaratory. In other words, he takes his own morality as a personal attitude, an 'existential' commitment he is willing to stand up for with his personality and life, and not as an impersonal, objective cognition. That non-cognitivism is widely and wrongly identified in Scandinavia with amoralism may be the result of the use of the unhappy term 'value nihilism', with which some Uppsala philosophers have designated their denial of moral cognition. It is to be expected that this distortion will continue to pervade popular discussion and it is excusable. But it is inexcusable in philosophical writers who are in a position to know better.[1]

Secondly, non-cognitivism has no connections with *moral indifferentism (relativism)*, if this is taken to mean that, because morality is subjective, one moral principle is as good as another, and that consequently no one is entitled to judge and condemn the behaviour or morality of others. This position is difficult to criticize because it is far from clear what it amounts to. But whatever its nature, nothing resembling it is implied by non-cognitivism. The belief that the two views are connected arises from confusing the content of a moral system with its foundation. Anyone who accepts a particular moral system must of course apply it when judging others' behaviour as well as his own. A moral system, by its very nature, concerns human behaviour universally, and the fact that others have adopted moral principles different from mine

---

[1] Bent Schultzer, *Direktiv Idealisme* [*Directive Idealism*] (1964). It is difficult to quote chapter and verse in support of the contention that this author subscribes to the grotesque popular misinterpretation of ethical non-cognitivism as moral nihilism. The book is written in a loose and chattering style, and although the author considers it to be his task to deliver the world from the curse of 'value-nihilism' (pp. 104, 108) he nowhere gives a precise account of the theory he wishes to combat. That the author regards a 'value-nihilist' (or an 'ideal-nihilist') as a man without ideals appears, however, from many pronouncements. I must repudiate as glaring misunderstandings what the author says on pp. 145ff. and 169ff.—without the slightest documentation—about my own elaboration of 'value-nihilism' by means of the theory of habit-formation and suggestion. Nowhere have I adduced the theory of habit-formation and suggestion as an argument in support of non-cognitivism as a logical analysis of moral discourse; it has been adduced by me only as a possible, although doubtful, psychological explanation of the natural illusion of objectivity characterizing moral consciousness, see, e.g., 'On the Logical Nature of Propositions of Value', *Theoria*, 1945, pp. 172ff., 208, the section under the heading: 'Whether the illusion of objectivity can be explained psychologically is without significance for the tenability of the logical analysis.'

is immaterial to the application of the principles accepted by me. This is true even on the theory that acceptance is constitutive, the expression of a personal attitude. The attitude and standpoint I have chosen are mine whatever the attitudes of others are. In support of my standpoint, of what I consider to be good and right, I must fight and condemn the opposing standpoints of others. By this I do not mean to advocate persecution (physically or in any other way) of people who disagree with me in moral questions. In most cases disagreement is compatible with respect for other people's diverging ideals. To deny this, as Hare has pointed out,[1] would be to miss the distinction between thinking that somebody else is wrong and taking up an intolerant attitude towards him. It cannot be denied, however, that toleration also has its limits.

Another point worth stressing is that the personal attitude which non-cognitivists consider to be the ultimate foundation of morality is by no means identical with an arbitrary whim. The moral standpoint which men adopt are fashioned by many common determinants that make for uniformity, at least among individuals of the same community or group. Fundamental evaluations are to some extent standardized by biological and physical features which all men possess. It is well known that countless attempts have been made to deduce from 'human nature' a true natural morality or natural law. What truth there is in these constructions lies in the impact of the common features of 'human nature' on existing morality. More important are the customs, conventions and accepted values of the society in which the individual grows up. Personal morality is never an arbitrary creation; it is the outcome of the evolving and critical elaboration of the traditions in which an individual was nurtured. Because of these common determinants and despite individual peculiarities and divergencies, moral attitudes display a considerable harmony, a harmony which has given rise to the view that moral ideals express a more or less imperfect cognition of objectively valid norms or values.

Finally, non-cognitivism does not eliminate moral reasoning by requiring that each moral judgment be based directly on a separate decision of attitude. For moral values and principles may often be organized in a hierarchy, so that values or principles at one level may be derived from those at a higher level together with factual premisses. If, for example, liberty is valued (higher level principle)

[1] Hare, *Freedom and Reason* (1963), pp. 49-50, 177.

and democracy is believed to be the form of government which best furthers liberty (factual premiss) it follows that democracy must be valued as the best form of government, unless the conclusion is neutralized by considerations based on other values and other factual premisses. In this way moral values may form a system, and the irreducible attitude of acceptance may be limited to a fairly small set of initial evaluations. It is probably not possible, however, to achieve the aim of the early utilitians, namely, the reduction of morality to a single value (pleasure or the satisfaction of needs).[1]

§ 17

Directives are normally used in communication by advancing them with directive function.

In this section we shall study the use of directives in communication. The question is whether it is possible with regard to directives to make a distinction similar to that between asserting and posing a proposition (levels 6 and 7 in the survey at the beginning of § 16).

The normal use of a directive in communication is to *advance* it to other people with a *directive function*, that is to advance it under such circumstances that it is—more or less—probable that it effectively will influence the behaviour of the recipient in accordance with the action-idea of the directive. In §§ 10–15 I have tried to explain how this is possible and I do not think I need go further into this matter.

The question remains whether directives also are used in communication without their normal directive function in a way somewhat similar to the use of propositions without their normal informative function—that is when a proposition is posed with a fabulating function. This question must be answered in the affirmative even if the fabulating use of directives does not in practice play a part comparable to the fabulating use of propositions in the literature of fiction and scientific hypotheses. As far as I am aware a fabulating use of directives occurs only in these situations: (1) when used for fun; (2) in children's games of make believe; and (3) in grown-up people's similar activity—dramatic performances.

Some other situations invite a similar interpretation. It could

---

[1] *On Law and Justice*, p. 305.

e.g. seem natural to consider the presentation of a draft statute or a draft resolution as a fabulating use of the directives involved. It is obvious, at any rate, that the directives in this situation are not advanced with directive intentions. Such an intention arises only at the moment when the statute is passed or the resolution adopted. But this interpretation would be a mistake. What is really going on in these situations corresponds to what, when speaking of propositions at the beginning of § 16, I called levels (1), (2), and (3). A directive is produced, considered and talked about, without any use being made of it. The draft is amended (the directive is reshaped), considered and discussed from the point of view, whether or not to make use of it (adopt the draft). The same is true of all situations in which people consider and discuss proposals for orders, applications, advice, legal decisions or any other kind of directive.

In a novel the characters utter directives as well as propositions, and in this case, likewise, no use is made of them. The author (fabulating) tells us that Mr. Smith commanded his children to do so and so. That means that the directive is mentioned, talked about, but not used.

We may conclude that although directives can be posed in fabulating speech, such use plays only a modest part in practice.

§ 18

The fundamental difference between indicative and directive speech is to be found at the semantic level. This difference conditions corresponding pragmatic difference of function, and is related to standard differences at the grammatical level.

In the second chapter, the structure, meaning and functions of indicative speech were analysed; and in the present chapter the same has been done for directive speech. If we compare the results of both analyses, they are seen to confirm our hypothesis that the distinction between indicative and directive discourse is reflected in differences at all levels of linguistic analysis, viz., at the grammatical, the semantic, and the pragmatic levels. The semantic level contains the most fundamental distinction; for the proposition, which is the meaning content of the indicative, is distinct from the meaning content of the directive. Both share the feature of being concerned with a topic describable in a phrase (in the directive the topic is always an action-idea). But in the proposition the topic is conceived as real, while in the directive it is held out as a pattern of behaviour. The proposition and the directive are two separate tools available for use in discourse, and the functions they are fashioned to perform must necessarily be as different as the tools themselves, just as the functions an axe is calculated to perform are by necessity different from those of a violin. The proposition's function in soliloquy is adjudicative, and is in dialogue informative or fabulating (see §§ 6–8). Directives normally are used only in dialogue, where their function is directive. Moral directives alone are used in soliloquy, where their function is adjudicative. Despite the fact that a formal resemblance permits us to use the term 'adjudicative' to describe a function of both propositions and directives, it should be obvious that this function is distinct in the two cases. For deciding on one's moral attitude and ideas is rather different from formulating and articulating one's conceptions of reality.

While semantic differences necessarily determine corresponding differences at the pragmatic level (differences, that is, of function in the use of propositions and directives respectively) the same is not true at the grammatical level. There is a standard grammatical form for directives as well as for propositions, but the correlation is not unambiguous. Directives are typically expressed by the use of the imperative mood or of some term with specifically deontic meaning; and propositions are typically expressed in the indicative mood, without the use of deontic terms. But though the imperative mood probably always carries directive meaning some crossings of meaning and grammatical form do occur. Sentences in the indicative which contain no deontic terms may, in certain contexts and with certain intonations, have directive meaning ('You will close the door'); conversely, sentences with deontic terms may in appropriate circumstances express propositions ('Parking here is forbidden', said to one by a friend).

Indicative and directive discourse, then, exhibit their differences at all levels of linguistic analysis, though in different ways. At the semantic level there is a clear distinction between indicatives and directives. Pragmatically, the function of indicatives is adjudicative, informative or fabulating, whereas directives have normally only directive function. The picture is not so clear at the grammatical level, but some forms of expression are especially suited to express either indicatives or directives.

Above in § 3, it was said that the terms 'descriptive' and 'prescriptive' seem inadequate for marking the fundamental twofold division of discourse we have in mind. We are now better equipped to understand why this is so.

The term 'descriptive' is unhappy, since both the proposition and the directive contain a descriptive element, namely the phrase which describes the topic (or action-idea), which is in one case thought of as real and in the other case presented as a pattern of behaviour. The difference lies, consequently, not in whether something is described, but in the attitudes with which the described topics are conceived. The proposition describes the world as it really is (or is believed to be): the directive describes it as a possible pattern of behaviour.

Similarly, the term 'prescriptive' is not to the point since it is ordinarily associated with particular kinds of directives (prescriptions, regulations, and quasi-commands), and is consequently inadequate for designating kinds of directives like requests, invitations, exhortations, entreaties and autonomous moral principles. The term 'directive' suffers, it must be admitted, from a similar defect but to a lesser degree only.

In § 5 I propounded the view that the element which distinguishes a proposition from an idea (the meaning content of a sentence from that of a phrase) is the thought of reality; and that this element is different both from 'nodding assent' to the sentence (Hare) and from asserting it. In § 6 I added that this view, if it is correct, is of far-reaching consequence as the foundation of a satisfactory analysis of the distinction between indicative and directive discourse. I hope that the reader will now be willing to endorse this estimate, especially if he compares the analysis given here with similar attempts made in the literature, for instance by Hare, Langford and Hedenius.

In § 6, it was mentioned that Hare confuses the indicative operator of a proposition—its 'neustic' element, the thought of reality, 'so it is' —with acceptance of the proposition, the 'nodding assent' to the sentence.

C. H. Langford and Marion Langford, like Hare, notice the fact that the command 'John, close the door' and the prediction 'He will close the door' have a descriptive element in common. 'When we consider', they write, 'what observations would serve to verify that the corresponding prediction was true, we see that the two sentences express precisely the same *idea* [my italics], namely that of John's closing the door. Of course, if John did not close the door, we should say that the person who made the prediction had been in error, but should not say this of the person who gave the command. That, however, is because, in ordinary circumstances, the indicative mood means pragmatically that the speaker believes what he expresses, whereas the imperative mood does not. To every imperative sentence there corresponds a synonymous indicative sentence with the same literal meaning but a different pragmatic meaning.' ('Introduction to Logic', *Philosophy and Phenomenological Research*, 1953-4, p. 565.) As the authors are not aware of the difference between the idea of a topic (expressed in a phrase) and the thought of the topic as real (expressed in a proposition), they are misled into the assumption that an imperative involves a proposition. This appears clearly from C. H. Langford's paper 'Moore's Notion of Analysis', *The Philosophy of G. E. Moore* (ed. P. Schlipp, 1942), pp. 333-4. Here a similar analysis is summed up in the following words: 'Now, the sense of an indicative sentence is a proposition, and therefore the sense of an imperative sentence is a proposition. Hence, to give a command is to express a proposition' (Cf. Mogens Blegvad, *Den naturalistiske Fejlslutning* [*The Naturalistic Fallacy*] (1959), pp. 140ff.). Since, on this view, there is no difference on the semantic level between an assertion and a command, it follows that the difference must be placed exclusively at the pragmatic level. It is the same meaning content, the same proposition, that in the one case is *asserted*, and in the other case *commanded*. This analysis seems to me obviously unsound because I cannot imagine how one and the same thing could be asserted as well as commanded. As the subject of assertion a proposition must possess the property of being either true or false; for 'to assert' means 'to present to others as true'. But exactly this property makes the proposition unfit for being commanded. A proposition is either true or false, only because it purports to state *what is the case*. To command means to express what *ought to be the case* although it is not so. Therefore, the notion of commanding a proposition is an absurdity: it means the same as saying that what is the case ought to be the case although it is not the case.

The analysis given by Hedenius, 'Befalningssatser, normer och värdeutsagor' ['Commands, Norms and Value-propositions'] in *Nordisk Sommeruniversitet 1954: Verklighet och Beskrivelse* [*Nordic Summer University 1954: Reality and Description*] (1955), pp. 179ff., is likewise distorted and contradictory because the author confuses the semantic with the pragmatic level of analysis. Hedenius operates with (1) the prediction 'You will close the door immediately', and (2) the command

'Close the door'. According to Hedenius (1) should be transcribed thus

⊢ *that you will close the door immediately*

where '⊢' is Frege's symbol of assertion, indicating that the subsequent proposition (expressed in a that-clause) is accepted and asserted. This means, expressed in Hare's terminology, that Hedenius identifies the phrastic element with a proposition and the neustic element with the assertion of this proposition.

Sentence (2) according to Hedenius should be transcribed thus:

! *Your shutting the door immediately*

where '!' is the symbol of the neustic element common to all imperative sentences. The phrastic element in this case is a phrase, not a sentence. The author further explains that the neustic element ('⊢', or '!') is identical with what he calls the 'factors of publication', that is, the circumstances from which it appears that the proposition, or the descriptive phrase, has been communicated in order to be accepted by the recipient, which in the case of commands means 'to be complied with'.

It should be noted that, on this view, the phrastic element of an imperative sentence is a completely neutral, descriptive phrase on a par, it is said expressly, with the current text-book example: 'the present king of France'. Therefore, in the phrastic element there is nothing of a commanding imperative nature. The commanding element is the outcome of the factors of publication by which the descriptive phrase is changed into an imperative sentence. On this ground it seems odd that Hedenius uses the term 'imperative' to designate the neutral, descriptive phrase (pp. 185–6). This, however, is more than a mere terminological oddness: it reflects a flaw in reasoning.

Hedenius rightly points out that it is possible, by omitting the neustic-asserting element in an assertion, to work out the proposition in its pure form. In that case one contents oneself with thinking of, or, so to speak, holding out for contemplation, the state of affairs with which the assertion is concerned, without taking any interest in the question whether or not this state of affairs does belong to reality. The proposition differs from the assertion in the lack of any decision on the attitude to take as to its truth or falseness, but its meaning is identical with that of the assertion, and in itself it is either true or false, independently of whether or not the speaker takes any interest in its truth value (p. 181). The author, however, does not see that a completely analogous reasoning applies also to imperative sentences, and that this fact knocks the bottom out of his analysis. For, with regard to commands also, it is possible to omit the neustic-commanding element, to disregard its

73

serious communication (publication) and to content oneself with think-ing of or contemplating the imperative—e.g., considering whether or not I should make use of it in a communication. It is obvious that the uncommunicated, merely contemplated, imperative is something more than a neutral, descriptive phrase. Even the unpublished imperative is according to its *meaning* an imperative and therefore it is only natural for Hedenius to use this term to designate the phrastic element. Con-sequently it must be admitted that there is a specific, imperative mean-ing independent of 'the factors of publication.' '!', the neustic symbol, is concerned with the meaning, not with the publication of it; it belongs to the semantic and not to the pragmatic level of analysis. To *assert* a proposition and to *advance* (publish) an imperative are pragmatic acts on the same footing. The proposition and the imperative—in my terminology: the directive—are semantic entities on the same footing. They have in common the descriptive phrase or, more correctly, the idea expressed in this (the phrastic element). They differ in having different operators in that the idea is conceived respectively as real and as pattern of behaviour (the neustic element). If '⊢' and '!' are to take up analogous positions, *either* both of them must stand for the pragmatic act, the assertion and the advancing respectively; *or* both of them must stand for the neustic factor in the semantic analysis, the thought of reality and the thought of a pattern of behaviour respectively.

§ 19

The distinction between indicative and directive speech is not exhaustive.

Though indicative and directive speech make up the two prin-cipal forms of speech, the division is not exhaustive. First of all, may I remind the reader that value judgments have been kept apart (see § 9).

Furthermore, there are such obvious examples of expressions which have neither indicative nor directive meaning as the ex-clamations 'Ouch!', 'Oh!', 'Damn!' and 'Wonderful!'. These have what is usually called *emotive meaning*. They describe nothing (and so have neither indicative nor directive meaning), but are verbal reactions which directly express an emotion. They are intimately related to mimicry and other biological reactions and lose their expressive function when detached from them. If one steps hard enough on a man's corns, he will utter a cry or a roar. But this is a biological and not a linguistic phenomenon. A Dane roars no differently from an Englishman. If, though, one treads more gently, the man may say 'Ouch!' or 'Hell!'; these exclamations

74

are linguistic utterances which depend on the language of the speaker. At the same time the man will probably react by withdrawing his foot and giving other indications of pain and disturbance. If someone were to say 'Ouch!' with no accompanying facial expressions or other bodily reactions but with a deadpan face as if he were saying 'Well', the utterance would lose its expressive force.

It is important to be aware of the ambiguity of the verb 'to express', for it has a bearing on understanding the special nature of emotive meaning. 'Ouch!' we have said to be the immediate expression of pain. What then is the difference between this utterance and the utterance of the statement 'I am in pain'? That there is a difference is obvious, for it is one thing to report one's emotions, and another thing to express them. When a young man in love expresses his feelings he does something different from reporting his state of mind. But the difference is blurred by the indiscriminate use of the word 'express' to designate the relation between linguistic form and meaning in the two separate cases. It is, nevertheless, clear that the word 'pain' "expresses" pain in quite another way than 'ouch'. The word 'pain' is suitable for evoking the *idea* of a certain experience; the statement 'I am in pain' is suitable for evoking a *belief* that a certain state of affairs, my being in pain, holds; but the exclamation 'Ouch!' is, like biological reactions, fitted to give vent directly to the experience and evoking in others a sympathetic response.[1]

These observations show that utterances with merely emotive meaning are located on the borderline between linguistic and biological phenomena. They play only a modest role in communication. Of greater importance are those utterances which carry emotive meaning while being primarily indicatives or directives.

Many words have both descriptive and emotive meaning. It is not unusual for two words to be used to describe nearly the same object, but with different emotional weight. (Examples are: 'leader'—'dictator', 'heroic'—'reckless', 'to uphold authority'—'to oppress', 'champion of liberty and right'—'rebel', 'practical politics'—'Machiavellianism'). Some words glitter like jewels

---

[1] This ambiguity has often been noted, see e.g. Hare, *The Language of Morals* (1952), p. 10; Charles L. Stevenson, *Ethics and Language* (1944), pp. 37ff.; 'The Emotive Conception of Ethics', *The Philosophical Review*, vol. LIX (1950), p. 299.

('our proud fatherland'), and others have a nasty smell ('pluto-cratic capitalistic monopoly'). There are words of many different degrees of warmth and cold, which have fine nuances of value in showing approval and disapproval, praise and blame, respect and contempt, admiration and scorn, love and hatred. Such words are appropriately used in persuasion, and are often particularly useful because their persuasive function is fused with their descriptive function. They go down easily without the hearer's being aware that he has been subjected to persuasion. Conversely, words which have strongly emotive content are used by different people to name different things. In Hitler's language, his dictatorship was 'true democracy', his police state the 'true' constitutional state, his capitalist economy 'true' socialism, and his regimentation 'true' liberty. Nor was Stalin prepared to give up the capital of good will that lies in the word 'democracy'. He called the Soviet Constitution 'the only perfect democratic constitution in the world', at the same time admitting that it 'upheld the regime of the dictator-ship of the working class'. The Communist press regularly uses a term with strongly emotive overtones, 'the will of the people', to designate the opinion of a small minority who make up only a few per cent of the population.

The emotive weight that accompanies an utterance may account for the meaning it expresses. The emotive weight in the com-manding tone of the utterance 'You will shut that door!' (perhaps reinforced by a specifically emotive expression 'You will shut that damned door!') makes it a directive.

Since the main concern of this study is the analysis of directives and norms, and not the function of emotive discourse, I shall not go any further into these problems.

I would like merely to remark that I no longer consider useful the con-cept *expressive* or *symptomatic* meaning, which I once used, following Jørgen Jørgensen.[1] I formerly assumed that every linguistic utterance has expressive meaning, that is, that each utterance is the expression or symptom of something. By this I meant that the utterance, as an integral part of a psychophysical whole, refers back to the experience which causes me to make the utterance. Whatever I say, my utterance must have been caused by emotional and volitional circumstances which

[1] *On Law and Justice*, pp. 6–7; Jørgen Jørgensen, *Psykologi pa biologisk Grundlag* [*Psychology on Biological Foundations*] (1942–6), pp. 455ff.

76

moved me to express myself, an urge to communicate ideas to others, or an emotion which spontaneously demands expression. I now see that this view is mistaken; for it confuses the semantic analysis of discourse with psychological inductive inferences. The consequence of this view would be that all human acts have expressive or symptomatic meaning. Even the act of killing, since it is an integral part of a psychophysical whole, refers back to the emotional and volitional state of mind which caused me to kill. But making such an inference is a different sort of thing from understanding the meaning of an utterance.[1]

[1] Influenced, probably, by the fact that grammarians treat the interrogative as co-ordinate with the indicative and imperative moods, 'questions' are often conceived as a semantic category on a par with 'indicatives' and 'directives'. In my opinion a genuine question is a directive, namely a request to give information. (There also occur rhetorical, pedagogical, ceremonial and possibly other kinds of spurious questions, whose semantic status I have not considered.) This description, however, is hardly sufficient. The question remains, what information? I refer to the interesting definition of a question as a propositional function by Felix S. Cohen in his paper 'What is a question?', *The Monist* 1929, reprinted in *The Legal Conscience* (1960), pp.3ff.

IV

THE CONCEPT OF A NORM

§ 20

From the point of view of the social sciences a norm is to be defined neither merely as a linguistic phenomenon (the meaning content which is a directive) nor merely as a social fact.

'Norm' is a term widely used in legal theory, sociology, linguistics, moral philosophy and logic, but there is no common agreement about its sense. It is in fact used most frequently without being defined at all. This is true, for example, of von Wright, although one of his books is chiefly concerned with norms. He is satisfied with an enumeration of various kinds of norms, namely, (1) the rules of games, (2) prescriptions, including legal rules, (3) technical norms, (4) customs, (5) moral principles, and (6) ideal rules. What these six classes of phenomena have in common is not easy to say, except for the fact that they seem to have something to do with directive meaning.[1]

For the concept 'norm' to be useful and productive in legal theory and the study of positive morality, its definition must meet certain conditions:

(1) norms must be intrinsically connected with directives, and

---

[1] Georg Henrik von Wright, *Norm and Action* (1963), pp. 1ff., especially pp. 15–16. The author defines his task thus: 'In this chapter I shall try to single out and briefly characterize some of the chief meanings of the word "norm" or, as we could also say, species or types of norms' (p. 1). It must be objected that to specify a concept is not the same as to indicate various meanings of the corresponding word. An isosceles triangle, e.g., is a triangle in exactly the same sense as any other triangle. If von Wright's six categories are 'species or types of norms' they all are norms in one and the same sense. But which one?

(2) the explanation given of the concept must make it possible to say that certain norms actually *exist*, or *are in force*.

The first condition is satisfied if norms are simply identified with directives; this is roughly the course Harald Ofstad takes. For him, all directives are norms, while the class of norms further includes any non-linguistic behaviour whose aim is to influence the conduct of others. He proposes the following definition of use of the concept of a norm:

'*X* advances a norm to *Y* (or *X*'s behaviour is normative with regard to *Y*) = def. *X* tries more or less strongly to dictate or guide *Y*'s behaviour'.[1]

This definition suffers from a number of defects which I shall only briefly indicate without discussion: (1) It is unreasonable to let the concept include all behaviour whose aim it is to influence the conduct of others. (The context makes it clear that the special terms 'dictate' and 'guide' are meant to stand for any way of influencing behaviour.) This would imply, e.g., that a man has advanced a norm if he gets someone drunk in order that he may disclose a secret. (2) It fails to distinguish proper effects from other effects, a failure which allows some purely informative utterances to count as 'the advancing of a norm'.[2] (3) As a definition of use it fails to provide an account of how the word 'norm' can be used in other contexts. (4) It is assumed that the norm may be linguistically formulated but left unclear whether it is to be taken as a speech-act (a pragmatic act), a sentence (which is a grammatical entity) or as a meaning expressed (which is a semantical phenomenon).

We need, however, to consider whether it is expedient as Ofstad does, to identify the concept 'norm' with the concept 'directive'. A definition on these lines may perhaps be useful in analytic moral philosophy, the field studied by Ofstad. But it will not serve the descriptive social sciences because it fails to meet the second condition which we listed above for a definition of a norm in legal theory or positive morality. This can be demonstrated from two points of view:

(1) The condition that the definition must make it possible to speak of the *existence* of a norm raises the question: How can a

[1] Harald Offstad, *Innföring i Moralfilosofi* [*Introduction to Moral Philosophy*], vol. I (1964), p. 22.
[2] Cf. above, § 7

directive be said to exist? A directive is the meaning content of certain linguistic constructions; it is, consequently, an abstraction which lacks independent existence, and exists only by virtue of the linguistic constructions which express it. If we now modified our definition and took a directive to be a linguistic construction which has directive meaning, it could be said to exist as a grammatical-linguistic phenomenon. We might, in that case, give as an example of a directive the sentence 'Peter, shut the door'. If a directive were, on the other hand, construed as a speech-act which consisted in the utterance of a sentence with directive meaning, the directive would exist as the *occurrence* of an utterance made by a certain individual at a particular place and time. But a concept defined in any of these ways would be of no use to the social sciences. For the subject matter of the social sciences, that which from their point of view can be said to *exist*, is made up of *social acts* not of either abstract meaning contents, or linguistic constructions, or linguistic acts.

(2) When in the social sciences we speak about the existence of a norm it is understood that by this we refer to a social *state of affairs*—i.e. to conditions which although changing, are of relative permanence and not merely a passing event. From this point of view many directives are ruled out as possible candidates for the norms studied in the social sciences. This holds with regard to all directives born out of a situation which is nothing more than an occurrence, a passing event. If, for example, a gangster orders the employees of a bank to hand over some money, these either do or do not comply with this directive. This is a situation describable in psychological terms as an event happening, and leaving no room for a term which refers to a state of affairs, a lasting condition. What could it mean to say that in this situation a norm has come into existence in any permanent or lasting sense?[1]

We may provisionally conclude that the concept 'norm' cannot be identified with the concept 'directive'. This is so, briefly, because a directive is a *linguistic* phenomenon (of whatever category—semantic, grammatical, or pragmatic), and the factual contexts which define many directives are passing events to be described in terms of individual psychology.

[1] Cf. below, § 22 c. Von Wright, *op. cit.*, pp. 116 and 126, however, uses the terminology that a norm (prescription) *exists* when an order has been advanced accompanied by effective sanctions.

Another approach, which we must now consider, defines the concept 'norm' in such a way that it designates not a linguistic phenomenon (a directive) but a factual social condition whose existence is established empirically.

Understandably, it is the sociologists who have made the attempt in this direction. While the lawyer is inclined to think of a legal norm as a meaning content (as a directive) abstracting from the social facts of the law in action, the tendency of the sociologist is to do exactly the opposite. Theodor Geiger distinguishes the norm from its verbal expression, or, as he says, the subsistent norm from the verbal norm. The subsistent norm, or norm proper, comprises a set of social facts which are revealed by the observation of behaviour. A norm of the pattern $s \rightarrow b$ ('in situation s behaviour b is to be carried out') exists, he says, if observation of the behaviour of members of a certain society shows that in the majority of cases either this pattern of behaviour is complied with or, if it is not, members of the society react by carrying out a sanction against the offender. This may be expressed in another way: a norm of the pattern $s \rightarrow b$ exists if the members of a society behave according to the pattern $s_1 \rightarrow r$, where $s_1 = s \, \& \sim b$ (the pattern '$s \rightarrow b$' has been violated) and r stands for the social reaction.[1]

Without examining Geiger's definition in detail, I will concentrate on its most important feature, namely, that the term 'norm', according to Geiger, denotes a set of observable social facts, that is, a certain regularity of behaviour. It is true that this definition makes sense of the notion that a norm can exist. But the definition is incompatible with certain other essential uses of the concept. One would not be able to say, for example, that a norm is *followed* or *applied*; that it is felt to be *binding*; or that it is *logically* connected with other norms which together make up a *system of norms*. These and other current uses of the concept 'norm' presuppose that a norm is a meaning content, and not a set of social facts. It is not surprising that Geiger is unable to evade these aspects of the customary meaning of the concept. As we have mentioned, he also introduces the term 'verbal norm', to mean the verbal expression of the norm proper; but on this point what he says is obscure. Are 'verbal norms' and 'subsistent norms' both species of the genus 'norm' (as equilateral triangles and right-angled triangles

[1] Theodor Geiger, *Vorstudien zu einer Soziologie des Rechts* (1947), pp. 23, 26, 32ff., 35, 47, 165.

are species of the genus 'triangle')? If so, then we are left in the dark as to how the concept 'norm' is to be taken. But it is difficult to see how one concept can cover two things as disparate as linguistic formulations and sets of social facts. The truth is, I think, that these things have nothing in common, though they do stand in a mutual relation just as crime and punishment, though different things, have certain relations to each other. If this is true, it is improper to use the same term 'norm' to designate these two distinct things. That Geiger does so seems to me a symptom of the impossibility of successfully defining 'norm' in such a way that it denotes simply a set of social facts.[1]

§ 21

A norm is to be defined as a directive which corresponds in a particular way to certain social facts.

On the basis of the remarks made in section 20, we may conclude that it is not possible to define the concept 'norm' (in a way useful to the social sciences) so that it denotes either simply a kind of meaning content (which includes all or only some directives), or simply a set of social facts. Both approaches must founder as too one-sided. We must then further conclude that a definition is required which integrates both aspects of the matter in the concept 'norm'. On this basis, I put forward the following definition: *a norm is a directive which stands in a relation of correspondence to social facts*, the nature of the relation to be specified subsequently. The only directives which can stand in the required relation are the impersonal directives with the exclusion of the autonomous moral directives; that is, those directives which have been called in the above survey (at the end of § 15) 'quasi-commands' and 'constitutive rules based on mutual agreement'.

Before I undertake the task of specifying what relation of correspondence is relevant, I want to stress the fundamental adequacy of the definition. The norm is said to be a directive, in the sense of a meaning content; to this extent the definition is adequate with regard to the use according to which a norm can be *followed* or *complied with*, felt to be *binding*, and *logically* related to other norms

---

[1] See my paper 'Om Begrebet "gældende Ret" hos Theodor Geiger' [On the Concept 'the Law in Force' in Theodor Geiger], *Tidsskrift for Rettsvitenskap*, 1950, pp. 244ff.

so that they together constitute a *system of norms*. But according to the definition a directive is a norm only if it corresponds to certain social facts, in a way to be specified. To say that a norm 'exists' means, then, that these facts exist; and to this extent the adequacy of the definition is secured with regard to that use of 'norm' which requires that norms can exist, and that statements to this effect form part of the description of societies.

Now, in undertaking the task of specifying how directives are related to social facts, I assume provisionally that we are concerned only with generally formulated directives, or rules (cp. below, § 22). It is, then, barely questionable that the fundamental condition for the existence of a norm must be that *in the majority of cases the pattern of behaviour presented in the directive* (s → b) *is followed by the members of the society*. If a rule is not effective in this sense, then it would be misleading to say that it 'exists', if such a statement is meant to be part of a description of social facts.

That a pattern of behaviour is on the whole *followed* does not mean that every member of the society generally acts in the same way in given circumstances. Usually the description of *s* is so qualified that the norm will concern only certain categories of the members of the society. Thus the directive that shops are to be closed at a certain hour relates only to those members of society who are shopkeepers.

That the pattern is *on the whole* followed involves a certain vagueness which makes it difficult to decide in some circumstances whether or not a norm exists.

This condition, however, is not of itself sufficient to provide an adequate definition. For it is necessary for the establishment of a norm that it be followed not only with external regularity, that is with observable conformity to the rule, but also with the consciousness of following a rule and being bound to do so.[1] If this requirement is not met (I shall subsequently return to the question of what it implies) then many patterns of social behaviour which differ essentially from those traditionally called norms would be included under the concept. I have in mind the following types of observable regularities of behaviour:

(1) *Patterns biologically or physically based.* Man's biological make-up and the general economy of nature effect conformity of

---

[1] H. L. A. Hart, *The Concept of Law* (1961), pp. 54-56.

behaviour in many ways. Most of us sleep during the night and are awake in daytime; we turn on the light when it becomes dark and wear more clothes when it is cold; we carry an umbrella or a raincoat if it looks like rain.

(2) *Technical patterns.* As we have mentioned earlier, some directives are offered as advice or directions for the most efficient performance of certain tasks and achievement of certain goals. When faced with similar tasks, people will to a great extent act uniformly and follow directions which are warranted by technology and tradition. This is especially true of professional undertakings. Bricklayers are trained in the time-honoured methods of building a wall or a chimney, gardeners learn how to graft and plant cuttings, tailors are taught the traditions of their profession.

(3) *Folkways* (habits which lack binding force). Because of uniform interests and traditions uniform habits grow up in the life of a people. In certain circles, under certain circumstances, it is usual to celebrate Christmas with a Christmas tree and gifts; to eat at set hours; to dance at the local inn on Saturday night; to get engaged before being married; to wear a wedding ring; to serve mustard with boiled cod; to have children baptized and confirmed. These patterns, without changing their substance, may become customs of a normative character merely by being deeply established.

These three and perhaps other classes of behaviour patterns are characterized by external conformity or regularity, without being internalized, that is, without being experienced as binding. This much is, I believe, commonly agreed. But agreement comes to an end when the question is raised of what is meant by calling a pattern of behaviour 'binding'. Two answers have commonly been given. Some writers have attached importance to the condition that the rule of action is experienced internally as *valid* ('binding' means arousing a feeling of obligation). Others have regarded as the decisive feature the external fact that violation of a rule is regularly met by a reaction (sanction) on the part of other members of society, the individual agent feeling himself in a position of coercion: either he follows the rule, or runs the serious risk of being exposed to punishment of some kind ('binding' means *'coercing'*).

On the former account, the criterion of a pattern of behaviour's having binding force lies in mental experiences and reactions either of the agent himself or of a spectator. A person who is in situation *s* (that is, a situation in which behaviour *b* is expected, in accordance with the supposed pattern) feels a special prompting or impulse to act according to the pattern. This impulse does not appear as a manifestation of his needs and interests; it may, indeed, conflict with these. Even though there exist no external hindrances to acting in violation of the pattern, and although his interests prompt him to act differently, the agent, under the influence of this impulse, does not feel free to do so. He feels himself to be subject to a peculiar kind of 'compulsion', but not a compulsion in the usual sense of a pressure stemming from the threat of sanctions—a threat of having inflicted on him some evil, which provides an incentive to act based on his interests and fears. The 'compulsion' that constitutes 'binding force' resembles the compulsion which arises out of the threat of sanctions in so far as the agent does not feel free, but rather feels under pressure to act in a way which conflicts with the way he would *like* to act. But it differs from external compulsion in that the impulse which prevents him from following his desires is not itself experienced as a manifestation of any need or interest; that is, it is not rooted in the fear of some evil or the desire for some good. For this reason, the compelling impulse has a stamp of unintelligibility and mystery, as if it did not arise from his own nature but was a dictate coming to him from outside.

This peculiar experience of being bound is manifested verbally in deontic words and phrases. Asked why he is acting against his own interest the agent will give answers such as 'because it is my *duty* to do so', 'because it is the *right* thing to do', 'because I *ought* to do it whether I like it or not'.

This admittedly sketchy account of the experience or awareness of duty and obligation must suffice here. No one has given a more penetrating analysis of this phenomenon than Kant, although he took the awareness of duty to be a revelation of the transcendental and not as one psychological phenomenon among others. For a further account of this subject, I refer interested readers to my earlier publications.[1]

How the spontaneous impulse which makes itself felt as a sense

---

[1] *Kritik der sogenannten praktischen Erkenntnis* (1934), Chapter VII, 1 and 2, and Chapter VIII, 2; *On Law and Justice*, pp. 364ff.

of obligation arises is a psychological problem which cannot be dealt with here.[1]

What the agent experiences immediately, a witness may experience by imagining himself in the agent's place. For him the impulse manifests itself as the *expectation* that the pattern in question will be followed. This 'expectation' is not, however, theoretical (like that expressed in 'rain is to be expected later in the day') but constitutes a *demand* (a deontic term). It shows itself verbally as an expression of *approval* or *disapproval* according to whether the demand is satisfied: he did *right*, or *wrong*, he *ought* not to have acted in that way. Verbal reactions of disapproval are often accompanied by adverse feelings, ranging from cool reserve to anger and indignation; and these emotions may be so strong that they lead to acts of violence, such as lynching. Although reactions of this kind are, we may suppose, produced mainly by the violation of the interests of the one who reacts, they may also be disinterested and caused by pure moral indignation. It is another question whether moral indignation can always be assumed to conceal hidden motives of self-interest (e.g., envy).[2]

I shall call any experience of obligation, rightness, wrongness, approval, or disapproval, the *experience of validity*. It must be made clear that this term designates certain psychological phenomena; 'validity' is nothing but the peculiar characteristic of these experiences. When I speak of the 'experience of validity', then, I am not referring to a recognition of 'validity' in the sense earlier discussed of a property inherent in moral principles, which cognitivists claim to exist and non-cognitivists deny. But it is not accidental that the word 'validity' is used to characterize these psychological experiences; for it is just the false interpretation of these experiences which has given rise to the idea of an objective quality of validity accessible to cognition.

According to the rival account of the 'binding' character of a behaviour pattern, what distinguishes a binding norm from non-binding conformity, or internal regularity from external conformity, is a set of observable facts: if the pattern of behaviour is violated, there regularly follows a reaction on the part of the society.

[1] See *Kritik der sogenannten praktischen Erkenntnis*, Chapter III, 8; *On Law and Justice*, pp. 364ff.
[2] Cf. Svend Ranulf, *The Jealousy of the Gods and Criminal Law at Athens*, vol. I–II (1933–4); *Moral Indignation and Middle Class Psychology* (1938).

This reaction comes either from individuals acting spontaneously or from the institutionalized organs of society created for this purpose (the police, the courts, and executive authorities). This is Geiger's view. According to him, as we have seen, $s \rightarrow b$ expresses an existing norm if the pattern $s_1 \rightarrow r$ is regularly followed, where s_1 stands for s & $\sim b$ ($s \rightarrow b$ is violated) and r signifies a reaction which has the character of a sanction. A norm exists, on this view, if compliance with its directed pattern of behaviour is guaranteed by *threat of coercion*. The experience of the norm as 'binding' is the internal reflection of this external fact.[1]

To some extent the two views lead to the same results. For the emotional and perhaps physical reactions of disapproval will in themselves constitute a sanction. The crucial question must then be one of approach: can the existence of a system of sanctions and, hence, of a normative system, be discovered merely by external observation of behaviour?

The answer is that it cannot. Not any disagreeable reaction is a sanction. The notion of a sanction is intimately connected with the feeling of disapproval. A merely external record of behaviour must lead to unacceptable results, by abstracting from the meaning of the reaction and its mental background. A person who earns a certain income is regularly met with the requirement to pay a certain sum to the Inland Revenue. Why do we not interpret this demand as a sanction (a fine) which shows the existence of a norm forbidding the earning of such an income? Why are customs duties not considered to be sanctions against imports, or the coercive measures taken with regard to the insane interpreted as sanctions against becoming insane? These and similar questions are not answerable on behaviouristic premisses; and this proves that a behaviouristic account of what it is for a norm to exist cannot be sustained.

The inadequacy of the account is especially obvious in the case of legal norms. Since legal sanctions are applied according to the decisions of the courts, the existence of a legal norm would have to be derived from an observed regularity in court decisions. But external observation is not sufficient for establishing such a regularity. For a long period of time a judge may display a certain

---

[1] 'That a norm is binding means: it is probable that either people comply with it or that violation of it calls forth an adverse reaction.' Theodor Geiger, *Vorstudien zu einer Soziologi des Rechts* (1947), p. 165, cf. pp. 26, 32ff., 47, 157ff.

typical reaction; he may, for example, regularly impose penalties for criminal abortion. But the pattern of reaction may change suddenly, if a new law has been passed. Nor can regularity be ascertained by recourse to the observation of a more general pattern of behaviour, viz., 'obeying the legislator'. For it is not possible, from the observation of behaviour alone, to identify the 'legislator' who is being obeyed. External observation alone might lead us to believe that it is certain individuals who are obeyed, that is, those persons named as members of the legislature. But one day there is a general election and the composition of the legislature changes. And so we go on, perhaps right up to the constitution; but even the constitution may be changed. A behaviourist interpretation, then achieves nothing. For the *change* in the judge's behaviour can be understood and predicted only by taking into account ideological facts, that is, only by assuming the existence of those feelings of validity, or ideology, which motivate the judge's decisions. Only on the hypothesis of the allegiance which the judge feels toward the constitution, its institutions and the traditionally recognized sources of law, is it possible to interpret changing judicial reactions as a coherent whole—as regularities constituted by an ideology.

Geiger's support of a behaviourist analysis is understandable as a generalization of views that are useful in anthropological investigations which concern descriptions of simple customs of a relatively constant nature. The sanction theory is based on the assumption that it is possible to observe how people actually behave in different situations, that certain patterns of behaviour are followed regularly, and that a reaction takes place if they are violated.

The use of the *indifferent* or *habitual* present tense ('the Chinese *eat* with chop-sticks'; 'they *honour* their ancestors') implies that the distinction between past, present and future is of no importance to the description at hand. This in turn implies that the described regularity has a *static* character, or, at least, that it is so static that the question of change can be ignored. 'That is how they behave'; people have acted in this way for a long time and will continue for a long time in the same way.

A sociologist inevitably has this way of thinking in his blood. A major branch of his science, cultural anthropology, occupies itself with describing the manners and customs of assorted peoples and groups, their mores and conventions conceived as static patterns of behaviour. In China people eat with chop-sticks and kiss with their noses; among Eskimoes such and such rules govern the division of a catch; in certain Indian tribes, if a man receives a gift he is obligated to make a return. In short, cultural anthropology deals with relatively constant patterns, a time-honoured customary order, determined by factors which change only slowly, like living organisms. This relative invariance allows anthropologists to use a method similar to that of the natural sciences: from past observations, together with the constancy of customs, they can make inductive inferences about the future. The indifferent or habitual present tense expresses this inductive inference.

But there is no room for such an approach when dealing with a dynamic order like a legal system. The future behaviour of the courts, as we have seen, cannot be predicted on the basis of past decisions alone. Judicial regularity is not external, habitual and static, but rather internal, ideological and dynamic.

There is another reason why the sanction theory will not do. As we have seen, according to that theory, the criterion for the existence of the norm $s \to b$ is that the pattern $s_1 \to r$ is regularly followed. But in this case, what kind of regularity is it supposed to be? Does the formula $s_1 \to r$ itself signify a mere habit without binding force, or a pattern of behaviour which itself has a normative character? The latter must be the case: People are *expected* to disapprove of contraventions of a norm. That $s_1 \to r$ is binding is especially obvious when r is taken to be the reaction of the courts to violations of legal norms. Geiger agrees with this.[1] If, however, $s_1 \to r$ is itself a norm, that is, a pattern of behaviour which is binding, then the theory entails the existence of a third norm, $s_2 \to r$ according to which sanctions are to be applied against whoever violates the second norm ($s_1 \to r$) which itself demands the application of sanctions against whoever violates the first norm ($s \to b$)—and so *ad infinitum*. Any norm requires as its basis an infinite chain of norms. A pattern of behaviour is said to be a norm, to be binding, only if it is backed up by sanctions. But the coercive measures themselves are taken in accordance with norms which have also to be backed up by sanctions applied in accordance with norms—and so on to infinity. A model which thus

[1] *Op. cit.*, p. 169.

implies an infinite regress cannot be adequate as a description of reality.

I have dwelt at length on Geiger's theory of sanctions, because we have to understand why it is unsound before we can see what social facts are referred to when we speak of the existence of a legal norm, or its being in force. The opinion is widely held that what constitutes the existence of a legal norm is the fact of the physical power behind the law, a power that will be exercised against offenders by the police, the courts and executive agencies. It is said that the law consists of rules which will be maintained, if the need arises, by means of physically coercive force—the use of violence. On this view, a law like the one which requires a buyer to pay the stipulated price depends in turn upon another rule which requires coercive sanctions to be used against the buyer who refuses to comply voluntarily. What is the nature of these secondary sanction-demanding norms? If it is said that they are themselves legal rules we land in the infinite regress mentioned already: secondary rules presuppose third level rules which presuppose fourth level rules, etc. If it is said, on the other hand, that the secondary rules are not themselves legal rules, we have on our hands the paradox that the rules which govern the judge's exercise of his office are not legal rules. In addition to these complications, the theory has the unfortunate consequence that large parts of what is normally considered the law are denied to be of a legal nature and are excluded from the province of the law. For it is a fact that there can be no enforcement of much of constitutional law, administrative law, and procedural law, in so far as these concern the competence and obligations of the highest organs of the state. Such is the case especially where there exists no judicial review of legislation.[1]

These complications and unacceptable consequences disappear, if we take the position that legal rules are not rules *maintained by* the exercise of coercion but rules *about* its exercise; they are rules which are in general not enforced but followed voluntarily, that is, in virtue of the feeling of validity which endows the rules with binding force. Legal rules are directed at those in authority, the organs of the state, and their source of effectiveness is the allegiance of officials toward the constitution and the institutions derived from it, together with the non-violent sanctions of

[1] *On Law and Justice*, pp. 52ff.

disapproval and criticism which are implied in this attitude. Legal rules govern the structure and functioning of the legal machinery. By 'legal machinery' I mean the whole set of institutions and agencies through which the *actes juridiques* and the factual actions we ascribe to the state are undertaken. It includes the legislature, the courts, and the administrative apparatus, to which belong the agencies of enforcement (especially the police and the military). To know these rules is to know everything about the existence and content of the law. For example, if one knows that the courts are directed by these laws to imprison whoever is guilty of man-slaughter, then, since imprisonment is a reaction of disapproval and, consequently, a sanction, one knows that it is forbidden to commit manslaughter. This last norm is implied in the first one directed to the courts; logically, therefore, it has no independent existence. The upshot is that, in describing a legal order, there is no need to employ a double set of norms, one demanding of citizens a certain type of behaviour (e.g., not to commit man-slaughter), and the other prescribing for the agencies of the legal machinery under what conditions coercive sanctions are to be applied (e.g., if manslaughter has been committed). At times, those drafting statutes employ the device of formulating a legal rule as a directive to the courts, leaving it to the citizen to infer what conduct is required of him. The criminal code is drawn in exactly this way. Nowhere is it stated in so many words that man-slaughter is prohibited. The prescription against this and other crimes is, rather, inferred from the appropriate rules of the criminal code which are directed to the judge. The Danish Criminal Code, section 237, thus simply states that 'he who kills another man shall be sentenced for manslaughter to imprisonment from 5 years and into lifetime'. More commonly, however, another device is employed. *Primary* rules (or substantive law) state how citizens are obliged to behave. It is impossible to infer from these rules alone how a judge is to decide in the case of a violation. According to the circumstances of the case, the judge may specify as a sentence some punishment (whose kind and severity is left unspecified by the primary law), or enjoin some performance or payment for damages. For this reason a set of *secondary* rules (the law of sanctions) is required to specify what sanctions may be exacted of those who violate the substantive law, and to make more precise the conditions under which various sanctions may be applied. Such rules are directed to the judge, instructing him how to decide different types of case. They are often expressed in terms of the *legal effects* that arise out of violations of substantive law; for example, when it is said that the legal effect of overdue delivery is to give the buyer a right to claim damages. This rule in fact amounts to a directive to the judge, requiring him to hold for the plaintiff when he sues in appropriate circumstances.

Are we to conclude from this that there are two sets of legal norms, one addressed to the citizens stating their obligations, and another addressed to judges, directing them to decide certain cases in certain ways?

From a logical point of view, we must answer in the negative: there exists only one set of rules, namely, the so called 'secondary' rules which prescribe how cases are to be decided, which, that is, basically prescribe the conditions under which violent coercion is to be exercised. For we have seen that primary norms, logically speaking, contain nothing not already implied in secondary norms, whereas the converse does not hold.[1]

From a psychological point of view, however, there do exist two sets of norms. Rules addressed to citizens are felt psychologically to be independent entities which are grounds for the reactions of the authorities. If we apply our definition of the existence of a norm, primary rules must be recognized as actually existing norms, in so far as they are followed with regularity and experienced as being binding. It is immaterial to the question of the existence of these rules that they are, in addition, sanctioned by the threat of coercion and consequently obeyed from mixed motives, both interested (fear of sanctions) and disinterested (respect for law and order). Confusion on this point might lead to the mistaken objection that our logical thesis that there exists only one set of norms implies that the law is obeyed solely from fear of sanctions.[2]

§ 22

Comments in further explanation of the concept 'norm':

(a) *Legal norms in particular*
(b) *Legislation and customs*
(c) *Generalization*

[1] *Op. cit.*, pp. 45–46, cf. pp. 66–69.   [2] *Op. cit.*, pp. 68ff.

(d) *Singular norms*
(e) *The relation of a norm to meaning and reality*
(f) *That norms have no truth-value*
(g) *The several senses in which norms have validity-values.*

We have arrived, tentatively, at the definition of a norm as a directive which corresponds to certain social facts in such a way that the pattern of behaviour expressed in the norm (1) is in general followed by members of the society; and (2) is felt by them as binding (valid). We must now further explain the definition and discuss its soundness.

(a) The requirement that the pattern of behaviour be felt as binding—and hence sanctioned by approval and disapproval and other spontaneous reactions on the part of the members of the society individually—does not preclude the bringing to bear, in addition, of *organized sanctions* on the person who acts contrary to the pattern. For this purpose rules are necessary which establish agencies with the power of deciding on behalf of society (i.e. with a force binding all members of society) as to whether a violation of obligatory norms has occurred, and, if so, what sanctions shall be applied. These agencies are the *courts*. If the exercise of sanctions is organized in this way we may speak of an *institutional order*. A well-developed institutional order includes further institutional agencies empowered to make general rules (legislative assemblies and governmental offices) and a great number of various agencies for the implementation and enforcement of enacted law and judicial decisions.

Law, as we explained above in § 13, in its broad sense, is an institutional order and thus differs from *convention* (courtesy, decency, conventional morality), which comprises those social rules whose only sanctions are unorganized disapproval and other non-violent reactions.[1] Whereas law is a social phenomenon which depends on the existence of social institutions, convention in principle is an individual phenomenon which depends on the unorganized and spontaneous reactions of each single member of society. We cannot, therefore, speak of 'Danish morality' as we speak of 'Danish law'. While the law may be determined more or less unambiguously, as the set of rules followed and upheld by the courts and other supreme agencies of the state, 'Danish morality'

---

[1] *On Law and Justice*, pp. 59ff.

can be nothing more than those moral convictions which are statistically predominant among the Danish population. This phenomenon is accordingly more vague and ill-defined than the law.

In primitive societies, where living conditions and social functions vary only slightly between individuals, fundamental values, attitudes and religious beliefs are for the most part uniform and harmonious. Tradition and custom, therefore, forcefully rule the life of the members in all its aspects. In modern societies this uniformity of attitude has broken down as the result of differences in social status, education and occupation, and social life, at the same time, has become extremely complicated. For these reasons many common social customs have ceased to exist or have lost their force. They have been replaced by legal regulations or by norms restricted in their force to smaller social groups (primary groups, professional groups, social classes and ethnic or religious communities).

Various kinds of law may be distinguished according to the sanctions attached to them. The modern state is essentially characterized by its possessing a monopoly in the exercise of violence, in internal affairs as a means of maintaining the legal order, and in external affairs as the instrument of power politics. What is called *municipal law* (the law of the political body organized as a state) is distinguished both from the law of private associations and from international law by the fact that its sanctions consist in violent coercion.

The law of *associations* is the law of organized private associations which exist within the jurisdiction of the state (limited companies, corporations, labour unions, trade associations, clubs, religious bodies and many other associations with varying structures and purposes). The sanctions of this type of law can never take the form of violent coercion, since this has been monopolized by the political authorities. It may consist in, e.g., organized boycott, temporary exclusion or final expulsion from the association, or the exaction of fines and other penalties as conditions for continuing membership. *Rules of games* are related closely to the rules of associations. A game may be regarded as a temporary association of persons whose aim is to amuse themselves by playing in accordance with certain rules. A rudimentary legislation exists in the players' agreement that such and such rules are to be followed.

There is often provision for a judge (or umpire, or referee) who can impose penalties. In this case also the highest sanction is expulsion from the 'association'; the judge may stop the game and expel the delinquent.

International law governs the society of states.[1] There exist institutional procedures both for the establishment of general norms and for the judicial decision of disputes. On our definition of law, therefore, international law is indeed law. But it has like the laws of associations, no institutional provisions for the exacting of sanctions by physical force. In the society of states there is, under present conditions, no monopoly of force; sanctions are therefore non-violent. Since expulsion from the society of states is in practice impossible, and since boycott is very difficult to organize, international law is less effective even than the law of associations; its sanctions have to consist almost entirely in moral disapproval. In modern times there have been attempts, albeit unsuccessful, to organize disapproval, boycott and even the use of military force through the law of a world organization. If it should eventually be the case that there evolved an effective disarmament of individual states and the concentration of the instruments of force as the monopoly of a supranational agency, international law would no longer exist. For under these conditions a world state would have been created, and the laws which govern the relations of formerly sovereign states would constitute a *municipal law*, the law of the world state. It would still be possible that what are now states would remain partly sovereign (self-governing) member states within a world federal state. The member states would retain internal jurisdiction and instruments of power which would be adequate to preserve law and order among their citizens, but insignificant compared to the power of the world state—a situation analogous to the relation between the American states and the Federal Government.

(b) A directive, as we have said, constitutes a norm on the condition that it corresponds with social facts, in the way we have described. This correspondence may be achieved in two different ways, either spontaneously or through the promulgation of the directive under such circumstances that it brings about this correspondence. In the first case we speak of custom, in the latter case, legislation.

[1] Cf. Alf Ross, *A Textbook of International Law* (1947), pp. 11ff.

95

Legislation[1] (in the broad sense of the word) is the establishment and promulgation of directives by agencies made competent to do so by existing rules. Rules of competence define what are the necessary conditions for creating a new legal norm. If an attempt at legislation does not satisfy these conditions the outcome is said to be *invalid* or *null and void*. A set of rules of competence constitutes a unity which may usually be divided into three parts: (1) those which determine *personal* competence, indicating what persons are qualified to participate in the procedure which creates new laws; (2) those which determine *procedural* competence, defining the procedure to be followed; and (3) those which determine *substantial* competence, indicating those matters with which the directive, issued by qualified persons in the manner prescribed, may concern itself.

Legislation has historically occurred only as part of a legal order, an order which, by our definition, depends on the organized exercise of sanctions in accordance with the decisions of the courts. There have existed and still exist systems which are backed by judicial but not legislative power (e.g., the primitive law of Denmark before the year 1200, or some kinds of the law of associations); the opposite, legislation unaccompanied by judicial power, is, however, unknown.

Laws which owe their existence to the acts of some legislating authority are called *statutory law or written law*, these terms taken in a broad sense, to include orders, rules, regulations and bylaws.

The norms which determine the competence of a certain authority A may themselves be written law, that is, they may have come into existence through the legislation of a higher authority A_1. The same is possible of the norms of competence which define the legislative power of A_1. Since the chain of authority must be finite, it follows that there exists a highest authority A_n, which is constituted by rules of competence not part of the written law. The norm or set of norms defining the competence of the highest authority may be called the *basic norm* of the system, which necessarily exists as unwritten law, or what we might call *implied law* or *customary law*.[2]

---

[1] *On Law and Justice*, pp. 78ff.; *Dansk Statsforfatningsret* [*Danish Constitutional Law*], vol. I (2nd ed., 1966), §§ 5 and 57.

[2] *Dansk Statsforfatningsret* [*Danish Constitutional Law*], vol. I (2nd ed., 1966), §§ 41 and 46.

We speak of *customs* when the correspondence between directives and social facts arises not through legislation but spontaneously as a product of an organic and unconscious evolution, a slow process of adaptation under the pressure of forces whose nature we little understand. In the case of customs, no operative role in the social pattern of events is played by the directive itself, or rather by any verbal expression and promulgation of the directive. There exists no authority whose function it is to enunciate the directive; anyone's account of the directive is correct and justified so long as it corresponds with the social facts which exist independently of any actual formulation of the directive.

Customs are *legal* and constitute *customary law*, if there are judicial authorities established to exercise organized sanctions in case of violation of the implied directives.[1] Otherwise, customs are *conventional*.

The transition from customary law to legislation is immensely important in the evolution of any society. Customary law is conservative; it relies on traditional and static patterns of behaviour. Those bound by it act as their fathers did. This does not mean that customs are unchangeable, for they may be adapted to changing conditions; this adaptation is slow and unplanned, lacking calculation and rational understanding of the requirements of a change in conditions. The German historical school of jurisprudence romanticized this evolutionary process, seeing it as the outcome of the organic growth of the 'national spirit' ('Volksgeist'), the spiritual substance which develops with a people and which is the primary basis of all law. At the same time it denied the legislator's vocation and power of interfering arbitrarily in this evolution. According to this doctrine, all the legislator is able to do is to listen to the growing legal consciousness of the people (as interpreted by academic jurists) and to further the spontaneous growth of the law. If the legislator misconstrues his mission and attempts arbitrary interference, his efforts will be frustrated and crushed by the inexorable forces of evolution.[2] We now know this philosophy to be fantasy. Experience has proved the possibility of using legislation for the conscious planning of social life. The doctrine of the historical school has this element of truth in it, that no legislator is omnipotent. However his competence is framed on paper, its

---

[1] *On Law and Justice*, pp. 91ff.
[2] *Theorie der Rechtsquellen* (1929), Chapter V; *On Law and Justice*, p. 344.

exercise will always in fact be contingent on the economic and ideological forces at work in the society. Legislation aiming at planning and directing social life is itself an effective factor, although only one among several.[1] Its source of effectiveness is the political myth, that allegiance which is felt towards a constitution and the institutions and authorities derived from it, based on the idea of a community and a common political power shared by all. To the extent that this acceptance of the political authority of the existing order is effective, citizens, even those who are out-voted, consider decisions taken by the competent authorities as their own decisions and are prepared to acquiesce in legislation which seems to conflict with their interests or ideals of social justice. But such acquiescence has a limit. If the divergence between the formal and the substantial legal consciousness, that is, between respect for law and order on the one hand and aspirations after justice on the other hand, goes beyond a certain limit, a critical situation develops. The law ceases to be accepted as valid and is obeyed, if at all, only from fear of sanctions; and thus the power of the legislator becomes precarious. The allegiance to government and law has given way to the spirit of rebellion. Whether this subsequently brings the issue in open conflict depends on a strategic estimation of the chances of success. If revolution would be premature, the tactical task is to undermine the existing social order by obstruction and propaganda.[2]

(c) We have defined the concept 'norm' in such a way that a norm exists if and only if the corresponding conditions are such that the norm is effective. Consequently, only those impersonal directives which we have classified as quasi-commands (legal and conventional rules) and rules of games can exist as norms. The question now arises: is it feasible, and useful, *to generalize* the definition in such a way that *any* directive is said to exist as a norm when its conditions of effectiveness are fulfilled? The definition we have so far operated with has been framed with the social sciences in mind. But it may turn out that this concept is a specific instance of a more general one. Let us consider the question with reference to personal directives and autonomous moral directives (see the survey at the end of § 15).

If such a generalization were possible, then, for example, a

[1] *On Law and Justice*, pp. 340, 351ff.
[2] *Op. cit.*, pp. 52ff.; *Why Democracy?* (1946), pp. 103ff.

norm whose content was 'Peter, shut the door' would be said to exist or to be in force if some person had effectively ordered Peter to shut the door. The effectiveness of this order, as we have seen, would arise either from fear of sanctions or from respect for authority. We would, accordingly, have to say that in the case of a bank-robbery there exists for the employees the norm 'Hand over the money', and that if Peter's father has ordered him to shut the door the norm 'Peter, shut the door' is in force.

In deciding this question, it will be useful to clarify why in the case of legal and conventional directives we require a term 'norm', implying that the directive is conceived not as an event in the life of an individual but as a state of affairs that exists independently of the reaction of the individual who is subject to the directive, that is, independently of the effectiveness of the directive in relation to him. The answer is that we need the concept 'norm' to express the social fact, which is independent of how any individual reacts, that it is *generally* effective among members of a social group. Regardless of whether a legal or conventional directive is effective with A, B or C as individuals, it may be the case that the directive is on the whole effective with regard to the members of the society. In this event, the directive appears to an individual as something which is given and which exists independently of his reaction to it.

Nothing similar can be said of personal directives. A command, for instance, is bound up with the concrete situation of personal contact between speaker and hearer. It is, against this background, either effective or not effective—that is all. So there is no reason to conceive the directive as existing, or as being in force independently of its effectiveness in a concrete situation.[1] If A, in situation s, commands B to shut the door, his command is either effective or not. If it is effective it may or may not be complied with. An analysis and description of the situation reveals this and nothing more. No purpose, then, is served by speaking of the effectiveness of a command as the existence of a norm to the effect that B is to shut the door. It is otherwise if commands regularly are issued to the members of a group; but in that case we really have to do with quasi-commands existing as norms within the group.

On the other hand, it may be reasonable to apply the objective

[1] On von Wright's dissenting opinion, see above, § 20 note 4.

existence expressed in the concept 'norm' to autonomous moral principles—only, however, if one assumes with the cognitivists that certain moral principles have an inherent property of validity that is accessible to cognition. It does seem natural to say of such directives that they exist as norms independently of their being accepted as valid. But since I cannot agree with the cognitivists I conclude that there is no basis for extending the concept norm to cover any directives other than quasi-commands and the rules of games.

(d) So far our assumption has been that a norm is a rule, that is, a directive posed in general terms. Can this assumption be maintained or must we abandon it? Current juridicial usage makes it seem natural to speak of *singular norms*, for example, a judge's directive to the defendant who loses a law-suit to pay so much money to the plaintiff, or a policeman's directive to move on, or the provisions of a contract which place a particular person under certain obligations. Singular directives, on the other hand, fail to satisfy the necessary condition that a norm exists only if it is on the whole followed and accepted as binding by the members of a community. As we have just pointed out, singular directives are either effective or not, and if effective are either complied with or not, and that is all.

All the same I find it convenient to abide by juridical usage. Singular directives and general rules make up a logical and systematic whole in such a way that it is natural to ascribe to some singular directives the same normative character which we ascribe to the general rules from which they are derived. But we must, accordingly, recognize that singular norms are essentially a secondary phenomenon whose existence is dependent on primary general norms.

We conclude that the definition of the concept 'norm' must be extended to include those singular directives which are derived from general norms as well as general norms themselves.

(e) Some difficulty has been caused by the question how a norm (or a rule or directive) is related to 'meaning' and 'reality'. Is a norm the *meaning* expressed by the linguistic formulation of the norm, as a proposition is the meaning expressed by a sentence in indicative speech? Black's answer is affirmative, adding, however, that this analysis is not illuminating, since the meaning does not appear from the linguistic construction as such but only from the use to which the construction is put.[1] Von Wright, on the other hand, denies that a norm is to be taken as the meaning of a linguistic construction. He does not intend, he says, to discuss the question in detail; but from his scanty remarks it appears that his reason for considering it inappropriate to identify 'norm' and 'meaning' is that he regards a norm as something which *comes into existence* through a particular use of a linguistic construction. It is the promulgation of a command or prescription, then, which brings a norm (directive) into existence by creating a certain relationship between the giver and receiver of the command. Not just any utterance of the prescriptive formula brings about such a relationship, but one that does bring it about also effects the existence of a norm.[2] Von Wright's reasoning implies that a norm consists in certain *psychological* (or in some cases sociological) facts, namely, the actual experienced relationship between the giver and the receiver of an effective command. Nowhere, however, does he say this explicitly. We have already pointed out, in section 20, that Theodor Geiger expressly (though inconsistently) maintains that a norm is primarily a subsistent norm, in the sense that it consists in certain social facts which are ascertained by the observation of social behaviour.

I hope that the preceding remarks and arguments have made it clear why one-sided definition of the concept 'norm', whether it identifies norms with meanings or with certain psychological and sociological facts, must fail, and lead only to difficulties—difficulties which are resolved by my own definition. A norm is a directive, and, to this extent, is a meaning content. But as Black points out, semantic analysis cannot distinguish one kind of directive from another, since every directive contains the same indiscriminating operator 'so it ought to be!' (see above, § 9). Only by distinguishing the situations in which they are issued and the sources of effectiveness located in these situations can directives themselves be distinguished. A directive is a norm, however, only on the condition that it corresponds in the necessary manner with social facts. A statement that a norm exists or is in force, consequently entails some statement about social facts. Any such statement, indeed, concerns the *meaningful interpretation of social facts*.

[1] Max Black, 'Notes on the Meaning of "rule" ', *Theoria*, 1958, pp. 107ff., 114ff., 160.
[2] G. H. von Wright, *Norm and Action* (1963), pp. 94, 117–18, 126.

(f) It is obvious and, as far as I know, undisputed that directives have no truth value (are neither true nor false), in most cases at any rate.[1] I cannot imagine that anyone would want to say that the order 'Peter, shut the door' or the rule of chess 'In a single move a king may be moved only one square' can be either true or false. Of the rule of chess it may be said that it exists (or is in force) in a certain community of two players; this assertion will be either true or false. But this is obviously not the same as ascribing truth values to norms themselves, just as black swans cannot be said to have a truth value merely because an assertion that black swans exist has a truth value.

Moral directives and norms, together with legal norms that are subject to moral evaluation, provide the only exception to the general agreement that exists on this matter. (I am disregarding the fact that technical directives may be called true or false if they can be interpreted as indicatives; see § 11.)

The logical character of moral directives is in dispute because of the fact that such directives, when they are accepted by an individual as principles of his autonomous morality (§ 15), are felt to have a stamp of validity independent of his personality and will, something which exists and is discovered by cognition as a quality inherent in the directive itself. We have already mentioned (in § 16) the radical divergence of opinion that exists between the cognitivists and the non-cognitivists concerning the interpretation of these experiences. Cognitivists regard such experiences as evidence of the objective validity of some directives, a validity which is independent of their acceptance and is accessible to cognition. Non-cognitivists reject this interpretation and maintain that the immediate stamp of objectivity which moral consciousness seems to perceive is an illusion whose origin can be explained psychologically. And this dispute is often taken to prejudge the question whether moral directives possess truth-values.

This is a mistake. The question whether a directive can have a truth-value is independent of the question whether a cognition of moral validity-qualities is possible. That a directive cannot have a truth-value follows analytically from the meaning of 'directive' and of 'truth-value'. The fundamental difference between a proposition and a directive lies, as we have seen, on the semantic

---

[1] See, however, Arne Næss, 'Do we know that Basic Norms cannot be True or False?' *Theoria*, 1959, pp. 31ff.

level. Both describe a topic (in the case of the directive an action-idea) which the proposition conceives as real ('so it is') and the directive presents as a pattern of behaviour ('so it ought to be'). To call an utterance true is, precisely, to accept that 'so it is'. Only propositions can therefore be true.

The soundness of this analysis would remain unaffected even if we were to accept the hypothesis that moral directives possess qualities of validity or invalidity. Let us assume that objective cognition has established the validity of the directive D. The statement 'D possesses objective validity' would then express a *true proposition*. But this is not the same as saying that D is a true directive. Truth value belongs to the proposition and not to the directive.

It may be objected that the distinction between the directive D and the proposition P: 'D possesses objective validity', is without practical significance since the two utterances have the same pragmatic function. If P is accepted as true, D is necessarily accepted as valid, that is, the person who believes P will feel bound to act according to D.

This objection is, in the first place, inconclusive; for even if tenable, it in no way threatens the thesis that truth-value belongs only to the proposition. In the second place, the objection is itself untenable. Whoever recognizes Hume's principle that no directive can be inferred from any set of indicatives will easily see that it is logically impossible to infer D from P. But even without Hume's principle, the untenability of the objection may be shown in the following way. Both directives and propositions may be used in communication to influence someone's behaviour. The functions of the two are, however, essentially different, since it is the immediate informative function of the proposition ('Your house is on fire', 'Your children have fallen through the ice') which is instrumental in bringing about the directive effect; no such mediation is true of the use of a directive. It is important to realize, however, that no information, of any kind, is itself sufficient to motivate a particular course of action. The driving force, the spring of action, must always be an interest or attitude of the agent. Information possesses motivating force only in so far as it is of consequence to some interest and attitude which it can activate. Information to the effect that a man's house is on fire, or his children have fallen through the ice, has no motivating force unless the hearer feels an interest in protecting, or an obligation to protect, his children or his possessions. In the same way, the information that a particular directive possesses a quality called 'validity' is not of itself sufficient to motivate action in a person who does not possess along with this information an attitude of respect toward what is 'valid'. One may accept the truth of P and at the same time not accept the validity of D in the sense of feeling obliged to act according to D.[1]

(g) I will end with some remarks about the use of the terms 'valid' and 'invalid' with reference to norms.[2]

In moral philosophy the term 'validity' is used to designate a supposed non-empirical quality which belongs to certain norms and which reveals itself to moral cognition *a priori*. No such cognition or quality, in my opinion, exists. But there do exist certain special experiences which we have called experiences of validity; it is an incorrect interpretation of these experiences which has given rise to the belief in the objective existence of a property of 'validity' (§ 21).

In directive legal speech (that is, the speech in which legal rules and decisions are expressed, as opposed to indicative speech *about* legal rules and directives) the terms 'valid' and 'validity' are used to indicate whether or not some *acte juridique*, a contract, say, or a will, has its intended legal effects. The conditions under which an *acte juridique* brings about legal effects are stated in legal rules, like the rule that a contract is invalid if it has been made under duress or fraud. Rulings on the validity or invalidity of an *acte iuridique* are therefore applications of those legal rules which are in

---

[1] Cf., *Kritik der sogenannten praktischen Erkenntnis* (1934), Chapter I, 2 and 'On the Logical Nature of Propositions of Value', *Theoria*, 1945, pp. 172ff., 203ff.

[2] The Danish language has two terms which usually both are translated by the English term 'valid', namely 'gældende' and 'gyldig'. Whereas 'gyldig' is used with a meaning close to 'valid', the term 'gældende' has a different function. 'Gældende ret' (German: 'geltendes Recht') means 'existing law', 'the law in force'. It refers without any evaluative connotation to the social facts we have described as constituting the existence of a norm or a system of norms. 'Gældende ret' is the opposite of *imagined* or *proposed* law, e.g., a draft. The term is used in indicative discourse to describe existing norms, especially in the dogmatic science of law, whose sentences may be formalized in the formula: 'D is "gældende" law in the society S', meaning that a directive D exists (or is in force) in the society S. I have allowed myself to trouble my English-speaking readers with these observations because the unfortunate translation of 'gældende' without explanation, as 'valid' has given rise to misunderstandings and pointless criticism; see, e.g., my review of H. L. A. Hart, *The Concept of Law* (1961) in 71 *Yale Law Journal* 1962, pp. 1185ff., 1190.

force in a specific case. To say of a will that it is invalid is to say that it fails to bring about the usual effects of a will, because of some aspects of its drawing. This is a legal decision which only the courts are competent to make. If someone other than an appropriate court, say, a lawyer, asserts the invalidity of a will, what he is doing is either (1) to predict from his knowledge of the law that the courts, if asked to decide on the matter, *will hold* the will invalid; or (2) to utter an exhortation (see § 12) that the will ought to be held to be invalid under current law. The former happens when a lawyer advises his client, the latter when he pleads a case in court.[1]

---

[1] In § 37, below, I mention a further sense which the expression 'validity' has in deontic logic.

V

AN ANALYSIS OF THE
ELEMENTS OF A NORM

---

§ 23

According to how the subject of a norm is determined a distinction is made between individual and universal norms. A norm is individual if its subject is determined as a closed class, by the use either of genuine proper names or of descriptions which are combined with an indication of time.

In this section and the following we shall analyse a norm and describe its constitutive elements. Since a norm is a directive of a certain kind, the analysis will to that extent be an analysis of directives, or, to be precise, of impersonal directives, which can alone be norms. While personal directives involve a speaker and a hearer and must be analysed accordingly, impersonal directives have no author and no recipient as such. This fact matters in determining who the subject of a directive is. It is often necessary, in order to know to whom a personal directive is addressed, to know its context; the subject of an impersonal directive, however, has to be explicitly indicated in the wording of a norm. A legal norm, for instance, is promulgated publicly to all and sundry; but whose actions in particular it concerns can be known only from what the norm itself says and not from the fact that it is addressed to everybody.

The analysis of a norm is concerned with the norm itself and must be kept distinct from the description of the factual background of the norm, that is, of those social conditions on which the existence of the norm depends. Because of his failure to provide a clarification of the concept 'norm', von Wright misses this distinction and consequently treats together what needs to be kept apart. For his analysis deals not only with those various elements which constitute the meaning of the norm—and this is the proper subject matter of the analysis—but also with the promulgation of the norm and the sanctions or authority that lie behind it, that is, with those facts which are relevant to the genesis and existence of the norm but not to its meaning.[1]

Since a norm is a directive, its meaning-content has to be characterized in general as an action-idea presented as a pattern of behaviour. And this provides us with a clue toward separating and describing those elements of the norm which determine its meaning. They fall into two classes: those which specify the action-idea and those whose function it is to indicate that the action-idea is presented as a pattern of behaviour. Or, if we use our formula $d(T)$ to symbolize a directive (§ 9), we can say that the former class is concerned with describing T and the latter class with signifying the operator d ('so it ought to be').

In sections 23 to 26 we shall examine those elements whose role it is to describe the action-idea. There are three elements with this function:

(1) An action must be performed by some definite individual (we limit our investigations to human behaviour and exclude the problem of 'legal persons'). A norm, therefore, must contain an element which determines its *subject*, that is, the agent (or agents) expected to behave according to the action-idea.

(2) Our expectations of how others should act depend upon the situations in which they are placed. One of the elements of the norm, then, must indicate the *situation* in which the norm is meant to be followed.

(3) And lastly, the norm indicates how its subject is to act under the specified conditions. The element of the norm which has this function I shall call the *theme* of the norm.

Before I undertake the separate description of these three elements, I want to make clear that the division is somewhat arbitrary, there being no sharp criteria governing it. Consider, for example, the formulation of a norm in which the subject is specified as 'fishermen of British nationality, over thirty years old, with an annual income of more than £1000'. Without changing the

---

[1] G. H. von Wright, *Norm and Action* (1963), pp. 70ff.

meaning of this norm, its formulation could be rewritten so that any of the properties attached to 'fishermen' are replaced by a further qualification of the situation. For instance, the subject might be specified merely by 'fishermen', and the question of nationality, age and income would fall under the description of the situation. Indeed, even the property of being a fisherman could be left out, with the subject being simply 'anyone' or 'everyone'. We normally think it natural that properties of a relatively permanent character (such as sex, date of birth, place of birth, name, blood type, nationality, and perhaps residence and occupation) should be included in the specification of the subject, and less permanent properties and circumstances included under the description of the situation—for example, where the subject is at the moment, what he is doing (e.g., driving a car), or has done (e.g., made a promise, committed a murder). The borderline, however, is vague, and for the purposes of logical analysis has to be drawn arbitrarily.

The distinction between situation and theme is similarly vague, for the description of the theme will to some extent imply descriptions of the situation. The theme 'shutting the door' can apply only to a situation in which the door is open, and 'paying one's debt' only when a debt exists. And 'not committing adultery' presupposes the marriage of one of the parties. But the theme could be so specified that what is in these examples only implied would need to be stated in the description of the situation.

The elements which indicate subject, situation, and theme may, in each case, be further analysed. We must decide which of these further variations are relevant to our present logical description. I want, first of all, to mention variations in the specification of the *subject*, namely, the distinction between *individual* and *generic determination*.

The subject may be determined individually, generically, or universally. This distinction is not so clear as is usually assumed. Von Wright calls a norm 'particular', with regard to its subject, when it is addressed to *one* specified person, and 'general' when it is addressed either to all men without restriction or to all men who satisfy a certain description. As an example of the first he mentions a command addressed to N.N. to open the window. A command which is addressed to a finite number of specified subjects, he adds, is to count as of the same kind.[1]

Von Wright's distinction is not clear. His only example of the

[1] *Op. cit.*, pp. 77–78.

individual determination of a subject is one which uses a name ('N.N.'); he mentions no other kind. And he fails to say what is the fundamental difference between individual and general determination. (It must be noted that the use of a name is often insufficient for singling out a particular person. Many people go by the same name). What distinguishes individual from general determination of the subject cannot lie in how many persons satisfy the description. For it is easy to give an example of a general description which is satisfied by only one person or by, at least, a definite number of persons: 'Those who, on January 1 1965, were licensed to import diamonds into Denmark', or, 'Those who on January 1, 1965, were Danish citizens'.

The distinction in question must, I think, be drawn in the following way. The subject is determined individually when it is specified as a *closed class*, that is, a class whose membership cannot logically vary with time. Such a class may be indicated by using either genuine proper names, that is, names which denote one and only one individual, or a description accompanied by some temporal specification. We are not, in fact, familiar with proper names which are, in our sense, 'genuine', unless, of course, we introduced the practice of registering a number for each individual as we now do for pieces of property and cars. In practice, then, we are limited to using the second method, at times combined with the use of proper names which are common to several persons. I will illustrate what I mean with some examples.

'Those who are licensed to import diamonds into Denmark' determines an open class. Even if we were to discover at some particular time that the class had, in fact, only one member, or only some definite number of members, it is 'open' to increase or decrease with time. On the other hand, a closed class is specified by 'Those who, on January 1, 1965, were licensed to import diamonds into Denmark'. The number of subjects (whatever it may be) is fixed for eternity, never to be changed; this is the result solely of the time specification. 'The owner of title no. 1 bo in the Land Register for the township of Rørvig' defines an open class; 'The present owner of the title no.1 bo etc.' a closed class. The time indication is, at times, implicitly understood. If to make clear what 'John Smith' I am referring to I say that he lives at 10, Park Road, I mean that he *now* lives there. Should several John Smiths live in the same place, I can specify my John Smith by giving his date of birth or his occupation. It makes no difference if these last properties define an open or a closed class. Once a class has been closed by a time specification it remains closed.[1]

It is always in principle possible to enumerate exhaustively the members of a closed class by referring to each with a genuine proper name or by using ordinary proper names combined with a time indication or other individuating descriptions. This is true, for example, of the persons who, on January 1, 1965, were Danish citizens. Regardless of the number of such persons and the practical difficulty of determining who they are, they are, as it were, specified individually. A norm which determines its subjects by using this description is logically equivalent to a set of norms each of which has as its subject a single person referred to by a genuine proper name or otherwise sufficiently identified.

Norms whose subject is determined individually are called *individual* or *singular* norms.

If the subject is not determined individually it may be determined either generically or universally. In the first case, the persons who count as the subject are members of an open class (or genus) defined by certain properties. In the second case, the subject comprises absolutely everyone. We have pointed out that the distinction between the subject and the situation which a norm determines is vague and must be drawn somewhat arbitrarily. I will include all qualifying conditions under the determination of situation. In this way, we have simplified the ways in which a norm may determine its subject; the subject is determined either *individually* (one or more persons who can, in principle, be identified) or *universally* ('everyone'). With regard to its subject, then, a norm is either individual or universal.[2]

---

[1] It is tempting to assume that individuating must necessarily be brought about by means of time-space-determinants. This, however, is a fallacy. The class of people who at a certain time stay at a certain place is not more closed than the class of people who at a certain time are red-headed.

[2] Hare, *Freedom and Reason* (1963), pp. 40, 48, seems to presuppose that a norm is universal when it concerns 'anyone' but does not seem to be aware of the vague and somehow arbitrary distinction between the determination of subject and the determination of situation. This appears from his contention that legal rules, because of their implicit reference to a particular jurisdiction, are not universalizable. On p. 36 it is said: ' "It is illegal to marry one's own sister" means, implicitly, "It is illegal (e.g.) in England to marry one's own sister". But "England" is here a singular term, which prevents the whole proposition being universal.' In my opinion nothing prevents the formulation of this norm as applying to anyone who is in a certain situation being, among other things, subject to English jurisdiction.

§ 24

According to how the situation is determined by the norm, we distinguish between occasional norms and rules. Rules are either hypothetical or categorical.

A norm may determine a situation individually, generically, or universally.

When the situation in which a norm is to be applied is defined as a closed class the determination of the situation is individual. This is the case when the norm contains a temporal specification such that what the norm prescribes is to be carried out at a definite time or a definite series of times, e.g., at 10 a.m. January 1, 1970, or when the statute comes into effect, or when the present king dies, or when each member of the present Royal Family dies. It is immaterial if further qualifications are added to the temporal specification in such a way that the norm may never need to be applied—for example if the norm prescribes how to act if the present king dies without a successor.

Since these norms contain an 'individual' specification of when they are to be applied, that is, a mention of one or more definite occasions after which they cease to have force, I call them *occasional* norms.

When the situation in which a norm is to be applied is defined as an *open class*, the determination of situation in the norm is said to be *generic*. In this case, the situation is defined by certain general characteristics without any time indications, when, for example, a norm contains the condition 'If a contract has been drawn between two parties, both legally of age, then ...'

When a norm is to be applied under all circumstances, that is, in any situation, its determination of situation is said to be *universal*. This must be qualified by the observation that the *theme* sometimes implies the presence of certain necessary conditions of the application of the norm.[1] For example, a directive to close the window is logically restricted to situations in which the window is open. And a norm which forbids killing presupposes the presence of opportunities to kill.

Norms which are generic or universal in their determination of relevant situations are called *rules*. Generic rules are called *hypothetical*, and universal rules *categorical*.

---

[1] Cf. G. H. von Wright, *Norm and Action* (1963), p. 73.

If we combine this classification with the classification according to subject determination, the result is the following table of classes:

A. *Occasional norms*, which are:
   (1) *Individual*, e.g., 'John Smith is bound to pay on demand a certain sum to James Brown.'
   (2) *Universal*, e.g., 'Everyone has to go into mourning when the present king dies.'

B. *Rules*, which are:
   (1) *Individual hypothetical*, 'John Smith is responsible for giving the alarm in case of fire.'
   (2) *Individual categorical*, 'John Smith is forbidden to enter the bar of the Red Lion in any circumstances.'
   (3) *Universal hypothetical*, 'If anyone borrows money he is required to repay it within the time specified.'
   (4) *Universal categorical*, 'Everyone is obliged never to kill another person.'

§ 25

According to how the theme of the norm is determined, we can distinguish between rigorous and discretionary norms.

The theme of a norm may likewise be determined either individually or generically; this distinction, however, is not so important here as it was with regard to the two other elements of the action-idea.

By an 'act' I mean the intentional production of a certain effect or change. An act is consequently individuated by its effect. 'Closing this window now' is an act determined individually, while 'closing a window' is determined generically, covering as it does the closing of any window at any time.[1] How and with what results the act 'closing this window now' is to be brought about is left open by the description; the description applies whether the left or right hand is used, whether one mounts a ladder or pulls a cord, whether one brutally smashes the glass or closes it gently, whether or not one makes a noise.

This shows that even if the theme of action is determined as an individual act it does not follow that there is only one way of

[1] G. H. von Wright, *Norm and Action* (1963), pp. 35ff.

complying with the norm. It is important to the agent what freedom of choice the norm leaves him, but the presence of this freedom does not depend straightforwardly on whether the theme is determined individually or generically. It depends also on how definitely the methods to be used and the consequences to be allowed are prescribed, whether explicitly or implicitly.

In other words, the distinction between the individual and generic determination of theme is quite vague and relative. For we might say that 'closing this window now' is determined generically as the class of acts which produce this effect regardless of what means are used and what consequences result. If these are limited in some way by the theme, one could always point out further differences in how the theme might be satisfied. A determination which rules out all freedom of choice is inconceivable.

Because of this vagueness and relativity I shall not distinguish categories of norms according to some distinction between the individual and the generic determination of the theme of the norm. I shall say, merely, that according to how precisely the theme is determined a norm is *more or less rigorous or discretionary*.

§ 26

Chains of norms. Commands and prohibitions.

In this section we shall continue to discuss the description of action-ideas.

(1) It may seem tempting and relevant, while considering the subject of a norm, to raise the question of *legal persons* (corporations and similar collective bodies). But since this would take us too far into the special province of the philosophy of law, I shall not deal with it here.[1]

(2) With regard to how a norm specifies the situation in which it is to be operative, I wish to mention briefly a device of great importance, which is used in connecting norms in a systematic unity, or system of norms. This device consists in specifying the condition of application of one norm as the condition that another norm has been violated. The two norms in question may have either the same subject or different subjects.

We have already referred to the fact (§ 21, s.f.) that legal norms

[1] These problems are discussed in *Towards a Realistic Jurisprudence* (1946), Chapter VIII, 6.

present themselves, from a psychological point of view, as two sets of norms, one directed to citizens, prescribing how they are to act, and the other directed to the courts (and other enforcement agencies), prescribing how they are to react to violations of primary norms.

This schema is, however, oversimplified. Consider, for example, the legal norm which requires the seller of personal property to deliver the goods in accordance with the stipulations of the contract. This norm does not specify exhaustively the conditions under which a judge should decide in favour of the buyer (as plaintiff), nor what the decision should be. If the norm did contain exhaustive instructions to the judge, it would have to deal with such things as what has happened since the violation is claimed to have occurred (Has the buyer brought his action within the proper time? Has the seller offered return or damages? Have proceedings been instituted in due form?) and would have to instruct the judge in detail on what he should require of the defendant (specific performance? payment of damages? sentence to punishment?). If each norm provided for all these conditions, it would be quite involved and unwieldy; furthermore, much material would be repeated endlessly from norm to norm. It is much simpler to separate norms into parts, and unite similar parts of different norms in a set of rules which constitute an independent whole. These separate sets may then be organized into a hierarchy so that the condition of the application of norms at one level is defined as the violation of norms of a lower level.

This is brought about in the following way.[1] One of these separate sets of rules, known as *substantive* or *primary* law, describes, motivated by considerations of public welfare, how the citizen is expected to behave, for example, that a seller is to deliver the stipulated articles in the proper time. Another set of these partial rules constitutes what may be called the law of *sanctions* or *secondary* law: These rules state the obligations[2] which arise from the violations of those obligations created by substantive law. They state, in other words, what sanctions are to be exacted of the citizen who has broken the law and make more precise the conditions under which sanctions are to be applied. Traditionally, the

---

[1] Cf. *On Law and Justice*, pp. 207ff.
[2] One does not say, however, that a crime entails an obligation to suffer punishment.

law of sanctions comprises the *law of damages* and *criminal law*; to these might be added those laws which specify the conditions under which a judge may direct what is called 'specific performance'. *Procedural law* or *tertiary law* forms a third set of rules; here we find a statement of further conditions which must be satisfied if judgment is to be given and enforced, that is, what procedure must be followed in determining and enforcing liability, and especially how an action is to be initiated, and what rules of evidence and procedure are to be observed in court.

These three sets of norms, taken together, may be interpreted as rules which prescribe for citizens the behaviour required of them and which instructs citizens how to go about using the legal machinery to obtain redress. But they may also be interpreted as norms prescribing how judges (and other agencies of enforcement) are to decide cases brought before them.

(3) It is of interest to note that the *theme* may be specified *positively* as the performance of an *action* (e.g., opening of a window), or *negatively* as an omission (e.g., not opening it, leaving it closed). Omission is not the same as the mere absence of activity. A man has not 'omitted' to help someone in distress, if he is far away and unaware of any need for help. 'Omission' logically implies at least that it was in the power of an agent to act positively in a situation.[1] There are other conditions which must be satisfied for non-action to count as omission; these, it seems, vary with the situation. I shall not, however, go into this difficult problem.

The positive and negative determination of the theme of a norm is not to be confused with the affirmative and negative formulation of the directive element of a norm. As we shall see later, an obligation to omit an action is not the same as the absence of an obligation to commit that act.

A norm which makes it a duty to behave according to a positively determined theme (the act *C*) is called a command (to perform *C*).[2] And a norm which makes it a duty to behave according to a negatively determined theme (not-*C*, the omission of *C*) is

---

[1] G. H. von Wright, *Norm and Action* (1963), pp. 45ff.

[2] The term 'command' in this book is thus used in two quite distinct senses: Here it is used as a term of modal deontic logic; above, § 10, it was used to designate one kind of personal, sender-interested directive.

called a prohibition (against the performance of C). By these definitions, we get the following identities:

command (C) = obligation (C)
prohibition (C) = obligation (not C)

or:

A command to undertake an act is the same as a prohibition against omitting that act, and conversely.

(4) Following von Wright, I wish now to mention that a theme may be determined either as the performance of an *act* or as an engagement in an *activity*.[1] Closing a window or killing someone is the performance of an act. To smoke or to run is to be engaged in an activity. An act is an event; an activity is a process. Von Wright points out the fact that norms which govern activities are secondary to norms which govern acts, in the sense that they are logically reducible to the latter. A prohibition against smoking is reducible to a prohibition against the act of starting to smoke (lighting a cigarette) together with the command to stop smoking if one has started (put out lighted cigarettes). On the other hand, it is not the case that every act can be defined as the beginning or end of some activity. The two concepts, then, are not on an equal footing; they are not mutually reducible. The concept of an act is primary and irreducible.

§ 27

In a formalized language the directive operator is expressed by the word 'obligation'. In legal language a number of other derivative modal expressions are used. Von Wright's assertion that 'permission' cannot be defined as the negation of obligation is disputed.

What distinguishes a directive from a proposition is its operator, which indicates that the topic (being an action-idea) is presented as a pattern of behaviour and not that it is thought of as real. I have represented the operator schematically by the words 'so it ought to be'. These words are themselves hardly ever used, in the expression of directive meaning. According to the situation in which the directive is issued and the background of factors which constitute its source of effectiveness, many different expressions are used, and they are often reinforced by facial and other non-

[1] *Op. cit.*, pp. 41–42, 71–72.

verbal means of expression. Choice of words, facial expression and behaviour all vary from situation to situation; consider, for example, ordering a bank clerk to hand over money; begging; asking a fellow traveller to close a window; putting forward a claim; giving advice; warning; admonishing. In some cases, the directive meaning is dependent on the tone of voice and situation in such a way that it is impossible to separate out definite linguistic elements as its expression. Imagine a shabby person approaching you in the street at night mumbling 'Just a cup of tea, guv'nor'.

Because of this variety of intentions and their expressions it is hardly possible to formalize ordinary directive speech. But the case is different if we confine ourselves to norms. Because their existential root lies in feelings of validity (see above §§ 16, 21, and 22g) their linguistic expression is to some extent uniform. Even though the wealth of linguistic and non-linguistic means of expression permits much variety in normative discourse, there are, all the same, a number of deontic expressions (§ 9) which are especially suited to indicate the directive operator in this kind of speech. All these words and phrases ('ought', 'must', 'have to', 'to claim', 'to have a right to', 'obligation', 'duty', 'right', etc.) have this feature in common: they mirror that feeling of validity and obligation which we have said is the existential basis of norms. For this reason it is possible, without too much violating our sense of idiom, to stylize normative language by introducing the term *obligation* as a standard symbol for the directive operator of a norm, that is, for the element which indicates that the action-idea, described by the determination of the subject, situation and theme, is presented as a pattern of behaviour ('so it ought to be').

If the analysis of directives and norms which is the basis of this study is correct, then we may assume that *obligation* is the fundamental directive category in which any norm may be expressed. I shall, at any rate, make this my working hypothesis. It does not rule out interpreting the concept of obligation differently according to the kind of norm in which it occurs. It is reasonable to assume that in legal, conventional, and autonomous moral contexts, 'obligation' will be interpreted according to the different ways in which norms are felt as valid.

There is no doubt, however, that many normative utterances employ terms other than 'obligation'. In legal language especially, we find such terms and phrases as: someone is *entitled* to something, has *permission* to do something, *may* do something, has a *claim* against someone, is *authorized* to act in a certain way. These and similar formulae obviously express something other than someone's being under an obligation. For our hypothesis that 'obligation' is the single and irreducible normative category to be maintained, we must show how these and similar formulae can be analysed in terms of 'obligation'. Since legal vocabulary is the most elaborate and articulate normative speech, and since the problems which confront us are discussed most thoroughly in legal theory, we shall in what follows be concerned primarily with the analysis of legal language. We must later discuss how what we say fits other examples of normative speech.

Before examining the normative modalities, some preliminary observations are in order. First of all, an obligation is normally a relation between two persons, that is, *A*'s obligation is normally an obligation to another person *B*.[1]

It is not, for the purposes of this study, necessary to account for how *B*, in the norm establishing *A*'s obligation, is identified. It is sufficient to point out, that if *A*'s obligation is completely defined with reference to subject, situation and theme, it will then implicitly and unambiguously be indicated who *B* is (if, as is usual, there is a *B*.) Secondly, it must be observed that any well-developed legal system, being institutional and dynamic, contains not only *norms of conduct*, which prescribe how to act, but also *norms of competence*, which provide how new valid and binding norms may be created through the performance of *actes juridiques*. Norms of competence are logically reducible to norms of conduct in this way: norms of competence make it obligatory to act according to the norms of conduct which have been created according to the procedure laid down in them. Like obligation, 'competence' is a relationship between two persons, between, namely, the person who is endowed with competence and the person who is subject to his power, who is, that is to say, under an obligation to obey the norms created by him in the correct manner.[2]

In the following table of legal-directive modalities, the first part comprises the modalities of norms of conduct and the second comprises those of norms of competence.

---

[1] See below, § 28. Cf. *On Law and Justice*, p. 163; *Towards a Realistic Jurisprudence*, Chapter VIII.

[2] *On Law and Justice*, pp. 32ff., 166ff.

The four modalities of the first part are the result of two simple logical transformations. We start in (1) with 'obligation' being ascribed to A; (2) is then introduced as, by definition, the negation of (1). We then introduce (3) and (4) to denote the same relation of obligation as (1) and (2), but seen from the point of view of B. (2) and (4) are *negations* of (1) and (3); and the expressions (3) and (4) are *synonymous correlates* of (1) and (2).

The four modalities of competence are related in the same way, with (5) being taken as the starting point. (5) expresses A's subjection to B, that is, his obligation to obey the norms which B has created in the proper way.

In the table, the symbol ' $=$ ' indicates that the expressions which it connects are synonymous and correlative, and the symbol ' $\sim$ ' indicates that the expressions it connects are contradictories. The formula 'obligation A–B (C)' is to be read 'A is, in relation to B, under the obligation to exhibit conduct C', where 'C' describes the situation and theme of A's obligation. The formula 'subjection A–B (F)' is to be read 'A is subject to B's dispositions (his norm creating acts) within the field F, where 'F' describes B's competence both in procedure and substance. The other formulae are to be read analogously.

Modalities of norms of conduct

(1) Obligation A–B (C) $=$ Claim B–A (C)

$\sim$ $\sim$

(2) Permission A–B (not–C) $=$ No-claim B–A (C)

(3) Claim A–B (C) $=$ Obligation B–A (C)

$\sim$ $\sim$

(4) No-claim A–B (C) $=$ Permission B–A (not–C)

Modalities of norms of competence

(5) Subjection A–B (F) $=$ Competence B–A (F)

$\sim$ $\sim$

(6) Immunity A–B (F) $=$ Disability B–A (F)

(7) Competence A–B (F) $=$ Subjection B–A (F)

$\sim$ $\sim$

(8) Disability A–B (F) $=$ Immunity B–A (F)

The first four modalities stand in relations of negation and synonymy and are, therefore, interdefinable. Any normative utterance which may be expressed by one of these modalities may be rewritten as any of the others. The same holds with the last four. Furthermore, any norm of competence may be transcribed as a norm of conduct, whereas the converse does not hold. This implies that any norm can, through logical transformations, be expressed, without change of meaning, by any of the four modalities of the norms of conduct. Among these four formally equivalent modalities, however, the modality of obligation is distinguished as fundamental; for it immediately expresses the specific directive operator which, when the directive is a norm, has its existential basis in the feeling of validity. The special position of the modality of obligation is shown in the fact that while a system is conceivable which contains only affirmative norms of obligation, the same is not true of the modality of permission. If there were no negative norms of permission, norms, that is, which state what is *not* permitted or what the agent is under an *obligation* not to do, then there would be no normative meaning whatsoever. Telling me what I am permitted to do provides no guide to conduct unless the permission is taken as an exception to a norm of obligation (which may be the general maxim that what is not permitted is prohibited). Norms of permission have the normative function only of indicating, within some system, what are the exceptions from the norms of obligation of the system.

It follows from this that we have need, in a formalized language, of only one, irreducible, symbol for the directive element of norms, and that it is most natural to let this symbol stand for obligation. In his deontic logic, however, von Wright operates with the two irreducible symbols O, for obligation, and P, for permission. He does so because he is in doubt whether 'permission' is an independent modality or not, and he positively rejects the view which I have expressed that permission is simply the same as the negation of obligation.[1] We must consider this fundamental problem more closely.

First of all, let us be clear about what the problem really is and what facts are decisive for its solution. Formally speaking, it is a question of definition. As I have defined 'permission' in the preceding table, the expression *is* identical with the negation of

[1] G. H. von Wright, *Norm and Action* (1963), pp. 85ff., 92.

obligation. Von Wright may object that a normative terminology constructed according to the table would be inadequate for formalizing actual normative discourse, since 'permission' is actually used in such a way that my definition is not a correct interpretation of it, and since, furthermore, it expresses a concept so essential that it cannot be ignored or written off.

Von Wright's argument is as follows. As man's skills develop and his institutions and way of life change, new kinds of act come into existence. A man *could not* get drunk before it was discovered how to distil alcohol. As new kinds of acts are originated, a legislator may feel it necessary to consider whether *to order* or *to permit* or *to prohibit* them for his subjects (my italics). If we presuppose the existence of a legislating authority, then, it is reasonable to divide human acts into two main groups, namely, acts which are and acts which are not (yet) subject to norm by this authority. That an act is subject to norm means that the legislator has decided on his attitude toward it by either *commanding, permitting,* or *prohibiting* its performance. Those acts which are not subject to norm (because the legislator has not yet decided on his attitude toward them) are *ipso facto* not forbidden and *in that sense* such an act can be said to be 'permitted'. It follows that it makes sense to distinguish between two kinds of permission, which von Wright calls *strong* and *weak* permission. Permission in the weak sense is identical with our concept of permission; it means simply that the act is not forbidden (because the legislator has not yet decided on his attitude toward it). An act is said to be permitted in the strong sense when the legislator has decided on the normative status of the act and has expressly permitted it. Permission in the strong sense is therefore not identical with the simple negation of obligation. Von Wright's conclusion is that it is impossible to define permission as the negation of obligation and nothing more.[1]

Von Wright's reasoning is obviously circular. It appears from the phrases I have italicized that he presupposes that a legislator's attitude toward an act is always manifested in some legislative act which either commands or prohibits the act (that is, makes it an obligation either to perform or to omit the act) or permits it, which implies that no obligation at all exists. Von Wright thus *presupposes* that to permit an act is an independent and irreducible

[1] *Op. cit.*, pp. 85–87.

normative decision which is distinct from regulating the act under an obligation, distinct, that is, from either commanding or prohibiting it. So what his reasoning should prove is really assumed in the premisses. Furthermore, this assumption that there are three different ways in which a legislator may react to emerging forms of behaviour is without warrant in real life. I have never heard of any law's being passed with the purpose of declaring a new form of behaviour (e.g., listening to the wireless) permitted. If a legislator sees no reason to interfere by issuing an obligating prescription (a command or a prohibition) he simply keeps silent. I know of no permissive legal rule which is not logically an exemption modifying some prohibition, and interpretable as the negation of an obligation. (Consider, for example, 'The owner of a house which is rented, is prohibited from entering the premises, except that he is permitted to enter in case of . . .'). If von Wright answers that in his opinion an act is permitted in the strong sense as soon as the legislator has decided on his attitude, this being neither to command nor to prohibit it, then he is confronted with the difficulty of having to say *when* a legislator has made up his mind even though no law has been passed.

Von Wright's curious reasoning would be more understandable if we took it to be concerned with family life and not with legislation, despite the fact that he speaks of legislative authority. It does seem sensible to say with regard to children that they cannot assume that whatever their parents have not prohibited is permitted. One would hardly accept the plea of a six-years-old boy that he is permitted to smoke since his parents have not forbidden him to do so. Because in this situation we are dealing with personal directives and not norms, I shall not venture to discuss the problem, except to hint that I am inclined to believe that our definition of 'permission' may be upheld in describing even these relations. For the peculiar characteristic which distinguishes such relations from legal relations is that children are subject to restrictive prescriptions that are rather indefinite and comprehensive in scope. It is for this reason that children are not entitled to conclude that an act is permitted merely because no express prohibition against it has been issued.

Von Wright, in the place we have mentioned, arrived at the conclusion that 'permission' means two different things. In the weak sense an act is permitted when it is not forbidden; in the strong sense an act is permitted when the legislator has considered its normative status and decided to permit it. Later in the same chapter he returns to the problem in order to explain in more detail what strong permission is. He says that it is possible to distinguish between various kinds of strong permission—permissions, as it were, of increasing degrees of strength. The weakest kind of strong permission occurs when the legislator does nothing more than declare that he is going *to tolerate* the act. My previous criticism is relevant here: I know of no legislative act which says this. A stronger kind of strong permission is said to occur when the declaration of tolerance is combined either with a prohibition (addressed to others) against *hindering or preventing* anyone from doing what is tolerated, or with *a command to enable him* to do so. When a strong permission of this kind occurs, the holder of the permission is said to possess, respectively, either a *right* or a *claim*. It is tolerated that a man enjoys the use of what he owns, and others are forbidden to hinder or prevent his doing so; and it is tolerated that a creditor receives what is due to him, and his debtor is commanded to enable him to do so.[1] By identifying 'permission' with 'right' and 'claim', von Wright, in my view, confuses the concepts. Neither in everyday use nor as a technical legal usage does 'permission' to undertake an act mean the same as the possession of a right or a claim. 'Claim' is the correlate of 'obligation'; and 'right' expresses no modality at all, but rather a concept used in the description of a complex legal situation.[2]

Finally, von Wright considers the idea that the declaration of tolerance which constitutes strong permission is meant by the legislator as a promise of his non-interference; and that the strongest kind of strong permission is, accordingly, identical with the constitutional guarantees of the liberties of the citizen.[3] His analysis and discussion of these legal phenomena are, however, manifestly inadequate. The idea of a promise made by a legislator to the citizen, creating a moral obligation which binds the legislator, is a figment of the imagination and has long since been abandoned in legal theory. The constitutional guarantee of certain freedoms has nothing to do with promises, but is a restriction of the power of the legislator, a disability which corresponds to an immunity on the part of the citizen. The legislator does not

[1] *Op. cit.*, pp. 88ff.   [2] Cf., *On Law and Justice*, pp. 170ff.
[3] *Op. cit.*, pp. 91ff.

promise not to use a power which he possesses, but, rather, his power (or competence) is defined in such a way that he *cannot* legally interfere with the liberties guaranteed. Any legislative act to this effect would be unconstitutional and therefore null and void. There is no need, however, to demonstrate any further the fallacies of this analysis of constitutional law. Against this analysis it must be maintained that the fact that certain liberties, that is, permissions to do or to omit at will, are *combined* with constitutional guarantees, in no way means that the term 'permission' occurs in a new and stronger sense.

Von Wright's fundamental view, that 'permission' is an independent normative modality not translatable in terms of obligation (commands and prohibitions), seems to me incomprehensible, in view of the way he interprets the term 'permission' in a subsequent section of his book, dealing with deontic logic. After a lengthy discussion, permission to do C is said to be identical with the negation of an obligation to omit C, that is, exactly what I believe it to be.[1]

I conclude that von Wright's argument for his contention that 'permission' (to perform a certain act) cannot be adequately defined as simply the negation of obligation (to omit that act) is unconvincing, and is rooted in fallacies about jurisprudence. I would like to add that the table of modalities given above is not my own invention but is a modified edition of one elaborated by Hohfeld and published in 1913;[2] and that I have used it for many years without encountering any instance of legal speech in which the term 'permission' (and derived expressions) could not without difficulty be interpreted as the negation of obligation.

§ 28

Comments on the table of legal modalities.[3]

It should be noted that the terminology of the table of modalities does not pretend to be identical with the terminology of actual legal speech. There simply does not exist an established and

---

[1] *Op. cit.*, pp. 136ff., 139.

[2] Wesley Newcomb Hohfeld, 'Fundamental Legal Conceptions as Applied in Judicial Reasoning', *Yale L.R.*, vol. 23 (1913), p. 16, and *Yale R.L.*, vol. 26 (1917), p. 710. These and other essays were reprinted after the death of the author in *Fundamental Legal Conceptions* (1923).

[3] Cf. *On Law and Justice*, pp. 161ff.

unambiguous usage. On the one hand, modal terms are often ambiguous: 'to have a right to' or 'to be entitled to' can designate a claim as well as permission or competence. On the other hand, a number of different terms are used to designate the same modality: the modality of obligation may be expressed not only by means of the word 'obligation' and its derivatives, but also by means of words and phrases like 'having to', 'it rests with (someone) to', 'to be incumbent on'. The system presented by the table is, however, not an arbitrary construction. It is rather, I should say, a *stylization* of actual usage, and it brings to light the fact that we actually do operate with terms that are mutually linked by negation and correlation. The adoption in practice of a fixed terminology in accordance with the table would be, of course, advantageous, but it is hardly likely. But even if lawyers adhere to traditional usage, an insight into the logical relations which connect the various modalities would be of use in the drafting of the law as well as in its interpretation.

It should be noted also that we are dealing exclusively with directive speech, that is with the speech in which norms are expressed or brought to bear in exhortations directed to a norm-subject (see § 12). Indicative speech about the existence or application of norms falls outside the scope of our analysis. Therefore, when I operate, in what follows, with sentences like '*A* is under an obligation to . . .', or '*B* is permitted to . . .' they are always to be understood to have directive meaning as when they are used in norms or exhortations.

Obligation and Claim

In so far as legal norms are conceived as norms for deciding cases that are brought before the courts and other enforcing authorities, no problem arises as to the interpretation of the term *obligation*. It simply expresses the attitude of being bound which is felt by those who obey the law out of respect for the authority of the law.

But in so far as legal rules are conceived as norms of conduct addressed to the citizen—and they are usually drafted from this point of view—the problem does arise of how the modality of obligation is to be interpreted. What does it mean to say that the citizen is under the obligation, in certain situations, to exhibit conduct *C*? The legal relevance of a norm addressed to the citizen lies entirely in the fact that the same norm is a rule laying down how the courts are to decide cases. It follows, therefore, that we need a statement of what forensic consequences are involved in the citizen's obligation, if the interpretation of that obligation is to be adequate to actual legal conditions. It is not sufficient to say that the conduct which the theme of the obligation specifies is the conduct which is desirable and expected in the eyes of society. What is legally relevant is not pious hopes but what is to be done when the agent does not fulfil his obligations (given that those conditions are satisfied which the secondary and tertiary rules require). It would naturally be desirable to define 'obligation' in such a way that the term was unambiguously bound up with a definite forensic reaction to the non-fulfilment of obligation. But this is not feasible if our stylized terminology is not to offend intolerably against time-honoured usage. On the one hand, we have to accept a use of the term which does not discriminate between cases in which the judicial reaction takes the shape of a sentence to punishment, a judgment imposing damages, and an injunction to specific performance. On the other hand, it must also be recognized that we cannot speak of 'obligation' in all cases in which one of these three kinds of reactions are in the offing. We do not, for example, speak of a breach of obligation in those cases in which damages are imposed according to the rules of strict liability or excusable impossibility. This is due to the fact, mentioned above in section 21, that not any disagreeable reaction is the sanction of a norm-creating obligation. If the reaction (such as, e.g., the imposing of taxes or custom duties) is not felt as the expression of public disapproval, it is not felt to be backing up any obligation. The same holds when damages are imposed according to the rules of strict liability or excusable impossibility; and this explains why in these situations we do not speak of a corresponding obligation—that is, an obligation to omit the dangerous activity or to perform what is impossible. In such cases liability to pay damages is not in the nature of a sanction but functions as a redistribution of wealth which is for various reasons judged desirable and legitimate.

According to what was said in § 26 (3), formulations expressing obligation may be transcribed in terms of commands and prohibitions according to the following rules. That an act is commanded is the same as that there is an obligation to perform it; that an act is prohibited is the same as that there is an obligation not to perform it. Therefore:

command C = def. obligation C
prohibition C = def. obligation not–C

from which follows:

command C = prohibition not–C
prohibition C = command not–C

B's claim is the correlate of A's obligation. Who is B? He is the person who satisfies two conditions: (1) it is he who exclusively is able by bringing a suit to start the legal machinery in order to obtain judgment imposing sanctions on A; and (2) he must be at liberty to bring his action or not as he likes.

When the creditor B at the day of payment demands the amount due of his debtor A he makes what we have called an *exhortation* (see § 12), that is, he brings the legal norm (or the obligation created by it) to bear on A by requesting him to live up to the obligations created by a system of norms, in this case the legal order, which both parties accept as binding. Anyone may exhort A to fulfil his obligations but B who is interested in A's fulfilling his obligations, has, naturally, a special incentive to do so.

In most cases an extra-forensic exhortation will be sufficient to make A fulfil his obligations. If this is not the case B, and only B, can bring the norm to bear on A by bringing a suit and this is a specifically legal phenomenon. It requires the existence of a legal machinery of adjudication and enforcement and presupposes procedural rules according to which B and only B is empowered, by *bringing an action*, to bring this machinery into action.

Normally the person who has the power to institute proceedings is also the person immediately interested in the agent's required behaviour. If A has promised B to pay him £100, against consideration, then B is the directly interested party as well as the person who has the power to institute proceedings. But it can happen that the two are not the same person. A, for example, may promise B to pay £100 to C. If it is assumed that B alone can institute proceedings, it will agree most with current usage to say that B alone has a claim on A; the definition formulated above has been made on that basis. B, who possesses the claim, is called the *proceedings subject*, and *C*, who is the directly interested party, is called the *interest subject*.

That *B* has the power to institute proceedings means that he is the one who is able to start the legal machinery moving with the aim of enforcing *A*'s obligation. It is another question whether *B* is free to institute proceedings or not as he likes or whether his exercise of this power is itself legally regulated and his freedom restricted by legal obligations. In private law *B* is usually free to exercise this power as he sees fit. His claim is in this way combined with the liberty to enforce it or not, since the purpose of the law is to provide him with an instrument for safeguarding his interests. This liberty is part of what we understand by private autonomy. It is part of the current conception of a claim and is therefore included in our definition, with the purpose of excluding from the definition situations in which instituting proceedings is an official act undertaken by a public servant in his function of serving the public interest, as is normal in criminal prosecution. The public prosecutor is not at liberty to proceed or not as he chooses but is legally obligated to exercise power in accordance with directions laid down by law. It follows that those obligations which are upheld solely by public prosecution under the threat of penalty are absolute, that is, no claim corresponds to them with regard either to the party whose interests have been injured, or to the state. Such a delimitation of the concept of a claim sees to harmonize well with current conceptions and usage.

Permission and 'no-claim'

From the table we see that permission to omit *C* means that there is no obligation to perform *C*, that is, that *C* is not commanded. It follows that permission to perform *C* means that there is no obligation to omit *C*, that is, that *C* is not prohibited. Therefore:

permission *C* = no obligation not–*C* = no prohibition *C*

If an act is neither prohibited nor commanded it is called a *liberty*:

liberty *C* = no prohibition *C* & no command *C* = no obligation not–*C* & no obligation *C*.

Permitted conduct and liberties thus have the common feature of not being prohibited. They differ in that a permitted act can be prescribed (I am permitted to do my duty), whereas an act which is a liberty cannot be prescribed.

If C is a liberty then not-C is also a liberty. Both formulas say the same thing, namely, that there is no duty with respect to either C or not-C.

That an act is a 'liberty' is the same as its falling outside the sphere of legal norms. It is legally indifferent. Neither its performance nor its non-performance results in legal reactions.

My liberty to go into the woods, to walk along the street, to smoke a cigar, or to wear a red tie means, therefore, that I am not in duty bound either to do or not to do these things; and that others (B or any others in relation to whom I have this liberty) have no claim on me.

It is impossible to enumerate the liberties that a person has. The sphere of liberty is defined negatively as everything that is not the object of legal regulation.

Certain liberties are, however, frequently mentioned by name, because they appear as exceptions; they are mentioned in such a way that the liberty either pertains to some single person or pertains to everyone, being an exception to an otherwise general rule. The first kind we call 'special liberty' or 'privilege', the latter 'general liberty'.

It is the property-owner's privilege to walk on his land. He is at liberty to do so and has at the same time the claim on others that they keep away. According to the Danish law on the preservation of natural amenities, people have the general liberty to walk over private land along the seacoast.

Another reason for naming particular liberties is the fact that the Constitution guarantees the citizen various liberties, as spheres which are protected from the intervention of legislation (religious liberty, freedom of the press).

When a liberty is common to all, as it usually is, its value to the individual may be problematical. That I have a liberty, after all, means only that others have no claim against me, that is, that no legal obstacles can be placed in the way of my enjoying the liberty. On the other hand *the liberty does not give me a claim against others to provide me with full opportunity to act as I please*. I am at liberty to sit on a bench in Hyde Park. But this liberty is of no use to me if the bench is occupied. I have no claim on others that they give up their seat to me. If the liberty of one person cannot be reconciled with the liberty of another, there will be a struggle. But there exists a certain amount of regulation of this struggle and thereby some protection for the one who first occupied a place, as a consequence of other claims which limit the means which may be used in displacing another person. If, for example, I am sitting on a bench, I certainly have no claim against others that they let me sit there. But I do have a claim against others that they do not attack my person, and this has the consequence that (legally) I cannot be driven away from the bench by force.

In business there is extensive liberty to operate in the market and to fight for customers. No one has a claim against others to leave his customers alone. But here, too, the legal order sets limits to the means used in the struggle of competition.

Subjection and Competence

Competence is the legally established ability to create legal norms (or legal effects) through and in accordance with enunciations to this effect. Competence is a special case of power. Power exists when a person is able to bring about, through his acts, desired legal effects.

The norm which establishes this ability is called a *norm of competence*. It states the conditions necessary for the exercise of this ability. These conditions usually fall into three groups: (1) those which prescribe what person (or persons) is qualified to perform the act which creates the norm (*personal competence*); (2) those which prescribe the procedure to be followed (*procedural competence*); and (3) conditions which prescribe the possible scope of the created norm with regard to its subject, situation, and theme (*substantial competence*). Among procedural conditions there will usually be one which prescribes how the norm is to be communicated to its subjects, or at any rate how it is to be promulgated, that is, how it is to be made public in such a way that the subjects of the norm have the opportunity to obtain information about the norm if they want to.

Those enunciations in which competence is exercised are called *actes juridiques*, or acts-in-the-law, or, in private law, dispositive declarations. Examples are: a promise, a will, a judgment, an administrative licence, a statute. An act-in-the-law is, like a move in chess, a human act which nobody can perform as an exercise of his natural faculties. Norms of competence are, like the rules of games, constitutive. (See above, § 14.)

Since a norm of competence prescribes the conditions for the creation of a norm it is a tautology to say that if an attempt is made to exercise competence *ultra vires* (outside the scope of the competence) no legal norm is created. This is expressed by saying that the intended act-in-the-law is invalid or that non-compliance with a norm of competence results in invalidity.

The power or competence of a person must be distinguished both from a liberty to exercise his powers as he pleases (but only, of course, *intra vires*) and from a duty to exercise it along certain lines. If there is such a duty there exists a *norm of conduct*, whose theme is the way in which the competent person is to exercise his power. It is important to understand this distinction between the norm of competence and the norm of conduct which regulates the exercise of this competence. Whereas exceeding the norm of competence, as we have said, results in invalidity, violation of the norm of conduct does not affect the validity of the *acte juridique* but involves a liability, like other violations of obligation. Such interacting of norms of competence and norms of conduct plays an important part in legal practice. An agent, for example, may be bound by his principal to exercise authority within certain limits, but the principal may nevertheless be unable to plead this, viz., that he has made such restrictions, against a third party who has relied on the agent's authority. A restraint which was privately placed on the ostensible authority of the agent and ignored by him will not exonerate the principal from liability, unless, of course, its existence is known to the third party of the transaction. But the exercise of power in disregard of these restrictions exposes the agent to an action by the principal. A similar rule applies to power in public law. Power is not assigned to public authorities to be exercised as they choose, but only in accordance with established rules or presupposed general principles. Here, too, it is frequently possible to distinguish between their competence and their duties with regard to the exercise of this competence; overstepping these norms results, not in invalidity, but in criminal or civil liability.

If the law were always carefully prepared and precisely drafted it would not be difficult to decide whether a given rule were intended as a norm of competence (resulting in invalidity) or as a norm of conduct regulating the exercise of this power (resulting in liability). But unfortunately such is not always the case. If, for example, a statute empowers the President of the Board of Trade to regulate the import of some commodities after previous submission of the matter to the Minister for Agriculture, it is not clear whether the required submission is intended as a restriction of competence with the result that such regulation is invalid if the submission is not made, or whether it is intended only as an obligation prescribed in a norm of conduct with the consequence that the President of the Board of Trade incurs a liability if he has not made the submission. This is a question of interpretation to be decided by the usual methods.

Subjection is the correlate of power or competence. The subjected person *B* is determined as anyone who according to the norms defining the substantial scope of *A*'s power may be the subject of a norm created by *A*. This term is linguistically awkward, since it is often used in a pejorative sense. I am here using it without any such implication. Citizens are 'subjected' to the power of the legislator, inheritors to the power of the testator, the party making an offer to that of the recipient, the successor to that of the transferror—all regardless of whether the particular disposition binds the subjected party or creates claims for him.

It is a conspicuous feature of the law of modern societies that the norms of competence in force can be divided into two distinct categories, different in their content and in the purposes they serve in the life of the community.[1]

On the one hand there are those rules of competence which create the power we call *private autonomy*. They are characterized by the following features. In the personal sphere they create a power for every normal adult individual. This power is in all important respects limited to the individual's ability to incur liabilities and to dispose matters concerning his own rights. When the dispositions of two or more individuals are coordinated they are enabled to 'legislate' by contract as far as their mutual relations are concerned. This power is not tied up with a duty to exercise it, or to exercise it only in a certain way. The individual is free to decide whether, and how, he will make use of his autonomy. The social function of private autonomy is to enable the individual to shape his own legal relationships, in accordance with his own interests, within the framework of the legal order. The power itself in

[1] *Dansk Statsforfatningsret* [*Danish Constitutional Law*], vol. I, § 5.

relation to a certain object is not a 'right' but is part of a transferable right. With the transference of the right the power is lost to the successor. The power that we are here considering may therefore be said to be *unqualified* (everyone has it), *autonomous* (it is used to bind the competent person himself), *discretionary* (it is exercised freely), and *transferable* (it can be transferred to a successor).

On the other hand, there are the rules of competence that create what we call a *public authority*. They have the following features. They create a power only for certain qualified persons. The required qualification consists in a designation in accordance with certain rules of law: in Denmark, Ministers have their power because of their nomination according to Article 14 of the Constitution, members of Parliament because of their election according to the Polling Act, and the King because of his hereditary right to the throne according to the Act of Succession. The substance of this power is a capacity to create rules that bind others (statutory enactments, judgments, administrative acts). The power is not granted with a view to its being used by the competent person freely and at his convenience. Its exercise is a duty, a public office in the widest sense, and when exercised it is a duty to use the power in an unprejudiced and impartial manner, for the furtherance of certain social purposes. These duties are more than merely moral duties; they are hedged in by sanctions and controls of various kinds. The power's social function is to serve the interests of the community—what is called the 'common weal'. Public authority is never part of a right and is therefore never transferable. At most, the exercise of power may be delegated to other persons, with the holder's own power left untouched. The competence which we are here considering may therefore be characterized as *qualified, heteronomous, in the public interest*, and *nontransferable*.

The distinction between private autonomy and public authority constitutes the basis of the traditional distinction between private and public law. Public law may be defined as the law which concerns the legal status of the public authorities.

Immunity and Disability

As we have seen, immunity and disability are negative modalities.

What has been said about liberty and 'no-claim' applies analogously to them. As negative terms they cover everything not subject to legal power; therefore it is not possible to enumerate and name specific immunities. Every person enjoys immunity with regard to every other person, provided that the other person is not furnished with power in relation to the first. Some specific 'rights of immunity' are, however, explicitly recognized, since they appear as exceptions. For example, it is said that foreign ambassadors enjoy immunity from the courts, and that citizens enjoy immunity from the legislature in those areas in which the constitution limits its competence.

The legal modalities have, until now, hardly been considered important as a subject of study. Usually 'legal relations' are merely divided in analysis into the correlative concepts of duty and right. This analysis is, however, unsatisfactory.

First of all, it has not been realized that the subject of the analysis is really the language of the law, and that the different modalities simply represent linguistic vehicles through which the directive content of legal rules is expressed. On the contrary, duties and rights have been regarded as metaphysical substances created by certain facts and creating in their turn legal effects. This metaphysical way of considering duties and rights to be substantial entities largely prevails in Continental and Anglo-American legal thinking, and has had unfortunate results for the treatment of practical legal problems.

Secondly, the duty-right division is too superficial. The term 'right' covers such heterogeneous concepts as claim, liberty, power (competence) and immunity; and 'duty' is not differentiated from the other passive modalities. The incompleteness of the duty-right analysis has caused the confusion which characterizes legal language, both in legislation and in the theoretical study of law.

Finally, it is an error to introduce 'right' as the correlate of 'duty'. The concept of a right is a systematic one in which a number of legal rules are united. It covers a collection of legal effects each of which may be expressed in the customary modalities. The right of ownership, for example, includes a set of claims, liberties, competences and immunities. A 'right' (such as ownership, the different *jura in re aliena*, copyright, etc.) is not a legal modality used in the expression of a particular legal rule, but rather a theoretical construct which serves the systematic presentation of the law in force.

To my knowledge, the American, Wesley Newcomb Hohfeld, was the first to investigate the problem of the legal modalities (*Fundamental Legal Conceptions*, 1923).[1] The account given here is largely inspired by Hohfeld, particularly in the idea that the modalities are connected by the logical relations of contradiction and correlation. My own attitude, however, differs from his. Hohfeld makes no attempt to interpret the modalities in terms of their legal functions, and he does not seem to realize that the modalities are really nothing more than linguistic tools of the law.

§ 29

It is possible to interpret the legal modalities in such a way that they have, to some extent, an application to non-legal normative discourse.

The preceding section dealt exclusively with normative modalities interpreted in relation to legal speech. I now turn to the question of the extent to which the table of modal expressions can be interpreted as covering non-legal normative speech also. The following observations are primarily intended to apply to moral speech, but they may very well also apply, *mutatis mutandis*, to speech in which other conventional norms, the norms of games and the like, are formulated or applied.

It is evident that non-legal normative discourse is on the whole more simple than legal discourse. (As we noticed earlier, if a system contains a judicial authority it is included under legal systems; see above, § 22 a). This is so, first of all, because those modalities which appear in the norms of competence do not apply to static systems which lack legislation and other kinds of norm-creating activity. To this there is, however, an important exception. A promise is also a moral phenomenon which is based upon conventional-moral norms of competence that create a 'private autonomy' similar to a legal institution but of a less formal and precise character. The modern discussion of the logical nature of the promise would, I believe, have been more simple and illuminating if more attention had been paid to the close relationship between moral and legal institutions. It would have been more

[1] See above, p. 124 note 2.

apparent, first of all, that the utterance of a promise is an act of directive and not indicative speech, that it is not a piece of information about the promisor's intentions, his volitional disposition or about any other past, present or future state of affairs; and, secondly, that the various acts which constitute the 'promising game'—making a promise, receiving it, fulfilling it, breaking it— are not natural acts but acts constituted by the norms of competence which create the 'binding force' of the promise, just as moves in chess are constituted by the norms of chess.[1]

Of the modal expressions found in norms of conduct it is obvious that 'obligation' and 'permission' occur also in moral speech. It is more doubtful whether the same is true of the modality of 'claim'. It has often been thought, mistakenly, that the conception of a claim (and of rights as the basis of claims) belongs in the province of law, whereas morality knows of obligations only. But it seems natural, especially in the case of a promise, to say that, through the utterance of the promise, the promisee acquires a claim on the promisor for the fulfilment of the promise. And there are other situations in which moral judgments are formulated in terms of claims, demands and rights. But it is certainly true that a moral claim is different from a legal one and it appears, in some respects, to be a weaker variant, displaying only a faint reflexion of the qualities of a legal claim. I shall mention four respects in which this is the case.

First of all, if a claim is to be advanced with weight it requires a considerable degree of precision. Whoever makes a claim must be able to say *what* he has a claim on, defining its subject matter qualitatively and quantitatively. Moral norms and obligations, however, are often formulated so vaguely that the conception of a corresponding claim appears hardly adequate. If one takes it as a moral obligation to love one's neighbour as oneself, to show mercy, or to give alms, it seems hardly feasible to construe the corresponding claims of definite persons in terms of a certain amount of love, mercy or alms. Love knows of no *quantum satis*. This is especially true of a morality which (like the Christian) is characterized by ideals of perfection and unrealizable demands— which set exalted tasks, requiring unending efforts—that is, a morality of the type we shall shortly characterize as 'idealistic'. It is less true of a morality which (like the Jewish) is marked by

[1] See above, p. 53, note 1.

136

detailed prescriptions and demands of strict observance, that is, a morality which we may call 'legalistic'.

It is easy to see why promising in particular has given rise to the idea of moral claims. For in this situation definite and precise expectations are caused in the promisee in accordance with the declaration.

Secondly, it is the possibility of instituting proceedings and enforcing a legal claim which makes it what it is—a *claim*; and this has no counterpart in moral life. A legal claim is, as we have seen, in one part an exhortation, in so far as it calls on the other party to fulfil his obligations under a given normative order. A moral claim may have the same function. But standing up for one's rights and claiming their fulfilment is more than mere exhorting. A claim is marked by the latent threat implied in the possibility of instituting proceedings. This element is completely lacking in moral claims.

Thirdly, the possessor of a legal claim has the power to dispose of it in a way which has no counterpart in moral affairs, apart, perhaps, from claims based on promises. The legal creditor may renounce his claim with the result that the debtor's obligation is extinguished. Furthermore, a legal obligation is usually actualized only if and only when the creditor presents his claim. As long as this does not take place the debtor incurs no liability by not performing on his own initiative. Moral obligations do not depend in the same way on the behaviour of the interested party. A moral obligation to love one's neighbour or to show mercy is not extinguished through renunciation, and no advancing of a claim is required to make it actual.

Finally, in some cases in which it is usual to speak about moral claims or rights there is hardly any corresponding obligation at all. This is so, for example, when human rights are proclaimed. When it is said that everyone has the right to education, the right to work, and the right to a standard of living adequate to the health and well-being of himself and his family, no one can be pointed out as the subject of a corresponding obligation. The intention of such declarations is to say that a social order which does not give everyone these rights is morally unjustifiable, and that therefore if actual conditions fall behind the ideal everyone is under the obligation of working to promote a better world. The claim involved in human rights is then nothing more than the expectation that everyone will do his best to further an evolution in the direction indicated by the ideals of human rights. This expectation is, however, so vague that it can hardly be recognized as a claim.

VI

DEONTIC LOGIC[1]

§ 30

The fact that norms (directives) are without truth-value does not rule out the possibility of a deontic logic.

The fundamental problem is whether it makes sense to assume the existence of a deontic logic, especially the existence of deontic inferences, that is, inferences in which one or more of the premises are of a directive nature. The problem may be described as what I have called *Jørgensens's dilemma*:[2]

On the one hand, logic is traditionally conceived as being concerned with sentences in so far as they express propositions, and especially with the relation between the truth-values of different propositions. The logical connectives are defined by means of tables of truth-values which determine unambiguously the truth-value of a molecular expression as a function of its constituent atomic expressions. To infer logically, therefore, means to relate the truth-value of one sentence to the truth-value of one or more other sentences. (For the sake of simplicity and since it is usual, though not correct, I will speak of 'sentences' instead of the 'propositions' expressed by sentences.) To infer S_2 logically from S_1, then, means that if S_1 is true S_2 is also true. Any logical inference, therefore, may be formulated as a hypothetical judgment of the pattern: If the premises P_1, P_2, . . ., P_n are true, then the

[1] It would have been more correct to use the term 'logic of directives' or 'directive logic'. As the expression 'deontic logic', however, seems to have gained general acceptance I stick to that. It is taken in a broad sense as concerned with all varieties of directive speech and not with ought-expressions exclusively.

[2] 'Imperatives and Logic', *Theoria*, 1941, pp. 53ff., reprinted in XI *Philosophy of Science*, 1944.

conclusion C is also true. It follows that a sequence of sentences can be recognized as a logical inference only on the condition that the premisses consist exclusively of sentences possessing truth-value, which therefore may be either true or false, and are actually one or the other. Since directives have no truth-value (see above, § 22 f) this condition is not satisfied if sentences expressing directives occur among the premisses, and this means that deontic inferences are excluded. One can, to be sure, construct rules of transformation according to which a directive D_2 is said to be inferred from another directive D_1. But it is impossible, since D_1 and D_2 are sentences without truth-value, to interpret such rules and to explain what it *means* to say that D_2 follows from D_1.

On the other hand, it seems to be immediately obvious that logical constants such as the logical connectives and the quantifiers are actually used in directive speech with a function similar to that which they have in indicative speech; and that reasonings actually occur which bear the stamp of logical inference even though one or more of the premisses are directives; for example:

> Take all the boxes to the station;
> This is one of the boxes;
> ∴ Take this to the station;

or:

> Any apprehended thief is to be sentenced to imprisonment;
> A is an apprehended thief;
> ∴ A is to be sentenced to imprisonment.

The dilemma, to put it briefly, consists in this: on the one hand it appears senseless to talk about 'deontic inference', on the traditional understanding of the concept 'logical inference'; while on the other hand it seems obvious that such inferences actually occur.

Placed in this dilemma, some writers, like Ingemar Hedenius and, following him, Manfred Moritz, have grasped the first horn of the dilemma, and said that deontic inferences cannot occur; and they have consequently maintained that the task lies solely in explaining what it is that actually goes on in so-called deontic inferences and how the illusion arises that logical relations may exist between directives.[1]

Hedenius' explanation is as follows: To any directive actually advanced there corresponds a parallel indicative which states the

---

[1] Ingemar Hedenius, *Om rätt och moral* [On Law and Morals], 1941, p. 122.

fact that the directive 'exists', that is, has been advanced. If A has advanced the directive to B:

(1) Take all the boxes to the station,

we have the following true parallel indicative:

(2) B has been ordered to take all the boxes to the station.

If we now add the further premiss:

(3) This is one of the boxes.

then (2) and (3) constitute the premisses of an indicative inference which has as its conclusion:

(4) B has been ordered to take this to the station.

By means of this indicative inference B is able to see the truth of the assertion involved in the conclusion, namely, that he has been ordered to take 'this' to the station, and this insight may cause him to act accordingly. But any directive conclusion such as

(5) Take this to the station

does not occur and cannot occur on the given premisses, or, indeed, on any premisses; for a directive, not possessing truth-value, cannot be part of any logical inference whatever.[1]

This line of reasoning has been elaborated by Manfred Moritz. In a study of fifty pages, he deals with the problem of how, if there are no deontic inferences, a judge, faced with a norm directed to all judges, is able to find out that the norm is directed to him also, and how he is able to take it as a guide to his decision.[2]

Common sense, for which I have preserved a healthy respect, seems to indicate that this is tilting with windmills. It is, besides, not difficult to see that the Hedenius-Moritz explanation is untenable, and that it presupposes the deontic inference that should have been explained away.

The sequence of indicatives:

(2) B has been ordered to take all the boxes to the station
(3) This is one of the boxes
∴ (4) B has been ordered to take this to the station,

is not a sound indicative inference and is nothing but an affected

---

[1] *Op. cit.*, pp. 124ff., 128–9, cf. 'Hypotetiska befallningar' ['Hypothetical Commands'] *Eripainos Ajatus*, XVII/1952, pp. 49ff., 74ff.
[2] 'Der praktische Syllogismus und das juridische Denken', *Theoria*, 1954, pp. 78ff.

manner of expressing the deontic inference according to which the general directive 'Take all the boxes to the station' implies that each of the boxes is to be taken to the station.

The indicative sentence (2) (that is, the parallel sentence which states the fact that B has received an order issued to him by A) refers to a historical fact; and so does sentence (4), the conclusion. The first fact stated is that B has received a command to take all the boxes to the station, and the second is that he has received a command to take this box to the station. Now, if we do not accept a deontic inference to the effect that the general directive entails the singular one, there is no logical connection on which to base the parallel indicative inference, that is, no connection which depends exclusively on the meaning of the terms employed in the two sentences. Sentence (2) states a historical fact, and so does sentence (4). Whether the first fact entails the second is, when deontic inferences are excluded, not a logical but an empirical question. Whether A, in commanding B to take all the boxes to the station, is able at the same time to command him to leave one of the boxes where it is, is—when deontic logic is ruled out—a psychological question to be decided on the basis of empirical observations. The inference of (4) from (2) is therefore not a sound *logical* inference.

We can also put our argument in this way. Hedenius' inference (2) & (3) → (4) (see above) derives its apparent soundness from an implied deontic inference, namely, that the general directive implies a singular one. If we consciously abstract from this and consider the constituent sentences of the inference strictly as indicatives, it will be seen that the inference is not in order as a syllogism. Where is the middle term? For it to be in order, the inference must be rewritten in this way:

(2a) All the boxes have the property that they are to be taken to the station

(3) This is one of the boxes

∴ (4) This has the property that it is to be taken to the station.

Written in this way, however, this can easily be seen not to be a genuine indicative inference. Sentence (2a) is not a genuine indicative, but a cryptic formulation of the directive that the boxes are to be taken to the station; and likewise with sentence (4).

Hedenius and Moritz then have failed in their attempt to

explain away the apparent deontic inference. I shall now argue that there is no reason to make such an attempt.

It is, to be sure, correct that the logical connectives and inferences which operate in directive speech cannot, if we accept that directives are without truth-value, be interpreted as truth-functions and truth-relations. Since they do actually function in directive speech the natural question is whether they might be *interpreted in some other way*. If it could be shown that the connectives, as they function in directive discourse, are definable by means of value tables analogous to those we know from ordinary logic, the only difference being that the two indefinables are interpreted as referring not to truth and falsity, but to another pair of values, then it would be unreasonable not to characterize the relations defined in this way as logical. Deontic logic would then be on a level with the traditional propositional calculus—a new interpretation of the same formal system, of equal status with the old.

The possibility of a deontic logic is now generally recognized[1] but there are great divergencies of opinion as to the interpretation of its values and its relation to the logic of indicatives.

Writing this Chapter I have had in mind primarily directive speech in the form of commands and quasi-commands (law and convention) but it is assumed that my reasoning and its outcome holds good in respect of all varieties of directive speech. I dare not deny, however, that specific inquiries could disclose peculiar problems when deontic logic is interpreted as the logic of, e.g., invitations, requests, advices, rules of games or moral principles and judgments.[2]

§ 31

In indicative logic external and internal negation are equivalent.

I have raised the question whether the value-symbols of deontic logic might be interpreted as standing for other values than truth

---

[1] The possibility of deontic inferences is still occasionally denied, see e.g., B. A. O. Williams, 'Imperative Inference', *Analysis* 23 (Suppl.) (1963), pp. 30ff. and G. B. Keene, 'Can Commands Have Logical Consequences', *American Philosophical Quarterly*, vol. 3 (1966).

[2] Cp. Lennart Åquist, 'Interpretations of Deontic Logic', *Mind* LXXIII (1964), pp. 246ff. He assumes many possible interpretations of deontic logic, among others a logic of commands, a logic of wishes, a logic of promises, a logic of decisions and a logic of intentions.

and falsity. I will, however, leave this question for the moment, for I believe that we shall be better equipped to deal with it after having studied the way the connectives actually behave in directive speech. In this section I start by investigating *negation*.

To understand the peculiarities of deontic negation it is useful first to consider negation in the traditional indicative logic. I speak of the Aristotelian two-valued logic, as the formalized system which corresponds to ordinary language with the highest degree of approximation.

In this logic, negation of the proposition p, symbolized by the formula $\sim$p, is defined by the following truth table:

p	$\sim p$
T	F
F	T

which means that $\sim p$ is false if p is true and true if p is false.

This definition conceals the fact that the negation of a proposition may mean two different things. Modern logistic theory has paid little heed to this fact, probably because the two kinds of negation are definable through the same table of value.[1] In deontic logic, however, the two kinds of negation are not equivalent, as we shall subsequently show, and for this reason it is important to draw attention to them.

$\sim p$ may express either the pragmatic act of rejecting p or a proposition on a par with p and dealing with a complementary subject matter. An example may clarify the distinction.

Let p stand for the proposition *Peter is at home*. The negation ($\sim p$), then, may express either the denial that it is the case that Peter is at home, or the acceptance and assertion of another proposition, namely, one which states that Peter is not-at-home, that is, that he is away. The distinction may be made clearer if we use the symbol $i(T)$ for a proposition. As we explained earlier (§ 5), T in this formula symbolizes a topic (Peter's being at home), while i indicates that the topic is conceived as real ('it is so'). If $p = i(T)$, $\sim p$ may mean either

$$\sim i(T)$$
or
$$i(\sim T)$$

which are called respectively *external* and *internal* negation.

[1] See at the end of this section.

External negation expresses my refusal to accept that things stand in the world in such a way that p forms part of its description. This refusal is expressed in a second-order proposition in uttering which I reject p as false. Internal negation, on the other hand, is itself a first-order proposition which states that things stand in the world in a certain way, namely, such that Peter is not-at-home, that he is away.

$i(\sim T)$ is called the complement of $i(T)$ and *vice versa*. The determination of $\sim T$ requires further analysis. It must suffice to say that T and $\sim T$ constitute a universe of discourse. If Peter is not at home he is out (either here or there). If he is not a British citizen he is either of some other nationality or stateless.[1] A proposition and its complement together exhaustively determine a certain dimension of predication (in the two examples, Peter's location and his national status respectively).

The single value-table of negation must therefore be replaced by two:

External negation

$p = i(T)$	$\sim p = \sim i(T)$
T	F
F	T

which is to be read as follows: If one accepts a proposition one cannot at the same time reject that proposition, and *vice versa*; or, more briefly, one cannot at the same time accept and reject the same proposition.

Internal negation

$p = i(T)$	$\sim p = i(\sim T)$
T	F
F	T

This is to be read: If one accepts a proposition one cannot at the same time accept its complement, and the same holds of rejecting

---

[1] A negation has meaning only if that which is subject to the negation itself has meaning. This is not the case if in the negated sentence, contrary to the rules of semantic logic (above, § 4), the predicate is incompatible with the subject. For instance, the sentence: 'My consciousness is coloured' does not express a true proposition; but its negation: 'My consciousness is colourless' fares no better. Cf. Jørgen Jørgensen, *Sandhed, Virkelighed og Fysikkens Metode* [*Truth, Reality and the Methods of Physics*] (1956), pp. 94ff.

a proposition; or, more briefly, one cannot adopt the same pragmatic attitude at the same time toward a proposition and its
complement.

The value table of negation, combined with the understood
assumption that any p is either true or false, defines two of the
principles of classical logic, the Law of Contradiction and the Law
of the Excluded Middle. The first means that p and $\sim p$ are incompatible, the second that they are exhaustive. Since $\sim p$ may
mean either $\sim i(T)$ or $i(\sim T)$ both principles must be restated, each
of them in two versions:

PCI (first principle of contradiction)
> *One must not at the same time accept and reject the same proposition;*
> or
> No proposition is both true and false.

PC II (second principle of contradiction)
> *One must not at the same time accept (or reject) both a proposition
> and its complement;* or
> No proposition can possess the same truth value as its com-
> plement.

PE I (first principle of exclusion)
> *(Being sufficiently informed)*[1] *one must either accept or reject a
> proposition;* or
> Any proposition is either true or false.

PE II (second principle of exclusion)
> *(Being sufficiently informed)*[1] *one must accept (reject) either a pro-
> position or its complement;*
> or, either a proposition or its complement is true (false).

These principles become easier to grasp if they are restated in
such a way that one principle states what holds with regard to one
and the same proposition, and the second states what holds with
regard to a proposition and its complement. The two principles
are to be called, respectively, the principle of external negation and
the principle of internal negation. We then have:

The principle of external negation: With regard to one and the same
proposition, assuming simultaneity,
> one *must not* (1) *both* accept *and* reject the proposition;

---

[1] This condition is important. It means that in accordance with classical logic we
disregard the lack of information which may make us consider a proposition as
neither true nor false, or accept (or reject) neither a proposition nor its complement.

(2) *neither* accept *nor* reject it;

one must   (3) *either* accept *or* reject it.

The principle of internal negation: With regard to a proposition p and its complement $(p)_c$, assuming simultaneity,

one *must not* (1) accept (or, respectively, reject)[1] *both p and $(p)_c$*;

(2) accept (or, respectively, reject)[1] *neither p nor $(p)_c$*;

one must   (3) accept (or, respectively, reject)[1] *either p or $(p)_c$*.

These two principles imply that $\sim i(T)$ and $i(\sim T)$ are equivalent. The external negation $\sim i(T)$ is the rejection of the proposition $i(T)$. It follows from the first principle that this proposition may not at the same time be accepted. If a proposition is not accepted its complement, *in casu* $i(\sim T)$, must, according to the second principle, be accepted. Therefore $\sim i(T) \equiv i(\sim T)$, as a simple consequence of the fact that the two kinds of negation have been defined through the same table of truth values.

$i(\sim T)$ is a proposition. Its external negation is $\sim i(\sim T)$. In virtue of the identity of external and internal negation we then have:

$$\sim i(\sim T) \equiv i(\sim \sim T) \equiv i(T),$$

which is called the rule of double negation.

The question arises of what really is expressed in these 'laws' or 'principles'. We have so far formulated them either as statements concerning the relations between the truth value of propositions or as norms which regulate the pragmatic acts of accepting or rejecting propositions. There seems to be a third possible interpretation of the principles, namely, as ontological statements of the following kind:

I The principle of external negation:

The world either is or is not in a certain state;

II The principle of internal negation:

The world is either in a certain state or in its complementary state.

It was once a temptation to interpret these principles, whether formulated in the first, the second, or the third way, as empirical statements whose truth or falsity must be established through the

---

[1] The parentheses could be omitted. That one cannot reject both p and $(p)_c$ is the same as that one cannot accept neither p nor $(p)^c$, and *vice versa*. That one must reject either p or $(p)^c$ is the same as that one must accept either p or $(p)_c$.

observation of facts, whether psychological, linguistic, or ontological. Nowadays it is agreed that such interpretation is untenable.[1] No experience could ever verify or falsify the principles. They are, in my view, *basic postulates or norms defining indicative speech* by prescribing the basic conditions which must be satisfied if indicative discourse is to fulfil the function of describing 'reality' and stating how 'the world' is or is not. If these postulates or norms are denied it becomes impossible to distinguish between what is posed in a discourse, that is, conceived as real (see § 5 and § 8), and what is not, and consequently between what can be accepted as true and what cannot. Therefore, either we accept these basic postulates or norms—or the rest is silence.

Before the development of mathematical logic the nature of negation was vigorously discussed. Sigwart attacks the view that the negative judgment *A is not B* expresses an act of thinking (*Denkact*) on an equal footing with the affirmative judgment; and this holds whether the negation is conceived as attaching to the predicate (*A is not-B*) or to the copula, the subject and the predicate being connected through a copula of a specifically negative character (*A is-not B*). His criticism is directed against Lotze, Brentano, Bergmann, Windelband and Rickert. According to his own views the negative judgment belongs to a logical level other than the affirmative: it turns against an attempted or accomplished judgment and declares the synthesis of subject and predicate conceived therein to be invalid. 'The judgment that *A* is not *B* means the same as: It is false, it is not to be accepted, that *A* is *B*. Negation is therefore, immediately and directly, a judgment about an affirmative judgment which is either contemplated or actually performed, and only indirectly a judgment concerning the subject of the affirmative judgment.' (Christoph Sigwart, *Logik*, vol. I, § 20, 4. My translation.) Expressed in the terminology we are using this means that he advocates an interpretation of negation on the pattern of external negation.

Modern philosophers have also occasionally touched upon the problem. Jørgen Jørgensen, contrary to Sigwart, maintains that the negative element is to be found in the theme that is subject to either acceptance or rejection, that is, he construes negation on the pattern of internal negation. In *A Treatise on Formal Logic* (Vol. 3 (1931), pp. 248–249), he writes: 'It must be pointed out, however, that our human understanding is actually only capable of drawing inferences from

[1] Jørgen Jørgensen, *Psykologi pa biologisk Grundlag* [*Psychology on Biological Foundations*] (1942–6), pp. 46ff., defends an empiristic interpretation of logic.

asserted objectives [presumably identical with what in my terminology are called "propositions"] and that even negative propositions—in contrast to interrogations—contain a positive element of assertion, in that they assert that the ("negative") objective therein contained is true. The proposition: "Peter is not taller than Paul" is just as assertive as the proposition "Peter is taller than Paul" and the difference between them can therefore not be sought in the "method of position" but must be looked for in the objectives.' To this the author adds the following note: 'Hence I must consider it misleading to characterize judgments as assertions or rejections of the content of propositions; for to reject the content of a proposition means asserting the corresponding negative, and where assertion is lacking, there is no proposition to be considered, The withdrawal of an assertion does not give a negative proposition, but simply the suspension of judgment altogether.' Hare, too, construes negation as internal negation (*The Language of Morals* (1952), pp. 20ff. Cf. 'Imperative Sentences', *Mind*, 1949, pp. 21ff., 34–35).

Of special interest is Gottlob Frege, 'Negation' in *Translations from the Philosophical Writings of Gottlob Frege*, ed. by P. Geach and M. Black (1960), pp. 117ff., expecially pp. 129ff. Also this author construes negation as internal negation. He denies that there are two ways of negating. To deny a thought (what I call a 'proposition') is the same as to affirm the contradictory thought. There is no 'external' negation because there are not two different ways of judging, of which one is used for the affirmative, and the other for the negative, answer to a question. Even in the case of a negative answer to a question, judging consists in acknowledging the truth of a thought. In my opinion this is contrary to the natural interpretation that to judge a proposition (thought) is to decide whether the proposition is true or not true, that is false. Frege's reasoning to sustain his interpretation rests on the assertion that if a negative judgment is assumed, expressed by saying 'it is false that . . .', assertoric force must always be attached to this locution. It is, then, possible to show that on these premises we would be forced to admit that we could not say, e.g., 'If it is false that the accused was in Berlin at the time of the murder, he did not commit the murder' (p. 130). I do not see, however, why assertoric force necessarily should be attached to the judgment 'it is false that . . .'. Frege gives no reason for his postulate. I am afraid he has been lured to believe that because the meaning of this locution is a judgment, it must necessarily be used with assertoric force. But so it is not. One can perfectly well tentatively consider a proposed judgment, use it interrogatively and hypothetically and in other ways with only fabulating function (above § 8).

Thus Frege's proof that there is no external negation must be deemed inconclusive. But I think that he is right in arguing that the assumption of two ways of judging (and two ways of negating) is *unnecessary*—that is in the logic of indicative speech with which this author exclusively is concerned. As we shall see in the next section this distinction, however, is the corner-stone in the construction of deontic logic.

§ 32

In deontic logic external and internal negation are not equivalent. Internal deontic negation is different from the corresponding indicative negation.

Turning now to a discussion of the function of negation in directive speech, I want to stress that utterances which state the existence of a norm or the fact that a directive has been advanced, since they are indicative utterances, fall outside the scope of the present investigation. Such utterances deal with historical, psychological and sociological facts, and must, even with regard to negation, be treated in logic exactly like any other indicative. It is, in my view, a mistake for von Wright to take deontic logic as dealing with (in addition to other things) utterances of this kind.[1] (We do, however, in § 38 below, explain how deontic logic has derivative consequences for this kind of indicative.) It has been mentioned several times already that one and the same sentence may, according to circumstances, express either a directive or an indicative which states the existence of a norm or the advancing of a directive. Its logical treatment will, then, vary with its meaning. When I operate, in what follows, with sentences like '*A* is under an obligation to . . .' or 'It is forbidden that . . .' they are always to be understood to have directive meaning as when they are used in norms or when someone, in deciding, exhorting, or claiming, applies norms. (See above, § 12.)

A few examples will show that external and internal negation

[1] In 'Deontic Logic', *Logical Studies* (1957), p. 62, von Wright writes: 'The system of Deontic Logic, which we are outlining in this paper, studies propositions (and truth-functions of propositions) about the obligatory, permitted, forbidden, and other (derivative) deontic characters of acts (and performance-functions of acts).' We find the same view in the author's latest work *Norm and Action* (1963), pp. 130ff., 133–4. Here, however, it is added: 'But the laws (principles, rules), which are peculiar to this logic, concern logical properties of the *norms* themselves, which are then reflected in logical properties of norm-propositions. Thus, in a sense, the "basis" of Deontic Logic is a logical theory of prescriptively interpreted O- and P-expressions', cf. below § 38.

are not equivalent in directive speech. To say that A is under no obligation to stay at home is not the same as to say that he is under an obligation not to stay at home, that is, to go out. In Danish[1] the sentence corresponding to 'You shall not stay at home' may, by the words being stressed differently, relate the negation either to 'shall' (external negation) or to 'stay at home' (internal negation). The imperative mood ('Don't stay at home!') presumably always expresses internal negation. We write

$$\sim\!d(T) \pm d(T)$$

to express that the two kinds of negation are not equivalent.[2]

I now, tentatively, establish a table of values for each of the two kinds of negation. The question what values are symbolized by the letters V and I is for the present left open, and so is the question what is meant by 'accepting' or 'rejecting' a directive. The establishment of the tables has been guided by the requirement that they should correspond approximately to the way in which negation functions in ordinary directive speech.

External deontic negation

$d(T)$	$\sim\!d(T)$
V	I
I	V

This is to be read as follows: If one accepts a directive one must not at the same time reject the same directive, and *vice versa*; or, more briefly, one must not at the same time accept and reject the same directive.

Internal deontic negation

$d(T)$	$d(\sim\!T)$
V	I
I	V or I

This is to be read: If one accepts a directive one may not at the same time accept its complement. *A corresponding rule does not hold*

---

[1] I have been informed that the same is not the case in English, cf. below p. 154, note 2.

[2] Lars Bergström, *Imperatives and Ethics* (1962), pp. 22ff., gives a survey of the views of various writers with regard to the question, how negation is to be understood in deontic logic, especially whether there are one or two types of negation of directives. Nicholas Rescher, *The Logic of Commands* (1966), pp. 104ff., makes a distinction between 'negation' and 'countermand' corresponding to our distinction between external and internal negation.

with regard to rejection. Rejection of a directive is compatible with rejection as well as acceptance of its complement.

A comparison with the account in § 30 shows that while the *principle of external negation* applies analogously to directives such is not the case with regard to *the principle of internal negation*. In deontic logic this principle must be reformulated as follows:

With regard to a directive *d* and its complement $(d)_c$ (assuming simultaneity)

> one must n ot (1) accept both *d and* $(d)_c$;
> but on e may (2) accept *neither d nor* $(d)_c$
> or (3) accept *either d or* $(d)_c$.

We may accept *principle I* (the principle of external negation), expressed in 'ontological' terms, as:

The deontic universe (or the universe of obligations) either is or is not in a certain state;

But we may not accept *principle II* (the principle of internal negation):

The deontic universe is either in a certain state or is in its complementary state.

To the tables of values and the principles based on them we may add the following comments.

(a) The principle of external negation is maintained unmodified. Accordingly, accepting a directive (as 'valid') is incompatible with rejecting it (as 'invalid'): it is a contradiction to do both. This harmonizes with the current view that one cannot say at the same time, with directive meaning, that *A* is under an obligation to perform a certain act and that he is not; or that one cannot at the same time command *A* to do something and not command him to do so.

All the same there is an essential difference between indicative and deontic external negation. Are we excluded from accepting that *A* is under an obligation to pay a certain amount of money to *B* and accepting at the same time that he is not, when reference is being made to different deontic universes, that is, to different normative systems and the obligations derived from them, for example, to Danish law and British law, or Danish law and the morality prevailing among businessmen? It should be kept in mind that, as stressed in the beginning of this section, we are talking about directives (norms), not statements about the existence of norms. The question before us is not whether it is an indicative contradiction to *state* that *A* is under an obligation under Danish law but not under English; but whether it is a deontic contradiction to '*accept*' both norms as 'valid' at the same time. (The meaning of these terms are still undefined.) It may also happen that *A* receives, at the same time, contradictory orders from different persons; one orders him to pick up the hat, the other to leave it where it is. If, in accordance with current thinking, we do not recognize any logical hindrance to accepting both norms or orders as valid, this means that the law of contradiction does not hold universally in directive discourse; it does not hold in relation to all simultaneous directives, but only with reference to a certain *system of directives*, that is, a sum of directives postulated as making up a coherent totality of meaning. Danish law, for example, is postulated as constituting such a unity. This postulate appears in certain principles which are accepted in the practice of the courts for the solution of apparent contradictions. These principles are known under the names *lex specialis*, *lex posterior*, and *lex superior* (*On Law and Justice*, § 26). Similar principles may in some circumstances apply as well to personal directives, for example, to those commands issued by parents to their children. It is hardly possible to say under what conditions the postulate may be made, but only that when it is made, explicitly or implicitly, the law of non-contradiction applies.

The contrast with indicatives on this point is perhaps not absolute. If there are, as we have hinted in § 5, different spheres of reality, does the principle of non-contradiction hold for propositions about states of affairs which belong to different spheres? Is it a contradiction at the same time to hold that the grass is green (in everyday world) and colourless (in the physical world)? Or does each sphere constitute an independent universe thus limiting the applicability of the law of non-contradiction?

(b) Internal deontic negation is similar to the corresponding indicative negation in so far as accepting a directive is incompatible with accepting its complement; i.e., there can be no obligation for the same person in the same situation to perform an act and not to perform it. This presumably harmonizes well with current views. If I order *A* both to pick up the hat and to leave it where it is, he will probably not indulge in reflections whether this 'order' expresses a consistent will or not (von Wright) but will simply reject my talk as nonsense, maintaining that although the noises I have made constitute a sentence they do not constitute a speech-act, since the sentence, by violating the fundamental rules which define directive speech, lacks meaning and does not order anything at all.

(c) Internal deontic negation *differs* from the corresponding indicative negation in that rejecting a directive is not incompatible with rejecting its complement. Nothing prevents rejecting that A is under an obligation to stay at home and at the same time reject-ing as well that he is under an obligation to go out. The deontic universe is in this case 'empty'; it is neither in one state or in the complementary state.

This implies that external and internal deontic negation are not equivalent: rejecting that A is under an obligation to stay at home is not the same as saying that he is obliged to go out. This has an important consequence. Whereas the external negation of a pro-position is itself a proposition (because it is identical with the internal negation of the proposition), the external negation of a directive is not itself a directive, but is, viewed in isolation, an empty sentence.[1]

To take an example: If I ask 'Is Peter at home?' and get the answer 'No', I have all the same received information, namely, that Peter is not at home, that he is out, and this is so because in this case external negation is equivalent to internal negation. But on the other hand, if I ask 'Am I under an obligation to stay at home?' and I get a negative answer, I have received no information at all about what is my duty and especially not the information that it is my duty to go out; for in this case external negation is not equiva-lent to internal negation. In Danish[2] the same is the case if I ask 'Shall (skal) I stay at home?' and get the answer 'No'. The sentence $\sim i(T)$ expresses a proposition because it is equivalent to $i(\sim T)$

---

[1] So Ota Weinberger, 'Ueber die Negation von Sollsätzen' [On Negation of Ought-sentences], *Theoria*, 1957, pp. 102ff., 126. Lennart Åquist, *op. cit.*, p. 251, and Edward Schuh in *Mind*, 1967, p. 123, are aware of difficulties in the interpretation of the formula $\sim Op$ in directive speech, i.e. when not taken as a statement of the fact that a command has not been given. Cp. Bergström, *op. cit.*, p. 28.

[2] I have been informed that the same is not the case in English, cf. above p. 151, note 1. This shows a very important difference in the logical behaviour of 'shall' (*skal*) in the two languages. This difference may perhaps explain why I have not, like Hare and others, felt any need to make a distinction between the logic of 'ought' sentences and the logic of ordinary imperatives, see R. M. Hare, 'Some Alleged Differences between Imperatives and Indicatives', *Mind*, 1967, p. 309f.

and says something about how the world is, about what is the case, namely, that Peter has gone out. The sentence $\sim d(T)$, on the other hand, does not express a directive since it does not say anything about how the world ought to be, that is, about what kind of conduct is required as a duty, these terms taken in the technical sense given them in this study (see above, §§ 9 and 27). The sentence is, considered in isolation, empty of meaning.

How is it then, one may ask, that external negation all the same occurs currently in deontic discourse? Well, sentences of this kind become meaningful when considered not in isolation but as a part of a coherent whole. They indicate permissions, that is restrictions (exceptions, partial annulment) of positive obligation-creating directives (commands, norms). Instead of saying 'Take nineteen of these twenty boxes to the station' I say 'Take these boxes to the station; you may, however, leave one', meaning that you are under no obligation to take more than nineteen. In legal language external negation is used to express exceptions to general rules. For example, 'The vendor shall deliver the goods to the buyer at the time stipulated. He may, however, retain them (that is, he is under no obligation to deliver them) if . . .'.

(d) Since $\sim d(T)$, considered in isolation, does not express a directive, it is tempting, with Weinberger, to say that it cannot be negated, that is, that the rule of double negation does not apply in deontic logic. This does not hold, however, if $\sim d(T)$ functions as a permission: negation of the permission means that the underlying directive is reinvested with binding force.[1]

(e) In what follows I shall use another, more usual, notation. Instead of $d(T)$ I shall write $O(p)$. 'O', like 'd', symbolizes the deontic operator and so stands not only for 'obligation' under a norm but also for the directive element of a command, a request, or advice. 'p' is a proposition describing a certain conduct. '$O(p)$' means then, the directive which directs that the subject is under an obligation (or is commanded, is advised) to behave in such a way that p becomes true. It follows that p is true when the directive is complied with. The directive 'Peter, shut the door', for example, is the same as the directive instructing Peter to behave in such a way that the proposition p (i.e., *Peter is shutting the door*) becomes true. It goes without saying that $\sim O(p)$ is the external and $O(\sim p)$ the internal negation of $O(p)$.

---

[1] So Bergström, *op. cit.*, p. 28.

Hans Kelsen until recently maintained, as a central point in his philosophy of law, that the principle of non-contradiction applies universally, that is, independently of whether or not the norms belong to different systems or kinds of norms. 'It is contradictory', said Kelsen, 'to contend that norm A (as a moral norm) and norm non-A (as a legal norm) are valid at the same time. That one is a legal and the other a moral norm does not preclude a logical contradiction, if the two have been established as norms, that is, in the same sphere of the "ought" and, consequently, in the same system of cognition.' (*General Theory of Law and State* (1946), p. 409; cf. pp. 373–5.) This contention is astonishing not merely because it so blatantly is at variance with current views and use, but also because it scarcely harmonizes with that non-cognitivism and relativism otherwise professed by Kelsen in moral philosophy. The explanation could be that Kelsen, as an inheritance from his neo-Kantian youth, has been captivated by the idea that normative utterances express a cognition. 'The principle of contradiction is quite as valid for cognition in the sphere of normative validity as it is in that of empirical reality' (*op. cit.*, p. 408). In my paper, 'Validity and the Conflict between Legal Positivism and Natural Law' (*Revista Juridica de Buenos Aires*, 1961, pp. 46ff.), I have tried to show that Kelsen's peculiar contention is related also to that concept of 'validity' by means of which he expresses the existence of a norm or a system of norms. I have maintained that this concept, in spite of Kelsen's indefatigable fight against Natural Law, involves the postulate that the legal order is inherently morally binding. Since my paper is not everywhere easily available and as I consider this point to be of central importance for the understanding and criticism of Kelsen's legal philosophy, I take the liberty of quoting:

> According to Kelsen the existence of a norm is its 'validity'; and that a norm possesses validity means 'that the individuals ought to behave as the norm stipulates'. But the norm itself, according to its immediate content, expresses what the individuals ought to do. What, then, is the meaning of saying that the individuals ought to do what they ought to do! We have analyzed this idea above. . . . We have seen that the idea of a duty to obey the law (to perform the legal obligations) only makes sense on the supposition that the duty spoken of is a true moral duty corresponding to a 'binding force' inherent in the law.
>
> Although this interpretation does not harmonize with the confessed empiricistic program of the pure theory of law, it is inevitable and must be taken as a survival of natural law philosophy of the quasi-positivist kind.

This interpretation is supported by the way in which Kelsen tries to explain the meaning of the reiterated admonition to behave as required by the norm. The meaning is, he says, that the subjective meaning of the norm is objective as well—which is the same as saying that the norm expresses a *true* demand: the individuals are not only 'commanded' to behave in a certain manner but they 'really', 'in truth', 'objectively' ought to do as claimed by the norm. But the idea of a true norm or an objective duty is exactly the idea with which the natural law philosophy operates, an idea which possesses meaning only on the assumption of objective, aprioristic, moral principles from which the true duties are derived.

That Kelsen is concerned with the traditional problem of the moral quality that distinguished legal order from gangster rule appears from the way in which he illustrates the idea of validity as having objective normative meaning. 'Not every act', he continues, 'whose subjective meaning is a norm is objectively one as well. For example, a robber's command to hand over your purse is not interpreted as a binding or valid norm.'

Only this interpretation makes it possible to understand Kelsen's peculiar view that it is logically impossible to regard a particular rule of law as valid and at the same time to accept, as morally binding, a moral rule forbidding the behaviour required by the legal rule. If legal validity is understood as a moral quality inherent in the established system, this view, puzzling in the light of empiristic principles, becomes well-founded. It should be noted that the assumption that the basic norm invests the factual order with validity is by Kelsen ascribed to what is called 'juristic thinking'. The presupposition is only revealed —and accepted—by the science of law. 'Juristic thinking' refers, I suppose, to ideas and beliefs commonly held by lawyers. 'Juristic thinking', however, is no trustworthy guide for logical analysis. It may be, and it is highly probable in the field of law and morals, that the common way of 'thinking' is saturated by ideological concepts reflecting emotional experiences but without any function in the description of reality, the task of legal science. In that case, the job of the analyst is to reject, not to accept, the idea of validity.

With admirable openness of mind, Kelsen has later revised his ideas in a way that, in my opinion, assumes the soundness of my criticism. He now writes:

'A norm, however, is neither true nor false, it is valid or non-valid. And there is no kind of parallel or analogy between the truth of a proposition and the validity of a norm. I stress this in deliberate contrast to a commonly accepted opinion, also for a long time defended by me. If there were an analogy or a parallel between the truth of a proposition and the validity of a norm, the principle of contradiction would apply to two conflicting norms in a way analogous to that in which it applies to two conflicting propositions. Just as only one of two conflicting propositions can be true while the other one must be false, only one of two conflicting norms could be valid while the other one must be non-valid. This, however, is not the case ... It is impossible to deny that conflicts of norms exist— that is, situations in which two norms apply, of which the one prescribes the performance of a certain action while the other one prescribes the omission of the same action. Conflicts of norms, especially between norms belonging respectively to a certain legal order and a certain moral order, occur only too frequently.' *Österreichische Zeitschrift für öffentliches Recht*, 1963, p. 2.

'In earlier works I have spoken about norms which are not the meaning-content of some act of volition. In my doctrine the basic norm was always conceived as a norm which was not the meaning-content of some act of volition but presupposed in our thinking. Now, gentlemen, I must confess that I cannot any more abide by this doctrine, that I have to abandon it. You may take my word for it, it was no easy thing to give up a doctrine that I had defended through decades. I have abandoned it seeing that a norm *(Sollen)* must be the correlate of a will *(Wollen)*. My basic norm is a *fictive* norm based in a *fictive* act of volition ... In the basic norm a fictive act of volition is conceived that actually does not exist.' *Op. cit.*, pp. 119–20.

The revision, however, cannot stop here. As shown above, § 8, fictions are of no use in cognition. Once it has been realized that the idea of a basic norm cannot be maintained as a necessary cognitive prerequisite, a postulate of 'legal thinking', and that it neither corresponds with any reality, one is bound to go the whole way: the doctrine of a basic norm must be abandoned.

§ 33

External and internal deontic disjunction are not equivalent. Internal deontic disjunction is different from the corresponding indicative disjunction.

When, in the preceding section, we made a distinction between external and internal negation, we were on firm ground. The distinction is clearly warranted in everyday language, in which external negation especially is in current use. If we turn now to disjunction, it is not obvious that a corresponding distinction between external and internal disjunction can be made, especially since it seems questionable whether an external version occurs in actual speech. Expressions such as 'You are either to shut the window or to open the door' are in undisputed use. But do we also know of the external version: 'Either you are to shut the window or you are to open the door'? Is $O(p) \, v \, O(q)$ different from $O(p \, v \, q)$?

In my judgment people are usually not conscious of any such distinction in everyday discourse, disjunctive deontic phrases being usually understood on the internal pattern, that is, as directing the subject to do either this or that. That an external version does however occur is shown by the following example.

In a certain factory precautionary measures varying with the circumstances are taken each night. Either the gate is closed or the dog is turned loose. The factory management employs a watchman to do this. Since, however, it does not consider the watchman sufficiently intelligent to decide for himself what to do on each separate night, it gives him the following instructions: 'A duty is incumbent on you every night, this being either a duty to close the gate or a duty to turn the dog loose. You will get further instructions each night as to which of these two measures you will take.' If on a particular night the watchman gets the instructions that the dog is not to be turned loose, he is able to infer that he is to close the gate:

$$O(p) \, v \, O(q)$$
$$\sim O(p)$$
$$\therefore O(q)$$

The inference may be expressed also by saying that $[(O(p) \, v \, O(q)) \, \& \sim O(p)] \to O(q)$ is a tautology.

If, however, the watchman were more intelligent, the management might have trusted him to decide for himself what measures to take each night. They might then have instructed him either to close the gate or to turn the dog loose, that is, issued the directive $O(p \, v \, q)$. It is not difficult to see that $O(p \, v \, q)$ is not identical with $O(p) \, v \, O(q)$. Whereas the first of these formulas means that the watchman is under an obligation which gives him a choice between p and q, the last formula means that either he is obliged to perform p, without having any choice, or he is obliged to perform q, likewise without choice.

A corresponding distinction in indicatives is unwarranted. The external disjunction $i(T_1)$ v $i(T_2)$ is identical with the internal version $i(T_1 v T_2)$.

The *value table of external deontic disjunction* is supposed to be analogous to the corresponding value table of indicative disjunction and, if so, looks like this:

$O(p)$	$O(q)$	$O(p) v O(q)$
V	V	V
I	V	V
V	I	V
I	I	I

As is well known, 'either-or' is, in everyday discourse, often used 'exclusively'. This is, I believe, the case in directive as well as in indicative discourse. In this case, the 'V' at the top of the third column should be replaced by 'I'.

The *value table of internal deontic disjunction* is presumably like this:

$O(p)$	$O(q)$	$O(p v q)$
V	V	I
I	V	I
V	I	I
I	I	I or V

This means that the disjunction is rejected if one of its constituent parts is accepted, or if both are so. But otherwise the disjunction may as well be accepted as rejected. That $O(p v q)$ is incompatible with $O(p)$, $O(q)$ and $O(p)$ & $O(q)$, and that it therefore behaves differently from external disjunction, is due to the fact that internal disjunction expresses a freedom of choice which is incompatible with a choiceless duty toward any of its constituent parts or toward both of them. If no such choiceless duty exists the disjunction is possible but not necessary.

On this basis two inferences are possible. They are expressed by saying that $O(p v q) \rightarrow \sim O(p)$ and $O(p v q) \rightarrow \sim O(q)$ are both tautologies.

The difference between indicative and deontic disjunction may be illuminated by some examples. Whereas in indicative logic p implies $p v q$ (if it is true that the letter has been posted it is true that it has either been posted or burnt), $O(p)$ does not imply

$O(p \, v \, q)$: the obligation to post a letter does not imply an obligation to either post it or burn it.[1]

As $O(p \, v \, q)$ implies that p is permitted and q is permitted (either
conditionally if p and q are meant as exclusive alternatives; or
unconditionally if this is not the case) it follows that $O(p \, v \, q)$ is
incompatible with $O(\sim p)$ and with $O(\sim q)$. Therefore the
inference

$$(D1) \quad O(p \, v \, q); \, O(\sim p) \, \therefore \, O(q)$$

or:

$$(D1) \quad \text{do } p \text{ or } q; \text{ do not do } p; \text{ so do } q.$$

is not valid because the premisses are incompatible, whereas the
corresponding indicative inference is indisputable.[2]

It has been suggested that a distinction must be made between
choice-offering and *alternative-presenting* disjunctions and that $(D1)$
should be valid if the disjunction is of the last mentioned kind.[3]
In my opinion this distinction is unsound and irrelevant. It is
unsound because the disjunction presenting p and q as exclusive
alternatives also offers the subject a choice, although a narrower
one as the choice offered when the disjunction is not-exclusive. In
that case the choice is among three possibilities: (1) p, (2) q, and
(3) $p \, \& \, q$. If the disjunction is exclusive the choice is limited to

---

[1] I pointed this out in my paper 'Imperatives and Logic', *Theoria*, 1941, pp. 53ff.,
reprinted in *Philosophy of Science*, 1944. Many writers have adhered to this point of
view. Hare, however, denies that at this point there is any difference between imperative and ordinary logic. He argues that, in accordance with a set of general conventions of communication, if a man says 'He has either posted the letter or burnt it', it
is 'implicated' that the speaker does not know whether the letter has been burnt or
posted. It follows that the disjunction is incompatible with the categorical assertions
that the letter has been posted; or that it has been burnt (*op. cit.*, see above, p. 154,
note 2). It may be so but it is irrelevant to the problem as I see it. Ordinary classical
logic disregards the speaker's lack of information, cf. above, p. 146, note 1. '$p \, v \, q$',
therefore, is defined in such a way that it is true if p or q or both are true. The incompatibility of $O(p \, v \, q)$ with $O(p)$ and $O(q)$ or both is not due to any lack of information.
Here is a fundamental difference between the logic of indicatives and the logic of
directives.

[2] A recent discussion has been concerned with the validity of this inference, see
B. A. O. Williams, 'Imperative Inference', *Analysis Supp.*, vol. 23 (1963), pp. 30ff.;
N. Rescher and J. Robinson, 'Can One Infer Commands from Commands?', *Analysis*,
vol. 24 (1963–4), pp. 176ff.; A. Gombay, 'Imperative Inference and Disjunction',
Analysis, vol. 25 (1964–5), pp. 58ff.; Lennart Åquist, 'Choice-Offering and Alterna-
tive-presenting Disjunctive Commands', *Analysis*, vol. 25 (1964–5), pp. 182ff.;
Yehoshua Bar-Hillel, 'Imperative Inference', *Analysis*, vol. 26 (1965–6), pp. 79ff.

[3] Rescher and Robinson, *op. cit.*; Lennart Åquist, *op. cit.*

(1) and (2). But still there is a choice and that makes the presumed inference invalid.[1]

It has been said that if William is told 'Take one of these pieces of cake, but don't take the larger' he knows perfectly well what to do. Whereas (*D1*) suffers from inconsistency, its seeming twin

(*D2*) do *p* or do *q*, and do not do *p*; so do *q*

is regarded as perfectly in order.[2]

I believe this to be correct although it must seem problematic why the premis of (*D2*)—'do *p* or do *q*, and do not do *p*'—must not be rejected as inconsistent. The explanation, in my opinion, is that the premiss, although using two phrases, contains only one directive whose theme of demand is described in a way synonymous with the use of phrase 'with exception of'. Consider the following sequence:

It is raining all over Denmark;
It is not raining at Funen;
∴ It is raining in Copenhagen.

This inference could be rejected because the premisses are inconsistent. But no objection is justified if it is put in this way:

It is raining all over Denmark with the exception of Funen; so it is raining in Copenhagen.

In the same way 'Take one of these pieces of cake, but don't take the larger' may be rewritten as 'Take one of the pieces except the larger', or 'Take one of the pieces marked 1, 2, 3 . . . n'.[3]

It may be asked whether $O(p) \ v \ O(q)$ is really a directive. One could argue that the external disjunction does not say anything definite about what the agent's duty is. The watchman does not know, before getting further instructions, whether to close the gate or to turn the dog loose. $O(p) \ v \ O(q)$, however, is not empty of meaning, as $\sim O(p)$ is. For, after all, the watchman knows that what is required of him is either the one thing or the other, and that in doing both, therefore, he will have safely performed his duty. $O(p) \ v \ O(q)$ is in this respect analogous to $p \ v \ q$. The indicative disjunction likewise fails to give definite information

---

[1] The example given by Rescher and Robinson, *op. cit.*, p. 179 note 1, is unconvincing, cp. Bar-Hillel, *op. cit.*

[2] Gombay, *op. cit.*, p. 62.

[3] In legal drafting it is a well-known device to put a general rule in one section and special exceptions in other sections.

about the state of the world. If, for example, I am told that Peter is either at home or at the University, I don't actually know where Peter is. All the same I know something—enough to find him if I look for him at both places.

§ 34

External and internal deontic conjunction are presumed to be equivalent and analogous to indicative conjunction.

In my opinion, $O(p) \ \& \ O(q)$ is equivalent in current use to $O(p \ \& \ q)$. It seems to come to the same thing whether it is said in the watchman's instructions:

'At closing time the following duties are incumbent on the watchman: (1) closing the gate; (2) turning the dog loose; and (3) putting out the light.'

Or whether the instructions say:

'At closing time it is the watchman's duty to close the gate, to turn the dog loose, and to put out the light.'

Whether the external or the internal version is used the conjunction is acceptable if and only if each of its constituent parts are acceptable. In this case, there is only one table of values, and this is presumed to be analogous to that of indicative conjunction:

$O(p)$	$O(q)$	$O(p) \ \& \ O(q)$ or $O(p \ \& \ q)$
V	V	V
I	V	I
V	I	I
I	I	I

Doubts may arise, however, about the case in which $p \ \& \ q$ constitutes a combination which has a meaning or justification not belonging to the sum of its constitutive parts taken separately. Consider, for example, the order: 'At the signal, put on the parachute and bail out.' This order could hardly be replaced by the sum of the two orders: 'At the signal, put on the parachute' and 'At the signal, bail out'. But this is probably due to the fact that the word 'and' in this context not only is a logical connective but also indicates a temporal relation. The combined order means that, at the signal, the agent is to put on the parachute and *then* bail out.

If the same temporal condition is incorporated in the second atomic directive ('At the signal, bail out after having put on the parachute') the transcription does not give rise to any difficulties.

The same is the case with other directives which have a combined theme. For example, 'Run to the grocer and buy . . .'; 'Look up Peter and tell him . . .'; 'Sell the property and distribute the proceeds . . .'. I have found no internal conjunction that could not, when attention is given to the double meaning of 'and', be identified without difficulty with an external conjunction of atomic directives.[1]

§ 35

External and internal deontic implications are not equivalent. Mixed values occur in the value-table of internal deontic implication.

Implication plays an important part in legal as well as in everyday language. The internal variety is used in every rule and in every universal occasional norm (§ 24). The external variety, that is, $O(p) \rightarrow O(q)$, is used frequently in legal language. Examples are: 'Everyone who is under an obligation to keep accounts shall employ a chartered accountant'; 'Everyone who is under an obligation to register shall at the time of registration pay a duty of . . .'; 'If a vendor has contracted to keep goods which he has sold, he is obliged to . . .'. In these and similar formulations the establishment of one obligation is tied up with the establishment of another obligation. The *table of external implication* may be taken to be identical with the corresponding table in indicative logic and consequently looks like this:

$O(p)$	$O(q)$	$O(p) \rightarrow O(q)$
V	V	V
I	V	V
V	I	I
I	I	V

[1] In his 'A Logic of the Doubtful. On Optative and Imperative Logic', *Reports from a Mathematical Colloquiem* (1939), pp. 53ff., K. Menger has argued that the identity of $O(p \ \& \ q)$ with $O(p) \ \& \ O(q)$ holds for commands but not for wishes. One may wish for a cigarette and a match without wishing for either by itself. The question falls outside the scope of the logic of directives, so I shall not discuss it. Cp. Lennart Åquist, 'Interpretations of Deontic Logic', *Mind*, LXXIII (1964), p. 252.

This table allows the following inference:

$$O(p) \rightarrow O(q)$$
$$O(p)$$
$$\therefore O(q)$$

which may be expressed also by saying that the expression $[(O(p) \rightarrow O(q)) \ \& \ O(p)] \rightarrow O(q)$ is a tautology.

Internal implication is expressed by the formula $O(p \rightarrow q)$, meaning that the agent is required to act in such a way that the implication $p \rightarrow q$ becomes true. If, for example, p stands for 'Peter has made a promise', and q stands for 'Peter is keeping the promise he has made', then $O(p \rightarrow q)$ means that Peter, if he has made a promise, is obliged to keep it. If we want to express the same obligation as holding not only for Peter but for everyone, a formula analogous to indicative implication is used. The indicative implication is written:

$$(x) \ (fx \rightarrow gx)$$

which means that for any person x it is true that if x is f (has made a promise) then x is also g (keeps the promise). The deontic implication is consequently written:

$$O[(x) \ (fx \rightarrow gx)]$$

which means that everyone is under an obligation to act in such a way that the indicative implication becomes true, the obligation, that is, to keep a promise if one has been made.

It should be noted that what implies the obligation to keep a promise which has been made ($O(q)$, or, respectively, $O(gx)$) is the factual circumstance that a promise has been made, that is, p or fx, and not an obligation $O(p)$ or $O(fx)$. It follows that the *value-table of internal deontic implication* has mixed values, in the sense that the truth-values of indicative logic appear side by side with the still undefined deontic values 'V' and 'I'. The table looks presumably like this:

p	$O(q)$	$O(p \rightarrow q)$
T	V	V
F	V	V
T	I	I
F	I	V

That truth-values appear side by side with deontic values is not surprising. It reflects the fact, well known in everyday language, that we are able to make an inference from premisses one of which is a hypothetical rule and the other of which is an indicative which states that the antecedent of the hypothetical has been realized. The inference is written:

$$O(p \to q)$$
$$p$$
$$\therefore O(q)$$

or is expressed by saying that the formula

$$[O(p \to q) \ \& \ p] \to O(q) \text{ is a tautology.}$$

For example:

Everyone who has made a promise is obliged to keep it[1]
Peter has made promise
∴ Peter is obliged to keep his promise

Inferences based on external and on internal implication should not, of course, be confused. The formulations:

$$O(p) \to O(q)$$
$$p$$
$$\therefore O(q)$$

and

$$O(p \to q)$$
$$O(p)$$
$$\therefore O(q)$$

are unwarranted. For instance:

If you are to love yourself you are to love your neighbour
You love yourself
∴ You are to love your neighbour.

and

Love your neighbour as you love yourself
Love yourself
∴ Love your neighbour.

[1] More precisely: Act in such a way that the implication, if anyone has made a promise he keeps it, becomes true. Even this formulation, however, is not quite satisfactory, since it is outside the power of any individual to make a universal proposition true. The sentence requires a still more precise formulation, but to seek one now would be too great a digression.

In a previous paper I pointed out that fallacies of this type occur frequently in the literature.[1] Such is still the case. Max Black, for example, accepts this inference as valid:

> All owners of cars are required to have operating licences
> All those having operating licences are to pay a fee
> ∴ All owners of cars are to pay a fee.[2]

Erik Stenius[3] makes a distinction between $O(p \to q)$ and $p \to O(q)$. The last of these expressions is in my opinion an impossible hybrid. Obviously it symbolizes neither an indicative nor a directive, and Stenius for this reason reckons it to belong to a third category called 'normative sentences'. By a normative sentence he means a sentence which is either a norm sentence, which I have called a directive, or a molecular complex of indicatives and norm sentences. According to Stenius the formula $p \to O(q)$ symbolizes a sentence like the following:

(S) If the lights are red, one is forbidden to cross the street

which is conceived as expressing a directive (a norm, in Stenius' terminology) that will come into force only under certain conditions. It is unclear what is meant by this. In the juridical sense, S, if promulgated as a law, enters into force at once. Furthermore, I

---

[1] 'Imperatives and Logic', *Theoria*, 1941, pp. 53ff., 67.

[2] 'Notes on the Meaning of a Rule', *Theoria*, 1958, pp. 139ff., 150. Cp. H. G. Bohnert, 'Semiotic Status of Commands', *Philosophy of Science*, vol. XII (1945), pp. 302ff., 313; E. J. Lemmon, 'Deontic Logic and the Logic of Imperatives', *Logique et Analyse*, 1965, pp. 39ff., 61. Also Mogens Blegvad, *Den naturalistiske Fejlslutning* [*The Naturalistic Fallacy*] (1959), p. 151, acknowledges inferences on this pattern. He argues that they meet the criterion of satisfaction. This is correct, but, in my opinion, is only another evidence of the inadequacy of this criterion for the construction of a deontic logic, cp. the note on the logic of satisfaction at the end of § 36. It is easy to invent instances showing that no inference is possible. Take the premisses: Everyone who has completed his eighteenth year shall undergo a certain vaccination; Everyone who has undergone this vaccination shall meet same day a week for a test. What should the conclusion be? If, in cases in which the conclusion is not senseless, a judge followed this pattern of reasoning he would commit serious injustice. Let us assume that the demand for a vaccination is a relative unimportant regulation sanctioned by only an insignificant fine; but that the demand for a subsequent test is of high importance—because the vaccinated person may present danger to other people —and therefore santioned by penalty of imprisonment. It would then be a serious injustice to sentence a young person to imprisonment because he had neglected his obligation to undergo the vaccination.

[3] 'The Principles of a Logic of Normative Systems', *Acta Philosophica Fennica*, 1963, pp. 247f., 256, cf. 249.

see no reason why such a prescription should not be written as $O(p \rightarrow q)$, since its meaning is exactly the prescription of a course of action such that $p \rightarrow q$ becomes true if p stands for 'the lights are red' and q stands for 'no one crosses the street'. S may also be understood, however, as an indicative implication which states that the fact that the lights are red implies the fact that the normative order N includes a norm forbidding crossing the street. In that case it should be written:

$$p \rightarrow i \, (O(q) \, \varepsilon \, N)$$

in which formula the last part symbolizes that the normative order N includes the norm $O(q)$.

A similar misconception is found in Ota Weinberger, who denies that $O(p \rightarrow q)$ represents a hypothetical directive.[1] This formula, he says, signifies that what is required as a duty is the implication $p \rightarrow q$ as a whole, and not q on the condition that p. If $O(p \rightarrow q)$ means obligation to act in such a way that $p \rightarrow q$ becomes true, then I do not understand this reasoning. For it is then obvious that given p, $p \rightarrow q$ becomes true only on the condition that q. $O(p \rightarrow q)$ therefore means the obligation to act q — $O(q)$ — under the condition that p.

§ 36

Psychological interpretations of deontic logic: Ross (1941) *and von Wright.*

In the preceding sections (§§ 32–35) we have met a number of deontological inferences symbolized in the following *tautological implications*:

External negation:	$O(p) \rightarrow \sim\sim O(p)$
Internal negation:	$O(p) \rightarrow \sim O(\sim p)$
External disjunction:	$[(O(p) \, v \, O(q)) \; \& \; O(p)] \rightarrow O(q)$
	$[(O(p) \, v \, O(q)) \; \& \; \sim O(q)] \rightarrow O(p)$
Internal disjunction:	$O(p \, v \, q) \rightarrow \sim O(p)$ and,
	$O(p \, v \, q) \rightarrow \sim O(q)$
External conjunction:	$O(p \; \& \; q) \rightarrow O(p)$
Internal conjunction:	$O(p \; \& \; q) \rightarrow O \, (q)$
External implication:	$[(O(p) \rightarrow O(q)) \; \& \; O(p)] \rightarrow O(q)$
Internal implication:	$(O(p \rightarrow q) \; \& \; p) \rightarrow O(q)$

[1] 'Über die Negation von Sollsätzen', *Theoria*, 1957, pp. 102f., 120.

By substituting a sign of conjunction for the sign of implication and negating the part following the connective, the same inferences are expressed using a series of *contradictory conjunctions*,

$$O(p) \ \& \ \sim O(p)$$
$$O(p) \ \& \ O(\sim p), \text{ etc.}$$

We may take it that these inferences and the value-tables for the connectives on which they are based are in harmony with current use in directive discourse.

We may now turn to the question which was raised but provisionally deferred at the beginning of § 31, namely, the question how the values V and I and the expressions 'to accept' and 'to reject' (a directive) should be interpreted. I shall take it as established that the deontic values cannot be truth and falsity. 'To accept' cannot mean 'to acknowledge as true', nor can 'to reject' mean 'to dismiss as false'.

In a paper published in 1941[1] I maintained that the deontic values should be interpreted as 'validity' and 'invalidity' and that a directive should be said to be valid when a certain, further defined, psychological state is present in a certain person and to be invalid when no such state is present. I considered especially two possibilities, namely, those of making validity dependent *either* upon the occurrence in a person acting as norm-giver (imperator) of a certain state of willing that his directive be obeyed; *or* upon the occurrence, in the subject of a directive of a certain state of willing to comply with the directive.

On these premises I came, and had to come, to the conclusion that apparently evident deontological inferences are not tenable as logical inferences because they are concerned with psychological conditions and because their truth, consequently, is of an empirical and not a logical nature. I showed this especially with regard to internal negation. The incompatibility of $O(p)$ and $O(\sim p)$, e.g., of the obligation to close the door and the obligation to leave it open, is, I said, not of the nature of a logical contradiction. Whether $O(p)$ and $O(\sim p)$ are compatible, that is, whether it is possible at the same time to order, or to accept, both directives, is a question to be decided by experience. And I added that if the saying turns out to be true that you will get a thrashing whether you leave the hat where it is or whether you pick it up, this counts

---

[1] 'Imperatives and Logic', *Theoria*, 1941, pp. 53f.

against the two being incompatible. Similar remarks, I held, can be made about the inference of internal implication which takes place when a hypothetical rule is applied to an instance covered by its hypothesis. Such an inference is likewise not logically binding since it depends on the psychological question whether a person who has commanded (or accepted) a general rule must also necessarily command (or accept) its application in a special case covered by the rule. It is not rare, I pointed out, for a person to lay down a general rule and still not apply it where he himself is concerned.

For these reasons I maintained that these apparently evident deontological inferences are really only of a pesudo-logical nature, being valid only on the tacit assumption of a premiss which ordinary unsophisticated people take for granted. That premiss is the premiss of *practical consequence* or *self-consistency* in the will which issues or accepts the directive. When this premiss is introduced the inferences are valid but are not of a directive nature. That $O(p)$ and $O(\sim p)$ are incompatible means, on this view, that a person with self-consistent will is psychologically unable to command at the same time both $O(p)$ and $O(\sim p)$ as directives within the same system.

More recently von Wright has taken over and elaborated this approach to the problem. When dealing with the problem of contradiction (incompatibility) between norms (which are assumed to be 'prescriptions', almost identical with what I have called commands and quasi-commands), von Wright discusses the question as it concerns *internal* negation. It is clear, he says, that it is logically impossible for one and the same agent to do and to omit the same thing on the same occasion. But is it logically impossible *to command* an agent to do and to omit the same thing on the same occasion, e.g., to shut the window and not to shut it, that is, to leave it open? Surely, it is said, one person can address to another person words to this effect and even threaten him with punishment if he does not obey. But does this mean that he has commanded him? The answer, von Wright maintains, depends upon what he calls the ontological problem of norms.[1]

When von Wright subsequently discusses the ontological problem it is still with internal negation in mind. 'Why is it, let us ask, that a command to open a window and a prohibition to do this, i.e., a command to leave it closed, contradict each other, are

[1] G. H. von Wright, *Norm and Action* (1963), p. 135.

incompatible'?[1] In our notation this is the question why $O(p)$ and $O(\sim p)$, that is, a directive and its complement, are incompatible.

One gets the impression that von Wright feels strongly about this problem. 'I wish I could make my readers see the serious nature of this problem', he says. To facilitate its understanding he uses illustrative drawings. One sees two men who represent the commander and the one commanded. The first man has in one hand a whip with which he drives the other man toward a certain object (shutting the window) and in the other hand he has a rope tied around the waist of the commanded subject by means of which he pulls him back from the same object (commands him not to shut the window). One cannot, says von Wright, maintain that such behaviour is impossible, even though it seems unreasonable and though a psychologist would perhaps speak of a man who behaved in this way as having a 'split personality'. To stamp $O(p)$ & $O(\sim p)$ as contradictory and incompatible is possible only if we relate the notion of a prescription to some idea about the unity and coherence of a will, the idea of a *rational*, or *reasonable*, or *coherent*, or *consistent* will (von Wright's italics). Contradiction (incompatibility) then occurs when two directives reflect an inconsistency (irrationality) in the will of a commanding authority, in the sense that it wills incompatible actions (shutting the window and leaving it open)'[2]

Finally, incompatibility is extended to include external negation, that is, it is extended to cover the situation in which an authority simultaneously commands and not-commands, that is, permits a certain act; in formal language, this is the issuance of the directive $O(p)$ & $\sim O(p)$.[3] Von Wright does not seem to be aware that the incompatibility in this case is of a different kind. If he had tried to illustrate this situation also by means of a drawing he would

[1] *Op. cit.*, p. 147.

[2] *Op. cit.*, p. 151.

[3] 'In terms of the will-theory of norms, the inconsistency of a set of commands means that one and the same norm-authority wants one or several norm-subjects to do or forbear several things which, at least in some circumstances, it is logically impossible conjunctively to do or forbear.

In terms of the will-theory, the inconsistency of a set of commands and permissions means this: one and the same norm-authority wants one or several norm-subjects to do or forbear several things and also lets them do or forbear several things. Something which the authority *lets* the subject(s) do or forbear is, however, at least in some circumstances, logically impossible to do or forbear together with everything which he wants them to do or forbear. This we count as irrational willing.' *Op. cit.*, p. 152.

have been confronted with the difficult task of drawing a man who is both using a whip and not using a whip. Although I consider the psychological interpretation of deontic logic to be a mistake, as I shall argue in the next section, all the same I consider it useful to elucidate the distinction that must be made between incompatibility based on external and based on internal negation. The incompatibility of commanding and permitting the same act is of a kind different from the incompatibility of commanding a certain act and its complement, that is, the omission of the same act.

$O(p)$ & $O(\sim p)$—or $O(p \rightarrow q)$ & $O(p \rightarrow \sim q)$ if the obligation as usual, is conditional on a certain factual situation—is perhaps not as unreasonable and inconceivable as von Wright seems to assume when he speaks of a 'split personality'. Let us imagine a group of people divided into two sections of almost the same strength, each comprising about thirty per cent of the population. Each of the sections is a fanatical religious sect passionately fighting the other section. The rest of the population is religiously indifferent. The A-sect possesses a sanctuary situated in a rather impassable part of the mountains. The A-sect has persuaded the indifferents to join in a political compromise which provides for legislation according to which any person is to be punished for passing the sanctuary without raising his hat. The B-sect considers this abominable and agitates for a law against idolatry which is taken to include the act of raising one's hat while passing the sanctuary of the A-sect. They succeed in persuading the indifferent party to join in such legislation as part of a general political settlement. At the last moment the A-sect intervenes and obtains the concession that the previous law concerning respect due to the sanctuary in the mountains shall remain in force.

The situation in this unhappy country is now such that it is a criminal offence both to raise one's hat and not to raise it while passing the sanctuary. The two conflicting norms, $O(p \rightarrow q)$ and $O(p \rightarrow \sim q)$, are both taken to be part of the law of the land. The situation is not impracticable. Most people now avoid passing the sanctuary for fear of exposing themselves to the criminal prosecution inevitable according to the wording of the law. Or people simply omit wearing a hat. Besides, the risk is not important. The police appear infrequently, complaints are usually so unprovable that no prosecution takes place, and the prosecution is in fact not too eager to take up even well supported denunciations. All the same, in the course of time a number of cases are proceeded with up to adjudication. The task of the judge is not difficult. If the accused has kept his hat on the judge will sentence him to punishment under the older law. If he has raised his hat he will be sentenced under the more recent law. Everyone is in fact satisfied. The *A*-sect never tire of stressing the criminality of keeping on one's hat. The *B*-section has carved the law against idolatry on the wall of their temple. And the indifferent have succeeded in pulling through two difficult political settlements.

Admittedly the case is fabricated and improbable, but it all the same shows that legislation on the pattern of internal negation— $O(p \rightarrow q)$ *&* $O(p \rightarrow \sim q)$—is conceivable. It could be formulated and enforced. But how could legislation on the pattern of external negation— $O(p)$ *&* $\sim O(p)$ or $O(p \rightarrow q)$ *&* $\sim O(p \rightarrow q)$—be conceived, that is, legislation which at the same time prohibits and does not prohibit (permits) the same act? In our fabricated example this would mean that the first law declares it forbidden and punishable to keep one's hat on, while the second law lays down that, all the same, this is to be permitted and consequently not punished. Such a formulation is nonsense and cannot be enforced since the judge cannot, indeed, both punish and not punish the same act.

This analysis may be criticized because I have made no distinction between the law as a norm directed to the judge and as a norm directed to the citizens (see above, pp. 90–92). If we take into account this distinction the analysis becomes more complicated.

In the first situation, that in which legislation is according to the pattern of internal negation, the law, if it is understood as a directive to the judge, directs him to punish anyone who passes the sanctuary with a hat whether he raises it or keeps it on. This norm is logically unexceptionable; it can be understood and complied with. It is another matter that such a law seems unreasonable, there being no purpose it could serve. Considered as a directive to the citizen the law's fulfilment is impossible since it is indeed impossible at the same time to raise one's hat and keep it on. But it is not excluded that the purpose of the law could be to prevent people from fulfilling the hypothesis under which the criminal prescription applies. The law as directed to the citizen then has the simple and logically unimpeachable content that it is forbidden under penalty to pass the sanctuary with a hat in one's possession.

On this reinterpretation, however, the subject matter of our analysis, a contradictory norm of the pattern $O(p \to q) \ \& \ O(p \to \sim q)$, has disappeared. The reinterpretation means that this conjunction is taken to mean the same as $O(\sim p)$, that is, the obligation not to bring oneself into situation p.

In the second situation—that in which legislation is according to the pattern of external negation—the law, if it is understood as a directive to the judge, directs him at once to punish and not to punish the same act. This is a request impossible to be fulfilled, and it cannot be reinterpreted in any sensible way. Considered as a directive to the citizen prescribing that the same act is at once both prohibited (and punishable) and not prohibited (and not punishable) the law is directively nonsense. It does not prescribe what cannot be fulfilled, for it does not prescribe anything at all; it is complete nonsense.

To sum up we may distinguish between different 'degrees of unreasonableness'.

A norm directing a judge *to punish* both a certain act and its complement ($p \ \& \ \sim p$) can be fulfilled, but it is *teleologically unreasonable* or purposeless if it is judged as a means of preventing people from committing the crimes in question. If the norm is hypothetical it can be reinterpreted as a prohibition against realizing the hypothesis.

A norm directing a person, either a judge or any other person, to *undertake* both a certain act and its complement is *directively unreasonable*, which means that it prescribes what is logically impossible, and its fulfilment is therefore logically impossible.

A norm formulation which at the same time prohibits and permits the same act is directively *pure nonsense*.

Note on the Logic of Satisfaction—In my paper 'Imperatives and Logic', *Theoria* 1941, I discussed another construction of deontic logic called the logic of satisfaction. On this view the logical values ascribed to directives are 'satisfied' and 'not-satisfied' corresponding with the values 'true' and 'false' of the logic of indicatives. A directive is said to be satisfied when the proposition describing the required conduct is true, i.e., $O(p)$ is satisfied when p is true. It is then obvious that there is a complete parallelism between the satisfaction value of the O-expressions and the truth-value of the corresponding p-expressions. On this basis a logic of directives may be constructed as an exact reflection of the logic of indicatives. Any propositional inference may be transformed into a directive inference by substituting the corresponding O-expressions for the given p-expressions.

A distinguished pioneering attempt to build such a logic was made by Hofstadter and McKinsey in their paper 'On the Logic of Imperatives', *Philosophy of Science*, vol. 6 (1939), pp. 446ff. A number of authors have followed their lead and elaborated the notion of satisfaction, so among others H. G. Bohnert, 'The Semiotic Status of Commands', *Philosophy of Science*, vol. 12 (1946), pp. 302ff.; A. Gombay, 'Imperative Inference and Disjunction', *Analysis*, vol. 25 (1964–65), pp. 58ff.; Nicholas Rescher, *The Logic of Commands* (1966), pp. 72ff., 88–89 and 124; E. Sosa, 'The Logic of Imperatives', *Theoria* (1966,) pp. 224ff. The last-mentioned author has formulated the following criterion of validity for pure directive arguments:

A directive argument is valid provided it contains a non-empty subset of conjointly satisfiable premisses such that: (i) if its members are satisfied then necessarily the conclusion is satisfied; and (ii) if the conclusion is violated then necessarily at least one of its members is violated.

A deontic logic on this pattern is incontestably possible. The question is, however, how it is to be interpreted. To infer one directive from another according to this logic means to say something about a necessary connection between the satisfaction of the directives in question. It may of course be of interest to know about the interrelated satisfaction values of directives, but it is surely not a logic of such content and relevance we have in mind in case of the practical inferences we make use of in everyday speech or legal reasoning. The immediate feeling of evidence does not refer to the satisfaction of the directive, but rather to something like its 'validity' or 'existence' or 'being in force'—however these expressions are to be understood. The inadequacy of a logic of satisfaction as a reconstruction of our actual practical reasoning appears from the fact that internal deontic negation, disjunction and implication, as shown in the preceding sections of this chapter, present peculiarities which distinguish them from their indicative counterparts. The divergency is demonstrated in inferences valid in the logic of satisfaction although not acceptable intuitively, e.g.:

$$O(p) \therefore O(p \lor q)$$

('Post the letter' implies 'post the letter or burn it');
or:

$$O(p \to q); O(p) \therefore O(q)$$

(Love your neighbour as you love yourself; Love yourself; Love your neighbour) which have been discussed above in § 33 and § 35 respectively.

Sosa, *op. cit.*, p. 233, admits it as an 'apparently undesirable feature' of the logic of satisfaction that it denies the validity of the inference from 'If it rains, close the window' to 'If it rains and thunders, close the window'. For the last directive is not necessarily satisfied if the former directive is so. The author, however, argues that this feature is no more than *apparently* undesirable because the main value of such a logic could lie in the disclosure of satisfaction interrelations. In that case, I add, such a logic should be provided with a warning: Not to be used by judges or other persons concerned with the administration of norms!

Recently A. J. Kenny in 'Practical Inference', *Analysis*, vol. 26 (1965–66), pp. 65ff., has invented a curious inverted logic of satisfaction called *the logic of satisfactoriness*. Whenever the logic of satisfaction permits the inference from A to B, the logic of satisfactoriness permits the inference from B to A. A plan is said to be satisfactory relative to a certain set of wishes, if and only if whenever the plan is satisfied every member of that set of wishes is satisfied. If it is the case that if A is satisfied B is satisfied, then it follows that if B is satisfactory A is satisfactory. The rules of this logic permitting inference from B to A are 'satisfactoriness-preserving' in the sense that they will ensure that in reasoning about what to do we never pass from a plan which will satisfy a definite set of desires to a plan which will not satisfy them.

Such a logic seems to me to be of little interest. To infer plan A from plan B means that A is a suitable means to the realization of B. This in itself is of little interest because in practical life the question will be whether plan A also is satisfactory in relation to other wishes. From plan B (to prevent over-population) we may infer plan A (to kill half the population) but the inference is hardly of any practical interest.

Whatever the interest, this logic does not fare better than the logic of satisfaction if evaluated as a reconstruction of our actual practical reasoning. On the one hand it permits such inferences as just mentioned. On the other hand it does not permit the inference 'Kill the conspirators; Brutus is a conspirator; so kill Brutus' (*op. cit.*, p. 74). Unfortunately it is exactly inferences on this pattern that play a prominent role in all practical reasoning concerned with the application of general rules to particular instances.

§ 37

Following Weinberger, the principles of deontic logic are interpreted as postulates defining directive speech. 'Validity' is not on an equal footing with 'truth' but is derived from the concept of 'acceptance' common to both ramifications of logic.

In a paper of 1957 Ota Weinberger criticized the psychological interpretation of that concept of validity which appears in the value-table of deontic logic. The incompatibility of $O(p)$ and $O(\sim p)$ does not depend on what is possible and what is impossible in a factual-psychological sense; it is not an assertion about possible states of will or courses of acts of will, but a logical principle. 'Validity' is not a psychological concept but a methodological concept of deontic logic. It expresses the way in which a directive is 'set' ('gesetzt'), and what this means is explained by analogy with the way in which propositions, the subject matter of indicative logic, are 'set' in indicative discourse.[1]

'A proposition', says Weinberger, 'is, in logical consideration, set [in our terminology: accepted] when it is regarded as true (asserted). As regards directives we need in complete analogy a concept expressing the setting of a directive in relation to logical analysis and logical deductions. This setting of a directive we shall call its validity. The sentences "We set a directive" and "We regard a directive as valid" are synonymous.' The author stresses that this explanation of 'validity' is not meant as a definition of the concept. 'Actually we do not say what validity is. We content ourselves with showing the logical properties of the validity of directives.' This the author does by means of a table which shows how the expression $O(p)$, $O(\sim p)$, and $\sim O(\sim p)$ are mutually related as to inference, compatibility and incompatibility.[2]

[1] 'Über die Negation von Sollsätzen', *Theoria*, 1957, pp. 102f., 111.
[2] *Op. cit.*, pp. 124, 128.

I am convinced, on the whole, of the soundness of this reasoning. Above, at the end of § 31, I have pointed out that the principles of indicative logic are not statements about the nature and organization of the world, nor statements about the psychological powers of man to accept contradictory propositions as true, but postulates defining indicative speech, that is, conditions to be satisfied if the discourse is to be able to carry out the function of describing the world and stating facts. If these postulates are violated it becomes impossible to distinguish what is posed in discourse, that is, conceived as real (see §§ 5 and 8) and what is not set, and it is consequently equally impossible to distinguish between what can be accepted as true and what cannot. Correspondingly, the principles of deontic logic, in my opinion, are postulates defining directive speech, that is, conditions to be satisfied if the speech is to be able to carry out the function of directing human behaviour. If these postulates are violated it becomes impossible to distinguish between what is posed in directive discourse, that is, conceived as what 'ought' to be real (see § 9), and what is not posed; and it is consequently equally impossible to distinguish between what can be accepted as valid and what cannot.

All the same, this analysis is not quite satisfactory. There is a difficulty in the way in which Weinberger puts 'validity' on an equal footing with 'truth'. According to Weinberger, 'setting' a proposition (or, in my terminology, accepting a proposition) means the same as regarding it as true; and 'setting' a directive means the same as regarding it as valid. However, while 'truth' is a quality ascribable to a proposition independently of its being accepted, since subject-independent methods of establishing its truth-value are available, the same is not the case with regard to 'validity'. What does it mean to say that a directive (e.g. the order to take the boxes to the station) is valid or not valid? And how do we establish which it is? A proposition can be accepted as true or rejected as false in soliloquy (§ 2). But as we have seen, a similar acceptance or rejection of directives does not normally occur (§ 16).

This difficulty, in my opinion, arises out of the belief that indicative logic is concerned with propositions regarded as true. But this can hardly be correct. When I maintain, for example, that p implies q, this does not imply that I have accepted p and q as true.

I have said nothing more than that p and $\sim q$ are incompatible, that is, that the expression p & $\sim q$ cannot according to its formal structure be accepted (in a sense quite different from the one used hitherto) as an indicative which describes the world. This is due to the fact that p & $\sim q$ can be shown to involve a contradiction and so does not pose anything at all. Let us write 'accept'$_2$ to emphasize that I am using this term in another sense than the one used hitherto. So far I have used this term to designate the act of acknowledging a proposition to be true (§ 6). Now I take it as designating the act of acknowledging a sentence as being fitted to express indicative meaning. Logic is not concerned with the conditions under which propositions are true or may be accepted as true, but with the conditions under which linguistic formulations may be accepted$_2$ as propositions, that is, as possessors of *indicative meaning*, and consequently as entities having the possibility of being either true or false.

Logic establishes indicative discourse in this way: it separates out expressions which, being either tautologies or self-contradictions, are without indicative meaning and are consequently precluded from being either empirically true or false, for which reason they are called, respectively, logically true or false.

The soundness of this interpretation of logic is supported by the fact that the demands of logic apply also to the speech of fabulation (see above, § 8), that is, discourse in which propositions are simply posed without being accepted or asserted. For even in a novel, writing 'it was raining and it was not raining' is ruled out. Since no proposition in a novel is taken to be true it is impossible in this connection to interpret logic as a set of statements about truth relations. The self-contradictory expression is rejected as being without indicative meaning and as consequently being unable to describe even an imagined world.

Correspondingly, the principles of deontic logic must be conceived as postulates which define directive speech, separating out sentences which, being either deontic tautologies or self-contradictions, are without *directive meaning* and are consequently unable to function directively. Such sentences cannot be accepted$_2$ as instances of directive speech. If, now, a directive which can *in this sense* be accepted$_2$ is called 'valid' and if a directive which cannot be accepted$_2$ is called 'invalid', it is obvious that 'truth' and 'validity' are not coordinate concepts. 'Validity' becomes a higher order concept and is applicable even in indicative logic, indicating that an expression is acceptable$_2$ as possessing indicative meaning. The concept of truth and the concept of acceptance$_1$ can be completely eliminated from indicative logic when this is interpreted as being concerned with the conditions under which combined sentences can be accepted$_2$ as having meaning; or, we could also say, the conditions under which the posing of one proposition is compatible with the posing of another one (cp. above, § 8). Correspondingly, deontic logic is concerned with the conditions under which the posing of one directive is compatible with the posing of another one. On this view, the two ramifications of formal logic are united in so far as they are expressed in the same system of concepts, one dealing with the formal conditions for indicative discourse, and the other dealing with the formal conditions for directive discourse.

Let me remind the reader, by referring to § 32 *a*, that logic applies to directives only on the condition that they belong to the same system, that is, are a sum of directives which are postulated as making up a coherent totality of meaning.

And referring to § 22 *g*, I wish to point out that the term 'validity', as expressing a fundamental logical concept, is used in a sense different from the senses mentioned in that place. It corresponds with acceptance$_2$ and not with acceptance$_1$.

I see the difference between von Wright's and my own views in this way: what in von Wright appear as ontological laws about the possible co-existence of norms in a consistent will, have been interpreted in this study as logical postulates defining directive speech. The difference may be illustrated by means of an example. The inference

> Take all the boxes to the station
> This is one of the boxes
> ∴ Take this to the station.

according to von Wright is based upon the ontological law that the two norms 'Take all the boxes to the station' and 'Do not take this box to the station' cannot co-exist in a consistent will, whereas he does not deny that they may actually co-exist in a will which is sufficiently irrational. The inference is consequently valid only on the assumption that the existential basis of its component directives is a rational will. To me the question of the compatibility of the two directives and the validity of the inference is not a psychological but a logical question. It follows from the deontic logic actually accepted in the directive speech of everyday language, that whoever poses the general directive 'Take all the boxes to the station' has also posed the implication 'Take this, which is one of the boxes, to the station' and that this excludes the internal negation that the box is to be left where it is. This follows simply from the way in which the words 'all' and 'not' actually function in directive discourse. As Hare strikingly puts it: 'If we had to find out whether someone knew the meaning of the word "all" in "Take all the boxes to the station", we should have to find out whether he realized that a person who assented to this command, and also to the statement "This is one of the boxes" and yet refused to assent to the command "Take this to the station" could only do so if he had misunderstood one of these three sentences. If this sort of test were inapplicable the word "all" (in imperatives as in indicatives) would be entirely meaningless.'[1] Of course it might happen that the headmaster, having just ordered all the boxes to be taken to the station, in the same breath adds that this box all the same is to be left where it is. This means that the first order has been partly cancelled and replaced by another order, but it in no way involves that the first order does not of itself imply the particular order regarding the particular box. In the case of apparently contradictory directives, unity of meaning is established by means of the principles of interpretation called *lex specialis* and *lex posterior* (§ 32 *a*).

My thesis, to put it briefly, is that there exists a deontic logic defining directive speech just as there exists an indicative logic defining indicative speech. According to deontic logic, whoever hears and understands the directive 'Take all the boxes to the station' by that has understood that the order covers this one of the boxes. Whoever disputes this has not understood the order. The implication is not conditional on any quality of the commanding will (von Wright), nor is it mediated through indicative-logical inferences whose integrating sentences are *F*-expressions, that is, indicatives which state the fact that a norm exists or that a directive has been advanced (Hedenius and Moritz; see above, § 30).

The deontic logic dealt with in this chapter is conceived as a

[1] R. M. Hare, *The Language of Morals* (1952), p. 25.

calculus of directives analogous to the usual indicative calculus of propositions. In section 27 we have dealt with the elements of a directive modal logic.[1]

§ 38

Deontic logic immediately concerns O-expressions (directives). It has, however, derivative consequences for the corresponding F-expressions.

$O(p)$ stands for a directive which prescribes an 'obligation' to act in such a way that the proposition p becomes true. It is usual to say that to a directive there corresponds an indicative. This may, however, mean two different things. The corresponding indicative might be p; or it might be $O(p) \; \varepsilon \; N$ (which expresses the fact that $O(p)$ exists or is *in force* in the normative order N, or, if $O(p)$ is a personal directive, the fact that $O(p)$ has been *advanced* in an interpersonal situation). Let us introduce the expression $F[O(p)]$ as equivalent to $O(p) \; \varepsilon \; N$.

Deontic logic is immediately concerned with O-expressions (directives). Here the question is raised whether it is also of indirect consequence to the corresponding indicatives of the type $F[O(p)]$.

F-sentences being indicatives, indicative logic unquestionably applies to them. Accordingly, one may construct the connections $\sim F[O(p)]$, $F[O(p)] \; v \; F[O(q)]$, $F[O(p)] \; \& \; F[O(q)]$, $F[O(p)] \rightarrow F[O(q)]$, and the tautologies and contradictions derived from them.

We note now that

$F[O(p)]$	corresponds with	$O(p)$
$\sim F[O(p)]$	,, ,,	$\sim O(p)$
$F[O(p)] \; v \; F[O(q)]$	,, ,,	$O(p) \; v \; O(q)$
$F[O(p) \; \& \; F[O(q)]$	,, ,,	$O[p] \; \& \; O(q)$
$F[O(p)] \rightarrow F[O(q)]$	,, ,,	$O(p) \rightarrow O(q).$

It is therefore to be expected that external deontic logic, that is, the logic based upon the value-tables of the external variant of the connectives, is identical with the usual indicative logic. And if the

---

[1] Von Wright himself seems to regard his deontic logic as a modal logic. In my opinion, what he has produced is partly a modal logic, partly a calculus of directives. Erik Stenius, likewise, in his 'Principles of a Logic of Normative Systems', *Acta Philosophia Fennica*, 1963, pp. 247ff., 249, seems to consider deontic logic to be a modal logic. In my view the two fields should be kept as separated in deontic as they are in indicative logic, cf. Hare, *op. cit.*, p. 27 note 1.

reader will check over the tables given above in sections 32–35 he will find this expectation justified.

The incompatibility of $F [O(p)]$ and $\sim F [O(p)]$, that is, the impossibility of posing at the same time that the existential fact exists and that it does not exist, corresponds with the incompatibility of $O(p)$ and $\sim O(p)$, that is, the impossibility of at once posing and not posing the same directive (within the same order).

On the other hand, in indicative logic, $F[O(p)]$, e.g., the fact that A has ordered B to pick up a hat, seems not to be incompatible with $F[O(\sim p)]$, that is, the fact that A at the same time has ordered B to leave the hat where it is. Whether these two facts can co-exist seems to be an empirical and not a logical question. Von Wright, as I have mentioned above in section 36, is of the opinion that they actually may co-exist, but only in the mind of a person whose will is not rational and self-consistent. Now let me remind the reader that the statement that a norm exists (or that a directive has been advanced) is not only a statement about the occurrence of social or psychological facts but also a *meaningful interpretation of these facts* (see above, § 22 e). By this I mean that stating $F [O(p)]$ (e.g., that A has ordered B to pick up his hat) is not stating only the linguistic fact that A at some time in relation to B has uttered some words; nor only the psychological fact that A has done so with certain intentions. It is also an interpretation of these facts as having *directive meaning* and this interpretation is restricted by the postulates of deontic logic. It follows that the formula $F [O(p)]$ *&* $F [O(\sim p)]$ is logically unimpeachable if it is taken to mean only that A has uttered the words 'Pick up the hat and leave it where it is'. It must, however, be ruled out as illegitimate if interpreted in directive terms as stating that A has given B the order to pick up the hat and leave it where it is. This interpretation is ruled out because according to deontic logic no such order is conceivable. Such a formulation cannot be accepted$_2$. In this way deontic logic has derivative consequences for F-expressions.

I believe that cognate ideas, though perhaps less clarified, lie behind von Wright's treatment of the question what kind of sentences deontic logic is concerned with, a treatment which I must admit I find rather hard to follow. Is deontic logic, von Wright asks, concerned with sentences interpreted as norms (directives or O-expressions) or with sentences interpreted as F-expressions, that is, indicatives stating the existence of norms (or the advancing of directives)? He admits that he does not know himself what is the best answer to this question. 'The "fully developed" system of Deontic Logic is a theory of descriptively interpreted expressions. But the laws (principles, rules), which are peculiar to this logic, concern logical properties of the *norms* themselves, which are then reflected in logical properties of norm-propositions. Thus, in a sense, the 'basis' of Deontic Logic is a logical theory of prescriptively interpreted O- and P-expressions.' (P-expressions are permissions.) The 'basis' to which the author refers, so far as I understand, is identical with the ontological theory (mentioned above in § 36) about the compatibility of norms, that is, whether they can co-exist in 'a rational or reasonable or coherent or consistent will.' Accordingly, the author says subsequently that the metalogical notions of (self-)consistency, compatibility, and entailment, which he has defined, are primarily relevant to the prescriptive interpretation, that is, to the norms themselves. 'They concern the logical properties of the norms themselves. The ontological significance of those properties, however, has to be explained in terms of the (possible) existence of norms. Hence this significance will be reflected in the descriptive interpretation too. For, on the descriptive interpretation, the O- and P-expressions express norm-propositions. And norm-propositions are to the effect that such and such norms exist.'[1] Although von Wright and I disagree as to the nature and foundation of deontic logic we seem to agree that this logic has derivative consequences for F-expressions.

[1] G. H. von Wright, *Norm and Action* (1963), pp. 133–4, 151, 165.

INDEX

absurdity, pragmatic, 29
acceptance, 15f., 61f., 169, 179
  declaratory and constitutive, 61, 64
act, 112
acte juridique, 56, 104, 118, 130
act-in-the law, 56, 130
action, 115, 127
action-idea, 34f.
activity, 116
admonition, 47
advice, 44f.
anecdotes, 30
applying (a norm), 37
as-if philosophy, 31
assertion, 19f.
authority, 41
  the highest, 96
  public, 52, 131, 133
autonomy, private, 132

binding force, 83f.
Black, Max, 101, 167
Bühler, Karl, 20

claim, 47, 118, 123, 125f.
  moral, 136
class, closed, 109
cognition,
  objectivity of, 62
  practical, 64

cognitivism, 65, 100, 102
command, 49, 50, 113, 115, 126f.
  coercive, 40
  authoritative, 41
communication,
  basic norm of, 19, 24, 33
  general theory of, 5, 6
competence, 96, 118, 130f.
complement, 145
conflict, teleological, 29
conjunction, 163f.
consciousness, legal, 98
contextual implication, 27
contradiction, 146, 169
convention, 52, 93
courts, 93

deontic expressions, 36, 117
descriptive and prescriptive, 7, 71
dialogue, 4
direction for use, 44f., 49
directives, 34f., 37, 69
  authoritative, 41
  autonomous, 50, 98
  existence of, 80
  hearer-interested, 44f.
  heteronomous, 49
  impersonal, 49
  personal, 38f., 48, 98f.
  sanctioned, 39f.
  speaker-interested, 38f.

International
Library of Philosophy
& Scientific Method

Editor: Ted Honderich
Advisory Editor: Bernard Williams

List of titles, page two

International
Library of Psychology
Philosophy &
Scientific Method

Editor: C K Ogden

List of titles, page six

ROUTLEDGE AND KEGAN PAUL LTD
68 Carter Lane London EC4

International Library of Philosophy and Scientific Method
(Demy 8vo)

Allen, R. E. (Ed.)
Studies in Plato's Metaphysics
Contributors: J. L. Ackrill, R. E. Allen, R. S. Bluck, H. F. Cherniss, F. M. Cornford, R. C. Cross, P. T. Geach, R. Hackforth, W. F. Hicken, A. C. Lloyd, G. R. Morrow, G. E. L. Owen, G. Ryle, W. G. Runciman, G. Vlastos
464 pp. 1965. (2nd Impression 1967.) 70s.

Armstrong, D. M.
Perception and the Physical World
208 pp. 1961. (3rd Impression 1966.) 25s.

A Materialist Theory of the Mind
376 pp. 1967. about 45s.

Bambrough, Renford (Ed.)
New Essays on Plato and Aristotle
Contributors: J. L. Ackrill, G. E. M. Anscombe, Renford Bambrough, R. M. Hare, D. M. MacKinnon, G. E. L. Owen, G. Ryle, G. Vlastos
184 pp. 1965. (2nd Impression 1967.) 28s.

Barry, Brian
Political Argument
382 pp. 1965. 50s.

Bird, Graham
Kant's Theory of Knowledge:
An Outline of One Central Argument in the *Critique of Pure Reason*
220 pp. 1962. (2nd Impression 1965.) 28s.

Brentano, Franz
The True and the Evident
Edited and narrated by Professor R. Chisholm
218 pp. 1965. 40s.

Broad, C. D.
Lectures on Psychical Research
Incorporating the Perrott Lectures given in Cambridge University in 1959 and 1960
461 pp. 1962. (2nd Impression 1966.) 56s.

Crombie, I. M.
An Examination of Plato's Doctrine
I. Plato on Man and Society
408 pp. 1962. (2nd Impression 1966.) 42s.
II. Plato on Knowledge and Reality
583 pp. 1963. (2nd Impression 1967.) 63s.

Day, John Patrick
Inductive Probability
352 pp. 1961. 40s.

2

International Library of Philosophy and Scientific Method
(Demy 8vo)

Edel, Abraham
Method in Ethical Theory
379 pp. 1963. 32s.

Flew, Anthony
Hume's Philosophy of Belief
A Study of his First "Inquiry"
296 pp. 1961. (2nd Impression 1966.) 30s.

Fogelin, Robert J.
Evidence and Meaning
Studies in Analytical Philosophy
200 pp. 1967. 25s.

Gale, Richard
The Language of Time
256 pp. 1967. about 30s.

Goldman, Lucien
The Hidden God
A Study of Tragic Vision in the *Pensées* of Pascal and the Tragedies of
Racine. Translated from the French by Philip Thody
424 pp. 1964. 70s.

Hamlyn, D. W.
Sensation and Perception
A History of the Philosophy of Perception
222 pp. 1961. (3rd Impression 1967.) 25s.

Kemp, J.
Reason, Action and Morality
216 pp. 1964. 30s.

Körner, Stephan
Experience and Theory
An Essay in the Philosophy of Science
272 pp. 1966. 45s.

Lazerowitz, Morris
Studies in Metaphilosophy
276 pp. 1964. 35s.

Linsky, Leonard
Referring
152 pp. 1967. about 28s.

Merleau-Ponty, M.
Phenomenology of Perception
Translated from the French by Colin Smith
487 pp. 1962. (4th Impression 1967.) 56s.

3

International Library of Philosophy and Scientific Method
(Demy 8vo)

Perelman, Chaim
The Idea of Justice and the Problem of Argument
Introduction by H. L. A. Hart. Translated from the French by John Petrie
224 pp. 1963. 28s.

Ross, Alf
Directives, Norms and their Logic
192 pp. 1967. about 25s.

Schlesinger, G.
Method in the Physical Sciences
148 pp. 1963. 21s.

Sellars, W. F.
Science, Perception and Reality
374 pp. 1963. (2nd Impression 1966.) 50s.

Shwayder, D. S.
The Stratification of Behaviour
A System of Definitions Propounded and Defended
428 pp. 1965. 56s.

Skolimowski, Henryk
Polish Analytical Philosophy
288 pp. 1967. 40s.

Smart, J. J. C.
Philosophy and Scientific Realism
168 pp. 1963. (3rd Impression 1967.) 25s.

Smythies, J. R. (Ed.)
Brain and Mind
Contributors: Lord Brain, John Beloff, C. J. Ducasse, Antony Flew,
Hartwig Kuhlenbeck, D. M. MacKay, H. H. Price, Anthony Quinton and
J. R. Smythies
288 pp. 1965. 40s.

Science and E.S.P.
Contributors: Gilbert Murray, H. H. Price, Rosalind Heywood, Cyril Burt,
C. D. Broad, Francis Huxley and John Beloff
320 pp. about 40s.

Taylor, Charles
The Explanation of Behaviour
288 pp. 1964. (2nd Impression 1965.) 40s.

Williams, Bernard, and Montefiore, Alan
British Analytical Philosophy
352 pp. 1965. (2nd Impression 1967.) 45s.

4

International Library of Psychology, Philosophy, and Scientific Method
(Demy 8vo)

PHILOSOPHY

Anton, John Peter
Aristotle's Theory of Contrariety
276 pp. 1957. 25s.

Bentham, J.
The Theory of Fictions
Introduction by C. K. Ogden
214 pp. 1932. 30s.

Black, Max
The Nature of Mathematics
A Critical Survey
242 pp. 1933. (5th Impression 1965.) 28s.

Bluck, R. S.
Plato's Phaedo
A Translation with Introduction, Notes and Appendices
226 pp. 1955. 21s.

Broad, C. D.
Scientific Thought
556 pp. 1923. (4th Impression 1952.) 40s.

Five Types of Ethical Theory
322 pp. 1930. (9th Impression 1967.) 30s.

The Mind and Its Place in Nature
694 pp. 1925. (7th Impression 1962.) 55s. See also Lean, Martin

Buchler, Justus (Ed.)
The Philosophy of Peirce
Selected Writings
412 pp. 1940. (3rd Impression 1956.) 35s.

Burtt, E. A.
The Metaphysical Foundations of Modern Physical Science
A Historical and Critical Essay
364 pp. 2nd (revised) edition 1932. (5th Impression 1964.) 35s.

6

International Library of Psychology, Philosophy, and Scientific Method
(Demy 8vo)

Carnap, Rudolf
The Logical Syntax of Language
Translated from the German by Amethe Smeaton
376 pp. 1937. (7th Impression 1967.) 40s.

Chwistek, Leon
The Limits of Science
Outline of Logic and of the Methodology of the Exact Sciences
With Introduction and Appendix by Helen Charlotte Brodie
414 pp. 2nd edition 1949. 32s.

Cornford, F. M.
Plato's Theory of Knowledge
The Theaetetus and Sophist of Plato
Translated with a running commentary
358 pp. 1935. (7th Impression 1967.) 28s.

Plato's Cosmology
The Timaeus of Plato
Translated with a running commentary
402 pp. Frontispiece. 1937. (5th Impression 1966.) 45s.

Plato and Parmenides
Parmenides' *Way of Truth* and Plato's *Parmenides*
Translated with a running commentary
280 pp 1939 (5th Impression 1964.) 32s.

Crawshay-Williams, Rupert
Methods and Criteria of Reasoning
An Inquiry into the Structure of Controversy
312 pp. 1957. 32s.

Fritz, Charles A.
Bertrand Russell's Construction of the External World
252 pp. 1952. 30s.

Hulme, T. E.
Speculations
Essays on Humanism and the Philosophy of Art
Edited by Herbert Read. Foreword and Frontispiece by Jacob Epstein
296 pp. 2nd edition 1936. (6th Impression 1965.) 32s.

Lange, Frederick Albert
The History of Materialism
And Criticism of its Present Importance
With an Introduction by Bertrand Russell, F.R.S. Translated from the German by Ernest Chester Thomas
1,146 pp. 1925. (3rd Impression 1957.) 70s.

International Library of Psychology, Philosophy, and Scientific Method
(Demy 8vo)

Lazerowitz, Morris
The Structure of Metaphysics
With a Foreword by John Wisdom
262 pp. 1955. (2nd Impression 1963.) 30s.

Lean, Martin
Sense-Perception and Matter
A Critical Analysis of C. D. Broad's Theory of Perception
234 pp. 1953. 25s.

Lodge, Rupert C.
Plato's Theory of Art
332 pp. 1953. 25s.

The Philosophy of Plato
366 pp. 1956. 32s.

Mannheim, Karl
Ideology and Utopia
An Introduction to the Sociology of Knowledge
With a Preface by Louis Wirth. Translated from the German by Louis Wirth and Edward Shils
360 pp. 1954. (2nd Impression 1966.) 30s.

Moore, G. E.
Philosophical Studies
360 pp. 1922. (6th Impression 1965.) 35s. See also Ramsey, F. P.

Ogden, C. K., and Richards, I. A.
The Meaning of Meaning
A Study of the Influence of Language upon Thought and of the Science of Symbolism
With supplementary essays by B. Malinowski and F. G. Crookshank
394 pp. 10th Edition 1949. (6th Impression 1967.) 32s.
See also Bentham, J.

Peirce, Charles, *see* Buchler, J.

Ramsey, Frank Plumpton
The Foundations of Mathematics and other Logical Essays
Edited by R. B. Braithwaite. Preface by G. E. Moore
318 pp. 1931. (4th Impression 1965.) 35s.

Richards, I. A.
Principles of Literary Criticism
312 pp. 2nd edition. 1926. (17th Impression 1966.) 30s.

Mencius on the Mind. Experiments in Multiple Definition
190 pp. 1932. (2nd Impression 1964.) 28s.

Russell, Bertrand, *see* Fritz ,C. A.; Lange, F. A.; Wittgenstein, L.

International Library of Psychology, Philosophy, and Scientific Method
(Demy 8vo)

Smart, Ninian
Reasons and Faiths
An Investigation of Religious Discourse, Christian and Non-Christian
230 pp. 1958. (2nd Impression 1965.) 28s.

Vaihinger, H.
The Philosophy of As If
A System of the Theoretical, Practical and Religious Fictions of Mankind
Translated by C. K. Ogden
428 pp. 2nd edition 1935. (4th Impression 1965.) 45s.

Wittgenstein, Ludwig
Tractatus Logico-Philosophicus
With an Introduction by Bertrand Russell, F.R.S., German text with an English translation en regard
216 pp. 1922. (9th Impression 1962.) 21s.
For the Pears-McGuinness translation—*see page 5*

Wright, Georg Henrik von
Logical Studies
214 pp. 1957. (2nd Impression 1967.) 28s.

Zeller, Eduard
Outlines of the History of Greek Philosophy
Revised by Dr. Wilhelm Nestle. Translated from the German by L. R. Palmer
248 pp. 13th (revised) edition 1931. (5th Impression 1963.) 28s.

PSYCHOLOGY

Adler, Alfred
The Practice and Theory of Individual Psychology
Translated by P. Radin
368 pp. 2nd (revised) edition 1929. (8th Impression 1964.) 30s.

Eng, Helga
The Psychology of Children's Drawings
From the First Stroke to the Coloured Drawing
240 pp. 8 colour plates. 139 figures. 2nd edition 1954. (3rd Impression 1966.) 40s.

Jung, C. G.
Psychological Types
or The Psychology of Individuation
Translated from the German and with a Preface by H. Godwin Baynes
696 pp. 1923. (12th Impression 1964.) 45s.

International Library of Psychology, Philosophy, and Scientific Method
(Demy 8vo)

Koffka, Kurt
The Growth of the Mind
An Introduction to Child-Psychology
Translated from the German by Robert Morris Ogden
456 pp. 16 figures. 2nd edition (revised) 1928. (6th Impression 1965.) 45s.
Principles of Gestalt Psychology
740 pp. 112 figures. 39 tables. 1935. (5th Impression 1962.) 60s.

Malinowski, Bronislaw
Crime and Custom in Savage Society
152 pp. 6 plates. 1926. (8th Impression 1966.) 21s.
Sex and Repression in Savage Society
290 pp. 1927. (4th Impression 1953.) 28s.
See also Ogden, C. K.

Murphy, Gardner
An Historical Introduction to Modern Psychology
488 pp. 5th edition (revised) 1949. (6th Impression 1967.) 40s.

Paget, R.
Human Speech
Some Observations, Experiments, and Conclusions as to the Nature, Origin, Purpose and Possible Improvement of Human Speech
374 pp. 5 plates. 1930. (2nd Impression 1963.) 42s.

Petermann, Bruno
The Gestalt Theory and the Problem of Configuration
Translated from the German by Meyer Fortes
364 pp. 20 figures. 1932. (2nd Impression 1950.) 25s.

Piaget, Jean
The Language and Thought of the Child
Preface by E. Claparède. Translated from the French by Marjorie Gabain
220 pp. 3rd edition (revised and enlarged) 1959. (3rd Impression 1966.) 30s.

Judgment and Reasoning in the Child
Translated from the French by Marjorie Warden
276 pp. 1928 (4th Impression 1966.) 28s.

The Child's Conception of the World
Translated from the French by Joan and Andrew Tomlinson
408 pp. 1929. (4th Impression 1964.) 40s.

International Library of Psychology, Philosophy, and Scientific Method *(Demy 8vo)*

Piaget, Jean *(continued)*
The Child's Conception of Physical Causality
Translated from the French by Marjorie Gabain
(3rd Impression 1965.) 30s.

The Moral Judgment of the Child
Translated from the French by Marjorie Gabain
438 pp. 1932. (4th Impression 1965.) 35s.

The Psychology of Intelligence
Translated from the French by Malcolm Piercy and D. E. Berlyne
198 pp. 1950. (4th Impression 1964.) 18s.

The Child's Conception of Number
Translated from the French by C. Gattegno and F. M. Hodgson
266 pp. 1952. (3rd Impression 1964.) 25s.

The Origin of Intelligence in the Child
Translated from the French by Margaret Cook
448 pp. 1953. (2nd Impression 1966.) 42s.

The Child's Conception of Geometry
In collaboration with Bärbel Inhelder and Alina Szeminska. Translated from the French by E. A. Lunzer
428 pp. 1960. (2nd Impression 1966.) 45s.

Piaget, Jean and Inhelder, Bärbel
The Child's Conception of Space
Translated from the French by F. J. Langdon and J. L. Lunzer
512 pp. 29 figures. 1956 (3rd Impression 1967.) 42s.

Roback, A. A.
The Psychology of Character
With a Survey of Personality in General
786 pp. 3rd edition (revised and enlarged 1952.) 50s.

Smythies, J. R.
Analysis of Perception
With a Preface by Sir Russell Brain, Bt.
162 pp. 1956. 21s.

van der Hoop, J. H.
Character and the Unconscious
A Critical Exposition of the Psychology of Freud and Jung
Translated from the German by Elizabeth Trevelyan
240 pp. 1923. (2nd Impression 1950.) 20s.

Woodger, J. H.
Biological Principles
508 pp. 1929. (Reissued with a new Introduction 1966.) 60s.